Representative Democracy

Representative Democracy

Legislators and Their Constituents

Michael L. Mezey
De Paul University

ROWMAN & LITTLEFIELD PUBLISHERS, INC.
Lanham • Boulder • New York • Toronto • Plymouth, UK

ROWMAN & LITTLEFIELD PUBLISHERS, INC.

Published in the United States of America
by Rowman & Littlefield Publishers, Inc.
A wholly owned subsidiary of The Rowman & Littlefield Publishing Group, Inc.
4501 Forbes Boulevard, Suite 200, Lanham, Maryland 20706
www.rowmanlittlefield.com

Estover Road
Plymouth PL6 7PY
United Kingdom

British Library Cataloguing in Publication Information Available

Library of Congress Cataloging-in-Publication Data:

Mezey, Michael L.
   Representative democracy : legislators and their constituents /
Michael L. Mezey.
      p.   cm.
   Includes bibliographical references.
   ISBN-13: 978-0-7425-4769-8 (cloth : alk. paper)
   ISBN-10: 0-7425-4769-8 (cloth : alk. paper)
   ISBN-13: 978-0-7425-4770-4 (pbk. : alk. paper)
   ISBN-10: 0-7425-4770-1 (pbk. : alk. paper)
   ISBN-13: 978-0-7425-6482-4 (electronic)
   ISBN-10: 0-7425-6482-7 (electronic)
   1. Representative government and representation—Case studies.
2. Legislative bodies—Case studies.   3. Legislators—Case studies.   I. Title.
JF1051.M38   2008
328.3—dc22   2008021753

Printed in the United States of America

♾ ™The paper used in this publication meets the minimum requirements of
American National Standard for Information Sciences—Permanence of Paper for
Printed Library Materials, ANSI/NISO Z39.48-1992.

For my grandchildren (in order of appearance)

Rebecca
Norah
Paul
Benjamin

Contents

Dedication   v

Figures and Tables   ix

Preface   xi

1. Representation and Democracy   1

2. Representation: A Theoretical Discussion   23

3. Constituencies and Interests   55

4. Earmarks and Errands   85

5. Representation and Public Policy   119

6. Interest Groups and Representation   145

7. Representative Government and Its Critics   169

8. Appendix: 30 Questions for Discussion   203

Notes   207

Index   229

About the Author   237

Figures and Tables

Figure 3.1   71

Figure 3.2   72

Table 3.1   68

Preface

Nearly forty years ago, the Rockefeller Foundation sent me to Thailand to teach in a program it had organized at Thammasat University in Bangkok. I had written my dissertation on the United States Congress and so was eager to learn what I could about the Thai National Assembly. A series of interviews with its members demonstrated that although Congress and the National Assembly could not have been more different in regard to their lawmaking roles, the representational activities in which Thai legislators engaged were remarkably similar to the work that members of the United States Congress did for their constituencies. Like their counterparts in Washington, Thai legislators ran errands for individual constituents, lobbied for funds for their districts, and acted as advocates for the people they represented.

These activities, which subsequent research seemed to indicate were common to legislators around the world, are in many respects the core of what we consider to be "representative democracy." The representational activities of legislators also are connected in complex ways with the strength and stability of the institutions in which they serve. Although legislative institutions derive their legitimacy in large part from the fact that they are representative bodies, the representational activities of their members, ironically, often have brought their institutions into disrepute. For example, some critics claim that legislatures and their members are too dependent on public opinion, and others argue that they are disconnected from the people they are supposed to represent. Still others claim that legislatures are overly influenced by interest groups, and some conclude that its representative nature renders the legislature unfit to play a central role in the policymaking process.

Clearly, then, the issue of representation raises normative questions about what the role of the legislature and its members should be, empirical questions about what it is that legislators actually do, and comparative questions about how and why the representational role of legislators varies across nations. Excellent theoretical discussions of representation include the seminal work of Hanna Pitkin, a vast literature of empirical studies focusing on the United States Congress, and a smaller body of work dealing with legislatures in other countries. Unfortunately, scholars conducting theoretical work and those doing empirical work often ignore each other, and those who study the United States Congress typically ignore relevant work on other nations.

The goal of this book is to bring together the theoretical, empirical, and comparative work on representation and representative institutions in a manner that will make this important subject accessible and useful to college students. The risk in writing such a book is that the final product will fall among the various subdisciplinary stools occupied by the representation theorists, by those who have mined the inexhaustible data on the U.S. Congress, and by experts in the politics of other nations. Each group is likely to believe that I have not done complete justice to its component of the discipline, and in some sense, I probably have not. On the other hand, as we try to teach our students in a brief fifteen-week period, we draw material from a variety of relevant approaches to our subject and try to synthesize it into a whole that is more meaningful to them than each of the individual parts. In the course of that enterprise, we summarize, simplify, expand, and omit as we decide what our students need to know, while keeping a list of recommended readings (see the footnotes in this volume) close at hand for those who wish to know more about something that we might have perhaps gone over too quickly. Finally, if we have done our work as teachers well, we have raised as many questions as we have answered. To that end, the appendix to this book includes thirty questions on representation and representative institutions that should spark thoughtful discussion among your students; at least they have with mine.

I have several debts to acknowledge. After I stepped down as dean of DePaul University's College of Liberal Arts and Sciences in June 2005, I wondered if, after more than a decade of administrative work, I had become permanently disabled from writing anything but strategic planning documents and bullet point memos asking for more money for my college. DePaul University was kind enough to give me a full year off to answer that question. The idea for this book, its original outline, and the early readings came out of that leave. Upon my return to the classroom for the 2006–2007 academic year, I had the benefit of a reduced teaching load that allowed me to get a good portion of the writing done. I am grateful to Fr. Dennis Holtschneider, C.M., president of DePaul University, for this time that I needed to return to the role of teacher and scholar.

I am grateful as well to Helmut Epp, provost of DePaul University, and Chuck Suchar, dean of the College of Liberal Arts and Sciences, for providing me with additional funds that allowed me to travel to Washington, D.C., to conduct interviews, acquire research materials, and pay the salary of a student assistant. I was able to hire a second student assistant with funds from the College of Liberal Arts and Science's Faculty Research and Development Committee. The two terrific students with whom I worked— Christine Scherer and Sarah Lawson—spent long hours with *The Congressional Record, Congressional Quarterly*, and a number of other sources tracking down the materials that have found their way into the many examples in the pages that follow. The book is immensely better because of their work.

Finally, I am grateful as always to my wife Susan, who when I left the deanship told me quite firmly that I could not just rest during my year off and teach when I returned. She knew that I would be happier in the long term if I identified a writing project and got to work on it. As usual, she was right. My grown children, Jennifer and Jason, and their spouses, Jonathan and Deirdre, continue to be a source of pleasure and pride to me, and they in turn have encouraged and believed in me. Their most important contribution, however, was to provide the four remarkable grandchildren to whom this book is dedicated.

Michael L. Mezey
Chicago, Illinois
April 2008

1

Representation and Democracy

Most nations, with few exceptions, are committed, at least rhetorically, to the concept of democracy. Derived from the Greek words *demos*—referring to the people—and *kratos*—referring to political power—democracy means, literally, that the people hold political power. Democracies are characterized by "popular sovereignty"; simply put, the people have the final say about the policies that govern their lives. Here in the United States, the speeches of our public officials and the everyday conversations of our citizens are filled with references to our democratic heritage, to self-government, to the will of the people, and even to our goal of fostering democracy around the world. And in the micropolitics of our personal and communal lives—parent teacher organizations, student government associations, neighborhood bridge clubs—phrases such as "let's vote on that" or "the majority rules" suggest the extent to which the bedrock principles of democracy are embedded in our political culture.

The practices and principles that characterize democracies are easy to summarize. Citizens, by majority vote, decide the public policies that will govern their behavior. All citizens have the right to vote, each citizen has one and only one vote, and all votes are counted equally. The power of the majority is limited only by the requirement that the political rights of the minority—rights such as freedom of speech and the press and the right to assemble—be protected. In other words, today's democratic majority cannot take steps to prevent today's minority from becoming tomorrow's majority.

This sort of direct democracy is characteristic of, for example, small local or private groups, the idealized New England town meeting, or the Athenian city-state—all members of the group gather together, consider policy alternatives, and decide by vote among them. But it is not characteristic of the politics of any modern nation-state. Rather, those nations that we typi-

1

cally refer to as democracies are more accurately described as republics. In republics, the people do not govern directly as they do in democracies; rather they affect political decisions indirectly by electing and influencing the behavior of representatives who actually make public policy and control its implementation. The requirements for a representative system compared with direct democracy are these:

1) public policy is made by representatives of the people and not by the people themselves;
2) these representatives are elected by citizens typically grouped into units called constituencies;
3) as is the case in a democracy, all adult citizens, with only rare exceptions, are allowed to vote for representatives, and all citizens have one vote;
4) representatives are accountable for their actions to those who elect them—their constituents—and can be replaced by them at the next election.

REPRESENTATION AND DEMOCRACY

Although in popular discourse terms such as republic, democracy, and representative democracy are used interchangeably, in fact they mean quite different things. Strictly speaking, representative systems are not democratic because self-government, which is what democracy means, is not the same thing as government by someone else, even if you elect that someone to do the governing on your behalf. Some political theorists have argued that representation frustrates democracy by removing political decision-making from the hands of the people and giving it over to a select group of citizens who actually govern. From this perspective, representation reduces democratic citizenship to the mere act of voting for one candidate or the other, thereby violating the democratic premise of popular sovereignty. The French theorist Jean-Jacques Rousseau argued that the general will of the people "cannot be represented; it is either itself or something else; no middle ground is possible."[1] More recently, the American political theorist Benjamin Barber asserted that representation "alienates political will at the cost of genuine self-government."[2]

Such arguments reduce the familiar phrase "representative democracy" to an apparent contradiction in terms. In most representative systems, decision-making by representatives is not just an alternative to decision-making by the people; typically, citizens in a representative system have no direct role in the making of public policy. When those who wrote the United States Constitution said in Article 4, Section 4, that each state in the Union was to be guaranteed "a republican form of government," their intention was not simply to guarantee representative government against the threat of executive tyranny but also against what at least some of the Founders viewed as the equally dangerous threat of democracy. It is ironic, therefore, that representative government, although "conceived in explicit opposition to democracy," today is seen as one of its forms.[3]

Those who defend representation as an authentic form of democracy offer several arguments in support of that view. Some note that true government by the people is a romantic notion that probably never existed; very few Athenians held the status of "citizen" that enabled them to participate in government, and some who held offices with significant power were elected to those positions.[4] Others make the point that democracy in its pure form is a practical impossibility in the modern nation-state, and still others argue that even if democratic government were somehow possible, it would not be a very good idea. However, none claim that all political systems that have representative elements are approximations of democracy. Forms of representation exist, for example, in China and Zimbabwe under Robert Mugabe, nations that few would consider democratic. Representation also can take place in a number of nondemocratic contexts, as when groups and individuals purport to, and sometimes actually do, represent people who have no voice in their selection—for instance, when Amnesty International claims to "represent" the interests of political prisoners, or when a delegate to the United Nations is said to represent the people of her nation.[5] The question then is what criteria a representative system must meet if it is to be considered a reasonable approximation of democracy, if not the genuine article.

First, political decision makers in a specific representative system must be elected by and accountable to the people. If few or no decision makers are elected by the people, then it is difficult to view such a system as even an approximation of democracy. For example, countries where elected representatives have very little influence on public policy (Egypt) are less democratic than those nations where all policymaking power is in the hands of elected leaders (Norway). Systems such as the United States, with independent and unelected judiciaries that can override decisions of elected representatives are, whatever their other virtues, less democratic than systems such as the British, where the elected parliament, and more specifically the House of Commons, is supreme. Systems in which a popularly elected lower house of the legislature shares power with a partially appointed upper house (Tunisia) are less democratic than systems in which there is either a unicameral legislature (New Zealand) or where both chambers are directly elected by the people (France). Countries in which all adults are permitted to vote (Canada) are more democratic than countries where women or other population groups are denied the franchise (Saudi Arabia).

As indicated earlier, democracy also requires political equality in the sense that all citizens hold equal political power. The familiar slogan that summarizes this idea is "one person, one vote." In the United States, the representational scheme that provides the 35 million citizens of California with the same number of senators (two) as the 650,000 citizens of Alaska makes the United States less democratic than those systems where each representative has about the same number of constituents. Similarly, the democratic criterion of political equality is subverted and the representative system is rendered less democratic to the extent that citizens who have significant financial resources are able to exert greater influence over representatives than those with fewer resources.

If we assume that elected representatives actually govern, the next issue is the degree to which the people influence the decisions that are taken by those whom they elect to office. Ultimately, if there is to be something resembling popular sovereignty, then citizens must be able to exercise control over the actions of those whom they identify as their representatives. However, representatives may not be consistently responsive to the wishes or the interests of the represented. For example, representatives may respond to the narrow interests and concerns of aggressive and attentive interest groups or to those groups with the financial resources to press their cases rather than to the interests of broader, less attentive and less moneyed publics, or they may act according to their own political and policy beliefs, with little reference to the wishes of those who have placed them in office. A representative may be more responsive to the views of his constituents on some issues than on others. He may be quite responsive to citizens' demands for federal government funding for new roads in their town but quite unresponsive to their views and interests on healthcare legislation.

Corruption or dishonesty can also play a role. Representatives at times have betrayed their constituents by acting in their own self-interest rather than in the interest of those whom they represent or in the interest of the nation as a whole. On the other hand, more innocent and complex factors can explain the variance between constituency views and representative actions, explanations that depend on different views about the proper role of the representative. Some argue that a representative always should vote in accordance with the wishes of those who elect him; others believe that he should use his own judgment about what is in the best interests of the constituency. Some contend that the duty of the representative is to act always in what he perceives to be the best interest of those who elect him; others say that if faced with a choice between what he believes to be best for his constituency and what he believes is best for the nation as a whole, his duty is to opt for the good of the nation rather than for the good of that segment of the nation that he represents.

Even if a representative has decided that it is his duty to reflect the views of his constituents no matter what his own views might be, it may be difficult, for a number of reasons, for him to discern what the real sentiments of the citizens are on a particular issue. It is not unusual for the opinions of citizens to be ill-informed; there is a great deal of evidence that most citizens in most countries pay little attention to the policy issues of the day or to the activities of those whom they elect to office. Even if the views of the constituency are clear, representatives, because they are more educated than the voters who elect them or because of their experience as political decision makers, may arrive at a different, more enlightened and refined view of the public interest than the view held by their less experienced and less knowledgeable constituents. In such a case, the duty of the representative may be to use his own judgment rather than rely on the less informed views of those who have placed him in office.

In sum, the views of the constituency and the actions of the representative could diverge for a number of reasons, and it is precisely because of this condition that the most passionate exponents of democracy are so critical of representative systems. Democratic principles make an unequivocal intellectual and philosophical commitment to the wisdom of the people and to their right and ability to determine for themselves what is and what is not in their best interest as well as what is best for the nation in which they live. Without such a commitment, it would make no sense to speak in terms of popular sovereignty or, in other words, of government by the people. When a political system places an intermediary between the people and political decision-making and leaves open the strong possibility that the intermediary may act for whatever reason contrary to the wishes, or worse the interests, of the people, the cardinal principle of democracy—popular sovereignty—is irretrievably undermined. Thus, for democrats, any data that suggest that representatives may and do deviate from the wishes of the people proves that democracy and representation are incompatible.

The truth of the matter, however, is a bit more complex. In fact, all representative systems have both democratic and undemocratic aspects to them and none can satisfy completely the strictest democratic criteria. On the one hand, the right of citizens to vote and their right to petition their representatives are clear democratic elements in most representative systems. On the other, every representative system recognizes, or at least accepts, the "undemocratic" prerogative of representatives to act contrary to the views of their constituents. Rather than thinking of democracy in absolute and dichotomous terms (a country is either democratic or it is not), it is more helpful to think in terms of a continuum running from more to less democratic with a number of stopping off places in between. Representative systems then can be arrayed along that continuum, with some systems, such as Russia, placed more toward the undemocratic end of the continuum and others, such as Denmark, much closer to the democratic end. In other words, it is a matter of gradations; it may be more reasonable to apply the apparently paradoxical term "representative democracy" to some political systems than to others.

WHY REPRESENTATION?

In ordinary parlance—that is, in discussions outside political science classes—we seldom distinguish between democracy and representative democracy and simply assume that our current arrangements are by definition democratic. But given our cultural and rhetorical commitment to "government by the people" and the various ways in which all representative systems in practice deviate from democratic ideals, why then has representative rather than direct democracy become the institutional norm for modern nation-states?

These questions have both practical and philosophical answers. Practically, the population size and territorial expanse of most nations combine to create insurmountable logistical barriers to the establishment of systems of direct democracy. In ancient Athens, the very small number of "citizens" easily could assemble and participate in their own government. In our more modern societies, all the members of parent teacher organizations or all adults of a small New England town can gather in one place to make decisions, but it would be very difficult for all of the citizens of even a relatively small nation to assemble in a similar fashion. And if the nation is large in terms of population and geography, no such gathering is even remotely possible. For the United States, with an adult population of more than 180 million spread over an entire continent, the only "place" where such a "gathering" could occur would be in cyberspace. The British thinker John Stuart Mill hoped for a government "in which the whole people participate" but concluded that representative government was "the ideal type of a perfect government," since "all cannot, in a community exceeding a single small town, participate personally in any but some very minor portions of the public business."[6]And even Rousseau, who as we have seen viewed representative government and democracy as antithetical, ultimately endorsed political systems based on representation in his works on the constitutions of Corsica and Poland.[7]

Even if one leaves aside the logistical challenges of providing everyone with an opportunity to participate in every political decision—imagine for a moment every citizen sitting at his or her computer in one great electronic chat room—how would such a large number of people engage in policy deliberation? Governing is not simply about choosing; it is about choosing wisely among competing alternatives. Deliberation refers to the process by which information on policy issues is gathered and shared, alternative approaches and opinions are aired and debated and their merits and draw-backs assessed, common ground is discovered, necessary compromises are entered into, and only then final policy choices are made. Such a process requires a forum and a set of procedures that allow discussion and debate to take place among advocates of various viewpoints. That in turn means some limit to the number of participants in the deliberative process. Several thousand, let alone several million, people cannot have a discussion. It is self-evident that the smaller the number of people involved in any decision-making process, the easier it is to deliberate and to come to a decision. A 100-member United States Senate should be a more effective deliberative body than a 435-member House of Representatives, which in turn must be more effective than the cacophony created by nearly 200 million citizens sitting at their laptop computers.

Numbers, of course, are not the sole determinant of effective delibera-tion; if the numbers get too small, then effective deliberation can be under-mined because all views may not be represented. But the willingness and ability of those who deliberate to be informed about the issue at hand and to listen to and consider the arguments of others is important. Even if somehow all citizens could participate in a deliberative process, would each be willing to take the time to learn and understand the policy issues on the nation's agenda and the various options among which they would be asked to choose? The data that we have on this is not particularly encouraging; virtually every study in virtually every nation shows that most people most of the time have very little information on even the basic facts about their political system, let alone the issues and policy options that it faces. In light of that, proponents of representation urge democrats to accept the fact that most people are so involved in their own private and personal lives—the world of family, work, and leisure—that even if they had the chance to par-ticipate, they would not choose to devote their time to the difficult and tedious work of collective, democratic decision-making, especially when dealing with complex and sometimes incomprehensible policy issues. Per-haps they might do so if a specific policy had a direct impact on their lives, but not when the policy area in question is one about which they know little and that has only a marginal effect on them. Farmers, for example, might well participate and do so with some knowledge when it comes to agriculture policy, but their participation would be unlikely to have the same commitment and quality if the issue was the space program or urban mass transit.

This lack of political interest and participation by the individual is often depicted as a civic failure, in some ways an abdication of one's citizenship responsibilities, and from a democratic perspective perhaps it is. But from another perspective, it may not be the best use of every citizen's time to ask him or her to become educated on every issue, big and small, central or marginal, so that each can have a voice on every policy decision. The French thinker Emmanuel Sieyes argued that a division of labor between representatives and citizens is appropriate to a modern commercial society in which people occupy their time with their personal economic affairs and do not possess the leisure time to devote to public affairs. As societies advanced and prospered, it was both right and inevitable that the business of governing should become a profession.[8] Writing nearly two centuries after Sieyes, the Austrian political economist Joseph Schumpeter suggested that the most society could ask citizens to do is to participate in the selection of their leaders and that the complexity of public opinion and the difficulty of matching those opinions with real policy options meant that it would be futile to seek substantive connections between citizen opinion and public policy.[9]

From this point of view, political systems operate best when policy decisions are left to professional politicians. If one supposes that the average citizen has neither the time, the interest, nor the capacity to participate directly in any but a few policy decisions, it makes sense to assign these responsibilities to a smaller group of people for whom public affairs would be a full-time responsibility, a vocation rather than an avocation. If one supposes further that wise public policy decisions emerge from a deliberative process, then it makes sense to assign these responsibilities to a group small enough to meet in one place and to deliberate effectively. For many defenders of representation, this view of how individual citizens wish to allocate their time as well as the argument for efficiency and effectiveness combine to trump the democratic arguments for the virtues of popular sovereignty and true self-government.

THE DANGERS OF DEMOCRACY

These practical objections to direct democracy and therefore the support for representative systems became increasingly persuasive as the populations of nations grew and as citizenship rights were extended to more inhabitants. Gradually, restrictions on the right to vote based on gender, race, or property disappeared and most nations moved toward universal suffrage. With more people possessing full citizenship rights, the impracticality of direct democracy became even more apparent. But not only practical arguments were marshaled against democracy. Even when participatory rights were more narrowly defined, philosophical objections to democracy existed.

These concerns were front and center during the deliberations over the design of the United States Constitution. Specifically at issue was whether ordinary people had the ability to make informed, intelligent decisions that would be in the public interest. Even at that time, when the right to vote was for the most part restricted to white male property owners, those who were skeptical about democracy argued that average citizens would be tempted to place their own self-interest above the common good. They also might be easy prey for demagogues who would move them in a particular direction by appealing to their passions and fears rather than to their reason. In that case, the end result of democracy might well be despotism rather than liberty for, as Alexander Hamilton wrote in The Federalist No. 1, "Of those men who have overturned the liberties of republics, the greatest number have begun their career by paying an obsequious court to the people, commencing demagogues and ending tyrants."[10]

In contrast, better educated citizens, those who occupied positions of wealth and privilege in society, were more likely to understand the complexity of public policy, to rise above their own petty interests, and to resist the wiles of those who would practice what James Madison referred to as "the vicious arts by which elections are too often carried."[11] Of particular concern to Madison and his colleagues was that the majoritarian principle that is an essential element to democratic systems could lead to a form of tyranny in which the wishes of the majority would subvert both the common good and the rights of the minority. At the time, the Founders' particular concern was less the civil rights and liberties of political or ethnic minorities that we think of today when we speak of "minority rights" and more the rights and privileges of those with property and wealth. The Founders feared that in a democracy this economically privileged minority would be threatened by the much larger number of citizens who had more modest economic resources. Vivid in their minds were the 1787 events in Massachusetts, where a group of farmers under the leadership of Daniel Shays marched on the state legislature to demand the issuance of paper money and the suspension of debts incurred during the Revolutionary War. To many of the Founders, Shays' Rebellion was a cautionary tale of the perils that popular sovereignty posed to both political stability and what they viewed as good government.[12]

In the case of the United States, then, those who framed the Constitution associated direct democracy with mob rule and with unwise policies. Elbridge Gerry of Massachusetts told his colleagues at the Constitutional Convention that "the evils we experience flow from an excess of democracy."[13] Madison spoke for most of the Founders when he wrote in The Federalist No. 10 that "Democracies have ever been spectacles of turbulence and contention; have ever been found incompatible with personal security, or the rights of property; and have in general been as short in their lives, as they have been violent in their deaths."[14] Alexander Hamilton added that "the people are turbulent and changing; they seldom judge or determine right,"[15] and his colleague at the Constitutional Convention, Roger Sherman of Connecticut, suggested that "the people should have as little to do as may be about the Government. They want information and are constantly liable to be misled."[16] William Livingston of New Jersey said that "the people have ever been and ever will be unfit to retain the exercise of power in their own hands."[17] A republic, in contrast, would minimize the evils that they associated with democracy because, according to Madison, decisions would be made not by the people, but by their representatives— "a chosen body of citizens whose wisdom may best discern the true interest of the country, and whose patriotism and love of justice will be least likely to sacrifice it to temporary or partial considerations."[18]

Thus, for the Founders, the practical obstacles to direct democracy were of less concern than its consequences. Citizens simply were not capable of being informed about various policy alternatives and the merits and implications of each. They would not be able to make an informed decision on what needed to be done and, more troubling, they would make self-interested rather than public-spirited decisions, decisions that might be influenced by the transitory passions of the day or by the machinations of demagogic leaders. These majorities could threaten the position of those with wealth and property, and as public opinion shifted, so would public policy, with instability and turbulence the inevitable result.

Representatives, in contrast, would be drawn from among the better educated and more prominent members of society and would more readily grasp the details of the policy questions before them. Their keener sense of, and stronger commitment to, the public good would enable them to see beyond their own self-interest, and therefore their decisions would be more likely to advance the public interest than would be the case if the people governed directly. And because the representatives themselves, like the Founders, would be drawn from society's wealthier classes, they would of course resist popular pressure for policies that would jeopardize their own economic positions—positions that the Founders believed coincided with the public good.

CHECKING THE LEGISLATURE

It is not too difficult to extend this critique of direct democracy to a critique of representative democracy, and several of the Founders did exactly that. If the people are unfit to make good public policy, they should be equally unfit to select good and wise people to act on their behalf. On this reasoning, the Founders were almost as skeptical about representative institutions as they were about direct democracy. They therefore took steps to restrict the powers of the new Congress, and especially the House of Representatives. These steps included a careful enumeration of legislative powers, the establishment of an independent and nonelected judiciary with the implied power of nullifying congressional actions that exceeded these enumerated powers, an independent, nonelected executive with the capacity to veto legislation enacted by the Congress, the addition to the Constitution shortly after its ratification of a series of political rights and liberties that Congress could not abridge, and, most importantly, the division of the Congress into two chambers with only the House of Representatives elected directly by the people.

The inclusion of a nonelected Senate composed of two senators from each state who the Founders expected would be appointed by their state legislatures served a number of purposes. It provided assurances to the small states that their interests would not be compromised by the actions of the House of Representatives, whose membership would be dominated by the larger, more populous states. It gave the state assemblies, the bodies that would be crucial to the ratification of the new Constitution, representation in the new government. And in requiring that all legislation be approved by both the House and the unelected Senate, the Founders checked the power of the House, the only branch of the new government elected directly by the people and therefore the only truly republican (or representative) national political institution. The analogy used by the founders was just as a saucer cooled hot tea, the Senate would serve to cool the ardor and passions of the people as expressed in the House.[19]

REPRESENTATIVE INSTITUTIONS AS CHECKS ON EXECUTIVE POWER

It is easy from our twenty-first century perspective to view the representative system created by the Founders of the American republic as antidemocratic and even at variance with the principles of representative democracy— given the significant powers placed in the hands of unelected or indirectly elected officials and the very limited number of people who were allowed to vote. But it is also important to note that for many people at that time, democracy was not the primary alternative to representation. Rather, those who wrote the Constitution were aware that representative institutions originated as an alternative to and a check upon unbridled executive authority, the gravest threat to individual liberty.

For much of world history, government had been the province of absolute rulers—sometimes kings who claimed the divine right to rule and sometimes tyrants who simply asserted their authority through force. Representative bodies arose as a means to counter these authoritarian rulers. The origin of representative institutions as both instruments of popular control and as checks on executive power is usually traced to Anglo-Saxon

England toward the beginning of the second millennium. There, kings consulted councils on matters of foreign negotiation, taxes, and laws. The members of these councils—upper level clergy and members of the nobility—were appointed to their positions by the King and, not surprisingly, they rarely blocked his wishes. Thus, these arrangements, although quite distant from representative democracy as we know it today, provided at least a potential check on the monarch because under some circumstances he might be asked to account for his actions to others.

The potential power of such councils became much more concrete when in June 1215, at a field by the River Thames called Runnymede, King John met with his barons, who were upset at his arbitrary actions, particularly in regard to the taxes that he was demanding to finance his war in France. In return for their continued loyalty and financial support, the barons demanded a charter that would limit the power of the monarchy and require the king to gain their consent on important matters such as taxation. This arrangement, memorialized in the Magna Carta, is considered to be the foundation of parliamentary power in England and the direct precursor to the House of Lords today, the upper house of the British parliament. For democratic theory, the Magna Carta embodies the embryonic notion that government could proceed only on the basis of the consent of the governed. Although at that time the "governed" was a small group of nobles, the Magna Carta established the principle that those from whom resources were extracted and on whose behalf decisions were made needed to be consulted and, by virtue of such consultation, consent to these decisions.

Over the course of centuries (to make a very long story very short) the number of people whose consent was required gradually increased (as the franchise expanded), the power of the monarchy in England gradually declined, and the power of Parliament gradually increased.[20] The British philosopher John Locke, writing in celebration of parliamentary independence achieved through the Glorious Revolution of 1688, asserted that the legislature, because it represented those whose consent the government required, must hold the supreme power "to make laws for all parts and for every member of the society, prescribing rules to their actions."[21] For largely the same reasons, John Stuart Mill viewed representative government as "the ideally best form of government" when compared with the despotism, benevolent or malevolent, associated with absolute monarchies and similar systems.[22]

In the American colonies, legislative institutions emerged as instruments of self-government in the earliest colonial times. In 1619, the Virginia Company authorized its governor to call together representatives of the plantations to make laws for their own government. Thus was born the Virginia House of Burgesses. This first legislative body in the New World soon claimed the sole right to impose taxes, a model that eventually was adopted in all of the colonies. When colonial control by chartered companies ended, the executive power in the colonies came to rest in the hands of royal governors responsible to the British Crown. As the actions of the king and his governors became increasingly tyrannical, the assemblies soon became the primary site of opposition to royal power. The colonists looked to them as the institutional means for checking executive power and articulating their grievances. In the words of James Wilson of Pennsylvania, they "were the guardians of our rights, the objects of our confidence, and the anchors of our political hopes."[23] As the colonies moved toward a break with Great Britain, the assemblies were said to "collect the common sense of the people" and, in the case of the Massachusetts Assembly, "The publicity of debates excited interest and accentuated the sense of crisis. The members, while framing their bold policies of resistance, challenged the people to support them."[24]

Because the prerevolutionary colonial assemblies were associated with resistance to tyrannical executive power, they became the center of power in the postrevolutionary colonies, and under the Articles of Confederation Congress was the dominant national political institution. Even though by the time of the Constitutional Convention many of the Founders had developed serious concerns about abuses of legislative power, they knew that if the new Constitution did not provide for a strong legislature, it would have little chance of being accepted by the states. Thus, there was no dispute with Madison's Lockean assertion that "in republican government, the legislative authority necessarily predominates."[25] And it was for this reason that Article I of the Constitution begins by vesting "all legislative powers herein granted" in the Congress. The Founders also were acutely aware, given their experience with the King of England and his royal governors, of the dangers of executive power, particularly in regard to issues of war and peace. Writing after the ratification of the Constitution, Madison said that

in no part of the constitution is more wisdom to be found than in the clause which confides the question of war or peace to the legislature and not to the executive department. The temptation would be too great for any one man. . . . The strongest passions and most dangerous weaknesses of the human breast: ambition, avarice, vanity, the love of fame, are all in conspiracy against the desire and duty of peace. . . . The executive is the department of power most distinguished by its propensity to war; hence, it is the practice of all states, in proportion as they are free, to disarm this propensity of its influence.[26]

This idea that there is an inverse relationship between legislative power and overbearing executive authority is borne out by contemporary events. For example, in the late 1970s, as Spain moved away from the authoritarian Franco period to a more democratic society, "Parliament was the place where all the advocates of renewal met," and parliamentary negotiations among the different political groups consolidated the fledgling democracy.[27] In the 1990s, as the nations of Eastern Europe terminated their Soviet-imposed authoritarian systems, the emergence of autonomous legislative institutions was taken as the surest sign that executive authority would be subject to checks and that the political freedoms associated with more democratic systems would be protected. In the case of Hungary, the 1989 Constitution, which served as a transitional document between the submissive rubber stamp legislature of state socialism and a more representative system, "created a very strong parliament alongside a relatively weak president and government."[28] Similarly, in Latin American nations such as Chile and Brazil, leadership by strongmen backed by the military always has come at the expense of legislative authority, and the resurgence of the legislature always has been accompanied by the ebbing of authoritarian control. And in the United States, scholars of American political institutions have observed a similar inverse relationship between presidential and congressional power, as periods characterized by the rise of strong, dominant presidencies seem to be followed inevitably by the resurgence of the Congress and the reining in of the presidency.[29]

It can be argued, as the Founders did, that representative institutions of the sort they created provide a stronger safeguard against tyrannical rule than more democratic systems. Demagogues who play on some combination of popular fears, biases, and ignorance often have come to executive power through direct election by the people. Popularly elected presidents, demagogic or not, always seem to argue that they are the only officeholders who truly represent all of the people which, they say, gives them a clearer sense of what the national interest demands than members of the legislature, each of whom represents only a small portion of the nation. Such leaders evoke broad popular support and have proven themselves adept at depicting their opponents in the legislature as self-seeking, bickering "politicians"—as representatives of special interests who either refuse to deal with the nation's problems or, when they do, act contrary to the manifest will of the people. During difficult times, and especially during times of severe economic distress or national danger, people have displayed a tendency to look for scapegoats and to turn to "the man on horseback" who promises to protect the country from its enemies within and without. Such men have a tendency to evolve into permanent fixtures, sometimes becoming near absolute rulers with no practical limits to their power. Adolph Hitler came to power in Weimar Germany through popular election at a time of economic distress, national humiliation, and growing alienation from representative institutions such as parliament and political parties. President Hugo Chavez in Venezuela came to power with mass popular support, and the steps that he has taken to reduce the authority of parliament suggest that he intends to stay in power for some time.

The designers of the United States Constitution were so concerned that someone could become president by appealing to popular emotions and using popular support to enhance his power that they rejected direct election of the president in favor of the Electoral College model that virtually removed the people from any role in presidential selection. George Mason of Virginia argued that allowing the people to choose the president was like referring "a trial of colors to a blind man."[30] They hoped that an established and well-respected representative institution composed of professional politicians with their own connections to the people could serve as a bulwark against power-seeking presidents. It is no coincidence, from this point of view, that as the presidential selection system that the Founders designed evolved into the functional equivalent of direct election by the people, the power of the American presidency increased.

Edmund Burke, the British theorist and parliamentarian and a person not known for his commitment to the common people, argued nonetheless that it was important for the members of the House of Commons to be elected because unless they owed their office to a power other than the king, they would not remain an independent force capable of checking the monarch and would instead be vulnerable to co-optation by him.[31] Those who wrote the United States Constitution also feared that the president would be able to co-opt and corrupt the members of Congress just as British kings had done to members of Parliament—that the office would be "the fetus of monarchy," as Edmund Randolph of Virginia put it.[32]

So despite misgivings about the abuses of legislative power, the Founders vested considerable policymaking authority in the Congress and gave the president no role in the selection or the salaries of representatives, little in the way of independent power, and only a conditional veto over congressional actions. Because the president, selected without congressional involvement, and the Congress, selected by the people without executive involvement, would share powers, each institution would have the ability to check the other, so that "ambition may be made to counteract ambition," as Madison phrased it in The Federalist No. 51, and threats to liberty from either institution would be averted.

However, one danger to liberty that the Founders did not anticipate was the expanded executive branch composed not just of directly or indirectly elected personnel, such as presidents, prime ministers, and cabinet members, but also a large and sometimes overweening bureaucracy. In all modern nations, the role of unelected civilian and military bureaucracies has grown. As knowledge has expanded and expertise has become increasingly important to the quality of public policy, civilian bureaucrats, although ostensibly under the control of elected politicians, have acquired enhanced discretionary power that can have a significant impact on the lives of citizens. Often, their elected political masters lack the expertise, the time, or the will (or sometimes all three) to supervise them effectively. On the military side, virtually every nation now has a standing army that functions in times of peace as well as war and that consumes a large portion of the national budget. Even though many nations, including the United States, have a commitment to civilian control of the military, in practice such control may be more apparent then real. And because the day-to-day supervision of the military falls to presidents and prime ministers, the power of the military may simply augment executive power at the expense of the legislature. In the United States, the president's power as commander-in-chief has given him extraordinary discretionary authority on issues of war and peace, essentially rendering the power to go to war granted to Congress in Article I of the Constitution a dead letter and creating what historian Arthur Schlesinger has referred to as an imperial presidency.[33]

In the United States as well as in other nations, strong military establishments and the heads of government with whom they are allied can be checked (at least in theory) by legislative leaders who ostensibly control the power of the purse, but exercising these checks often has proved to be difficult. In Latin America, Asia, and Africa, on numerous occasions military forces have closed representative institutions, including legislatures. In Thailand in 2006, a government was disbanded and its prime minister driven into exile by a military coup, something of a tradition in that nation. In spring of 2007, the Turkish military issued a thinly veiled threat of a military coup to dissuade the Parliament from selecting a president whose views on religious issues they found threatening to the secular nature of the state. The fact that the military had carried out such coups before lent credibility to its threat.

All of this suggests the seemingly love-hate relationship that representatives and representative institutions have had with democracy. On the one hand, as we have discussed, representation has been seen as a significant deviation from democratic practices, as vitiating, both in theory and in practice, the fundamental democratic principles of popular sovereignty and rule by the people. On the other hand, representative institutions have played a key role in limiting, and on occasion eliminating, the power of authoritarian leaders, in checking abuses of executive power, and in creating and maintaining political systems characterized by fundamental liberties essential to democracy such as freedom of speech and the right to vote. Although democratic purists will continue to argue that representative systems are by definition undemocratic, it is difficult to think of modern political systems that we normally (albeit perhaps erroneously) classify as democratic apart from their representative institutions, and it is undisputed that when forces in a society seek to restore authoritarian rule, among their first steps is to either intimidate or close down the legislature.

REPRESENTATION AS A BETTER DEMOCRATIC FORM

To this point, representative systems have been depicted as either a "second best" alternative to a more preferable but impractical model of direct democracy or as an alternative approach that trades some elements of democracy for other desirable ends such as more informed public policy, more efficiency in government, protection against the political dangers of a government too reliant on the will of the people, or a bulwark against the potential tyranny of those with executive power. However, when compared with direct democracy, representative systems also can be viewed as a different and even superior democratic form. Representative systems can foster informed public discourse that can serve to educate citizens on public policy issues and "give value to democratic politics."[34] As representatives link citizens with their governments, they ensure that political decisions are taken in the context of public opinion and the public interest. As society changes and opinions shift, the actions of the people's representatives can reflect these changes and thus enhance the responsive capacity of the political system. Such responsiveness is in many respects the very essence of democratic politics.

This perspective rejects the view that representative systems alienate citizens from their politics by simply reducing them to voters. Rather, representation makes a nation more authentically democratic, not simply because of its capacity to constrain excessive executive power, but also because of its capacity, through the interactions between representatives and their constituents, to connect government with a large and diverse society composed for the most part of people with low to moderate levels of political interest and involvement. As such, representation provides a different and perhaps a more effective means to achieve popular control of political decision-making than the methods of direct democracy.

This line of reasoning focuses attention on several questions about the relationship between representatives and those whom they represent. How and to what extent are representatives responsive to the concerns and interests of broader publics? What exactly are the responsibilities that representatives have to those who put them in office? Need they follow their constituents' wishes to the letter or do they have some degree of autonomy in what they do? Is acting as their constituents would wish the only way that representatives can fulfill their responsibilities? To what extent does a representative system serve the interests of the nation's citizens, rather than deteriorating into an oligarchy in which those in power make decisions without any reference to the people at large become co-opted and coerced by the presidents, prime ministers, and bureaucrats whom they are supposed to control?

There is a rich theoretical literature dealing precisely with these questions of the ideal relationship between the representative and the represented. This normative approach to representation will be the focus of our discussion in the second chapter of this book. These theoretical treatments of representation exist in parallel with an equally rich empirical literature that tries to determine how the representative relationship takes place *in practice*. How do representatives determine exactly who it is they are supposed to be representing and what their wishes and interests might be? What exactly do representatives do as they discharge their duties? Should representation be viewed simply in terms of legislators responding to the policy priorities of their constituents or are there aspects to representation that do not involve major policy decisions? What constraints do the represented place upon their representatives; do voters hold them accountable for their actions; and if so, how?

REPRESENTATIVE SYSTEMS

The answers to some of these questions, particularly those concerning the behavior of representatives and the manner and extent to which they respond to their constituencies, are determined in part by electoral systems, political party systems, and interest groups, as well as by the way in which different representatives in different political systems understand the term "constituency." These elements, taken together, suggest a representative *system* composed of several interacting institutions, understandings, and practices that provide a context for, and therefore complicate, the simple, dyadic relationship between elected representatives and their constituents.

For example, a member of a legislature who comes to office in a nation where each legislator is the sole representative for his constituency— referred to as a single-member district system—is likely to have a different relationship with his constituents than a legislator in a nation where representatives are elected from multimember districts via a system of proportional representation. Similarly, representatives in nations where political parties are relatively weak and incapable of imposing discipline on their members in the legislature are likely to view representation differently and act differently from their counterparts in nations where parties are strong and highly disciplined. Someone who is the sole representative of a constituency in a system with weak political parties is likely to view the piece of real estate that constitutes his geographic constituency as the focus of his representational efforts. A legislator who is one among several representing the same constituency and who functions in an environment characterized by strong, disciplined political parties is less likely to be focused on his corresponding piece of real estate and more likely to be concerned with his political party and its interests. And in nations where interest groups have easy access to individual legislators—typically nations with weaker political party systems—representatives will need to take the views of these groups into account as they play their representational roles, unlike their counterparts in nations with stronger political parties that typically insulate individual representatives from such groups.

THE PLAN OF THE BOOK

The empirical literature on representation and representative institutions informs the chapters that follow the theoretical discussion in chapter 2. Although the emphasis is on the United States Congress, a comparative perspective incorporating findings and insights from analyses of other nations also is included. Representation is truly an international concept, and representative institutions of some sort exist in virtually every nation in the world. An understanding of how representation works in Washington, D.C., will be enhanced by an understanding of how it works in London, Caracas, and New Delhi. Many of the representational practices that occur in the United States are unique to the Congress, but some are found in other nations as well. More importantly, the impact of different electoral and party systems on how representation takes place can only be appreciated when one looks at electoral and party systems other than one's own.

Chapter 3 addresses descriptive representation. Some suggest that the extent to which the composition of a legislature reflects the demography of its nation is a key indicator of the degree to which the institution is representative. For example, can Belgium be viewed as a representative democracy if its legislature does not reflect the ethnic balance between its Flemish and Walloon populations? Or is the U.S. House of Representatives, where women constitute fewer than 20 percent of the membership, less democratic than the Norwegian Storting where women comprise 38 percent of the membership? Or how democratic can any legislature be when in nearly all instances its membership is drawn from the more economically privileged sectors of society and where there are seldom representatives from lower rungs of the socioeconomic ladder? Beyond demography, the larger question is the extent to which the composition of the legislature reflects the various political and economic interests and divisions of the entire nation. Are all views and interests abroad in the land represented by people who will speak and act on their behalf? Is each view and interest represented in proportion to its strength within the society as a whole?

The heart of the argument that representative systems are a proxy for democracy is the notion that representatives are responsive to the wishes of their constituents. As explained in chapter 4, such responsiveness is most evident when representatives are asked to deal with specific problems that individual constituents or groups of constituents bring to them, particularly problems that they may have encountered with the bureaucracy. Representatives are also expected to act as advocates for the needs of their constituencies; they are asked to seek government funding for local projects such as highways, schools, and hospitals or provisions in legislation that will protect and advance locally important economic interests and enterprises. Representatives from around the world report that they spend a great deal of time responding to these narrow constituency concerns, many of which do not require an act of the legislature as a whole or may require relatively minor modifications in legislation.

Chapter 5 addresses the extent to which constituency attitudes, as opposed to other factors, affect the public policy decisions of representatives. It can be argued that a representative institution does not behave very democratically if its members pay little or no heed to the wishes or interests of those whom they represent when it comes to deciding issues that are before the legislature. Although the members of the Supreme Soviet in the former Soviet Union were elected by the people and reflected more than most other legislative institutions the demography of the nation, the actions of these representatives were determined by the wishes of the leadership of the single legal political party, not by those who, at least formally, elected them. Although members of the British Parliament devote considerable effort to dealing with the individual problems of their constituents, the positions that they take on major policy issues are determined largely by their party leaders. And in the United States, the actions of representatives may have little to do with the wishes or interests of the electorate.

Chapter 6 explores the role that interest groups play in representative systems, both as enablers of and barriers to the responsiveness of representatives to citizen views and interests. Constituency attitudes are not conveyed to representatives solely by individual citizens, but also by organized groups. Labor unions, professional organizations, and trade associations may aggregate the views of the individual citizens who affiliate with them and press these views on representatives. Instead of (or in addition to) an individual constituent urging a legislator to support an increase in the minimum wage, a union to which that constituent belongs may lobby for such legislation on behalf of all of its members. Instead of an individual hospital administrator pressing his representative for more generous Medicare payouts to his facility, a national group of hospital administrators may organize to present such proposals to representatives. Organized groups, in other words, can be more effective than individual citizens at articulating constituency views, and in that sense they may enhance the responsiveness of public policy to citizen opinion.

On the other hand, interest groups also may magnify the influence of minority interests. If the views of physicians, as articulated through the activities of the American Medical Association, have more influence on health policy than the views of the vast majority of citizens, who are consumers rather than providers of health services, then the public policy results may be contrary to the majoritarian principle that is an integral part of democratic political theory. Such a situation can move a representative system toward the less democratic end of our continuum by rendering problematic the argument that representation is an effective proxy for direct democracy. And to the extent that financial resources rather than numbers determine the success of an organized interest's efforts to influence representatives, the activities of interest groups may further undermine the supposed democratic nature of a representative system where, presumably, each citizen's voice is equal.

Finally, chapter 7 addresses the criticisms that have been leveled against representative institutions, some of which already have been noted. In most countries, popular approval of the legislature as an institution and often of the individual members themselves is relatively low. In the United States, Congress is typically the least well regarded of our national political institutions. There are those who view legislatures as slow to act, inefficient, and uninformed when they do act, and therefore inferior to powerful executives as effective policymaking bodies. Some argue that representatives are too reliant on public opinion—that is, too responsive to their constituents—and are inclined therefore to do what is popular rather than what is necessary. Adherents to this point of view typically argue for the merits of bureaucratic states or strong presidential systems presided over by popularly elected chief executives. Others criticize representative institutions and their members as being too removed from the opinions of their constituents and therefore unfaithful to their democratic obligation to represent those who elect them to office. They tend to view legislators as estranged from the citizenry, overly dependent on financially powerful interest groups, and operating more in their own interests or in the interests of the rich and powerful rather than in the interests of the public at large. Advocates of this view typically argue for more democracy—for reforms that would reduce the autonomous role of representatives and increase the decision-making influence of the average citizen.

The argument in chapter 7 is not necessarily that these critics and their remedies are all wrong (although some clearly are), but that the merits of representative systems, whatever their deficiencies, outweigh their problems and that reforms can address many of these deficiencies without discarding the idea of representative democracy. Chapter 7 also explores the argument that it is precisely the connection between legislators and their constituents—the idea of representation itself—that most provokes the critics, particularly those who prefer more authoritarian alternatives. In brief, to the extent that each representative acts in an *individually responsive* manner to the wishes of his constituents or the wishes of interest groups or party leaders whom he, for one reason or another, views as objects of his representational activities, he makes it less likely that the institution will discharge its *collective responsibility* to produce good public policy in the interest of the nation as a whole. If that is the case, then the very actions that representatives take to meet the democratic expectation that they be responsive to their constituency undermine the reputation of the legislature and provide support for the arguments for greater executive control. On the other hand, the actions of representatives may well be at odds with the views of those whom they represent because representatives *are* better informed than average citizens and *are* better able to judge the merits of competing policy proposals. Although these deviations from constituency views may result in better public policy, they also provide grist for the democratic argument that representative systems undermine the principle of popular sovereignty. It may be then that representatives are in a no-win situation; by doing exactly what we would expect them to do—being better informed than average citizens but at the same time being responsive to their demands—they provide ammunition for those who would shift power away from legislatures toward executives and for those who would shift power away from legislatures toward the people.

2

Representation: A Theoretical Discussion

It should be clear from the preceding chapter that the degree to which a representative system can be viewed as an approximation of democracy depends on the nature of the relationship between the representative and the represented. To understand that relationship, we need to understand exactly what the term "representation" means, a task that is considerably more complex than a simple parsing of the word would suggest. Literally, the term means "to make present again" ("re" being the prefix for "again" as in repossess or reenlist). But exactly who does the representative "make present again," how does he do that, and under what constraints does he operate?[1]

PRINCIPAL-AGENT THEORY

If a representative system is to be thought of as more rather than less democratic, then the issue of popular sovereignty needs to be addressed. Specifically, in what sense can it be said that the people govern if in fact it is their representatives who govern? One answer, and the starting point for a great deal of the theoretical and empirical literature on representation, is that government by the people is approximated if citizens control the actions of their representatives. From this perspective, representatives are the agents of a larger body of citizens and their job is to carry out the wishes and advocate the interests of those citizens. For the many practical reasons discussed in the previous chapter, the citizens of the modern nation-state cannot be physically present to govern themselves. But they can be "made present again" through their representative, and their presence is manifested by the control they exercise over the behavior of the representative whom they have empowered to act on their behalf. The formal term for this approach to understanding representation is *principal-agent theory.*[2]

To understand what is meant by principal-agent theory, consider the relationship between a professional baseball player and the person whom he employs as his agent. What does the player, whom we may refer to as the principal, expect from the agent in return for the 10 percent of every deal that the agent normally collects from the player? Naturally, when negotiating contracts, arranging endorsement deals, and managing the money that the player earns, the agent is expected to respond to the wishes of the player and to act in the player's best interests.

Why do players employ agents when it would be perfectly legal and acceptable for them to negotiate their own contracts and handle their own money? They do so for some of the same reasons that have been used to justify political systems where decisions are made primarily by the people's representatives as opposed to direct democracies that rely on citizens making their own decisions. That is, the player may not have the expertise to understand the complex details of professional sports contracts and may not have the negotiating skills to go head to head with the business executives, accountants, and lawyers who run professional sports teams. Even if the player has the expertise, he may not wish to spend the time that would be required to represent himself in an effective manner. By employing an agent and authorizing the agent to act for him, the player can use his time to train, to improve his skills, and to enjoy the money that he is earning.

The expectations that the player has for his agent are clear-cut. She is expected to act in the best interests of the player and to follow the player's wishes when those wishes are communicated to her. If she does not think that in a particular instance it is a good idea to follow the wishes of the player, she needs to be able to explain to her client why she disagrees with him. The most compelling explanation that she can muster in such circumstances will cite the player's best interests—"I do not want to do what you asked me to do because I don't think that what you want is best for you." If her argument is unpersuasive and the player persists in his views, no matter how misguided they may appear to her to be, the agent needs to follow the wishes of the player.

Although an agent may have a good reason for proposing actions contrary to the *wishes* of her client, an agent who acts contrary to the *interests* of the player—say by colluding with the team's owner on contract terms that are clearly disadvantageous to the player—is deemed to have behaved unethically and may be vulnerable to legal action on the part of the aggrieved athlete. At a minimum, the agent who shirks her responsibility to pursue her client's best interests is likely to be fired.

The key points in the relationship are these: the agent, rather than the principal, is the person who *decides what to do and acts*, unless she has specific contrary instructions from her client; the agent has this capacity to act because her principal—the player—*authorizes* her to act on his behalf, typically through a signed contract; the agent acts in the *best interest* of her client; and the player holds the agent *accountable* for what she does—that is, he can ask for an explanation of what the agent has done and dispense with her services if he is not satisfied with either the results of the agent's work or with the quality of the explanation offered. In any case, when there are differences of opinion between the player and the agent, it is the view of the former that prevails.

If we move the principal-agent model from the world of professional sports to the sport of professional politics, the principal becomes the citizen and the agent becomes the representative. In a representative system the citizen-principal has no role in deciding public policy questions; rather, he authorizes the representative-agent to act in his stead. The same questions about the relationship between the baseball player and his agent apply to the relationship between the citizen and his representative. In brief, what are the responsibilities of the elected representative (agent) to the citizen (principal) he represents, and how is the representative held accountable for his actions?

At first glance, the parallel is simple and apropos. The representative is the agent of those who elect him to office; he is authorized to act on their behalf not with a signed contract of the sort that a player would have with his agent but through an electoral process. In his work in the councils of government, he is bound to represent the opinions and interests of those who have elected him. The heart of the principal-agent approach to representation is the idea of constituency control: information, opinions, wants, and needs flow from the constituency to the representative, and he is expected to respond. Responsiveness can take a number of forms: introducing legislation that constituents favor, voting on specific bills in accord with the opinion of the constituency, speaking out on behalf of the interests of one's constituents, seeking positions of influence within the legislature so that one can work more effectively for one's constituents, and providing specific services for individual constituents and for constituency based interests. As was the case with the athlete and his agent, the opinions of constituents ought to prevail when they are in conflict with the opinions of the representative, and when the representative deviates from the opinions of the constituency, such deviations need to be accompanied by explanations phrased in terms of the interests of the constituency. Constituents judge the sufficiency of these explanations when the representative seeks reelection; it is at that point that he is held accountable for his actions. All participants in the relationship are presumed to be guided by self-interest.

Constituents are interested in having their views and interests faithfully represented in the political decision-making process, and the representative has an interest in continuing in office. If his constituents do not think that the representative is being responsive to them, he can be replaced in the next election.

WHO ARE THE PRINCIPALS?

From a democratic perspective, the principal-agent model makes a great deal of sense. The representative system offers a reasonable facsimile of popular sovereignty, but only if the people's control over those who are representing them is at the heart of the representative relationship, just as the athlete ultimately controls the actions of his agent. However, applying the principal-agent approach to political representation reveals a number of important differences from the player-agent model. For starters, our political agent—the representative—has multiple principals rather than a single person. These multiple principals are usually referred to as a constituency, and although that term can mean a number of different things, it is always a collective term encompassing a large number of people.[3]

In its most common usage, constituency refers to a demarcated geographic territory and to those people who live within its boundaries. In the United States, constituencies are created by aggregating city blocks, precincts, towns, cities, and counties; for members of the United States Senate (as well as members of the House of Representatives from sparsely populated states such as South Dakota and Wyoming), constituencies are defined as their entire state. Outside the United States, territories composed of towns, provinces, or regions also have been the building blocks of constituencies. In Israel and the Netherlands, all legislators are elected on a national list, so in essence each member of these two parliaments has the nation as a whole as his or her constituency.

These geographic constituencies are heavily populated. Districts of members of the U.S. House of Representatives contain nearly 700,000 citizens—many more than the single client that the athlete's agent needs to consider, and a group large and diverse enough to have a variety of opinions and interests. Although legally and formally the representative may see this entire geographic entity and all who live in it as his constituency, politically he is likely to view the constituency in more nuanced terms. The political scientist Richard Fenno hypothesized that representatives view their constituencies as a series of concentric circles, with all who live in the district as the largest circle. The circles then get smaller if, for example, the representative thinks only of those who regularly vote for him as his constituents; although legally he represents all of the constituency's residents, he may be less responsive to the views of those who never vote for him, perhaps because of their unwavering loyalty to a political party other than his or because they disagree with his positions on most issues.[4]

In some contexts, he may think of an even smaller circle composed of a group of district leaders—people of influence such as local officeholders, executives of major corporations, union leaders, journalists, and clergy—as his most meaningful constituency because their views can influence the opinions and voting decisions of larger publics or because the welfare of their businesses can affect the economic well-being of the entire constituency. Also, as "attentive" members of the public, these people are more likely to be aware of the policy issues before the legislature, what the representative is saying about these questions, and how he votes. Finally, an even smaller circle may contain the representative's core group of supporters— those who contribute campaign funds to him or help him raise funds from others, those who organize his reelection campaigns, and those who are his closest friends and advisors on political and policy issues. Although these core supporters usually reside or work in the constituency, there may well be exceptions, particularly in regard to those who contribute campaign funds.[5]

The ease with which members of the U.S. House of Representatives conceive of their district primarily in geographic terms (no matter how broadly or narrowly they define its population politically) is to some extent the product of the single-member district system under which nearly every member of every legislature in the United States is elected. In practice, a piece of territory is marked off on a map by those responsible for drawing district lines—the state legislature, or in some cases independent commissions—and that piece of territory is the legislator's, and only his, to represent. In the case of the United States Senate, two representatives (i.e., senators), typically elected during different election years, are assigned to the same constituency. In political systems that elect legislators under a system of proportional representation, several legislators, elected simultaneously, are responsible for representing the particular territory that defines the constituency.[6] As examined below, the relationship between representatives and the represented in such multimember district systems will be different from the relationship that characterizes single-member district systems, but the same territorial definition of constituency, with all of the potential nuances suggested by Fenno, applies.

Even though most representatives are elected from geographically defined constituencies, in some nations they may view their most important principals as the political party organization to which they belong and to which they owe their nomination and election to office. In highly disciplined political party systems, the representative's first obligation is to vote as his party leaders direct. Although such representatives also have obligations toward those who live in the geographic area that they represent, when it comes to policy issues they are more accurately conceived as agents of their party leaders rather than of their constituents. And because voters in these political systems often tend to think of the party as the institution that represents their opinions and interests in government, it can be argued that the party rather than the individual legislator is more appropriately viewed as the agent of the constituency.[7] In that case, when the representative supports the position of his party leadership, he may in fact be responding to the wishes of his constituents.

Similarly, under certain circumstances representatives may view organized interests rather than their constituents as their principals. These interests may have a strong presence in the representative's district—perhaps a union to which many of the residents belong or the trade organization that lobbies for the largest employer in the district. Or an interest group may have contributed money to, or otherwise supported, the representative's election campaign or the campaign of the political party to which the representative belongs. Such groups need not necessarily be based in the representative's geographic constituency. Campaign contributors do not respect political boundaries, and in the United States very few members of Congress rely exclusively on funds raised in their own constituencies. And from a less pecuniary point of view, the representative may have an ideological attachment or personal sympathy to a particular interest group and its positions, even though that group could have few if any members or supporters in his district.

No matter how broadly or how narrowly the representative conceives of his constituency, the number of citizens, opinions, interests, and voices is still quite large. Even if the representative views a smaller subset of the constituency as his most important principals, there are still many principals, perhaps with conflicting views and interests, and only one agent. This makes the job of the representative much more complicated than his counterpart who represents the professional athlete. The latter must contend with only one principal with one set of opinions and interests; the former has multiple principals with multiple opinions and interests.

The multiplicity of the principals in the representative relationship has significant implications for authorization—a key component of the principal-agent approach. It is not much of a stretch to view the representative as being authorized to act by those who elected him, but what form does authorization take for those who voted for the representative's opponent? As residents of the constituency, they are entitled to representation, but the mechanism by which they have authorized the representative to act is a bit more abstract, turning perhaps on their decision to participate in the election or their tacit commitment to the constitutional rules that encourage them to abide by the results, whether or not the results are pleasing to them. This is a particular problem in nations such as the United States and

Great Britain that elect their representatives under a single-member district system. In such winner-take-all systems, those who vote for the losing candidate must rely entirely on the winning candidate for representation. In the more commonly used proportional-representation systems, each constituency is represented by several legislators allocated among the political parties in proportion to their votes. Parties that do not gain a majority or plurality of the votes still may elect one or more of their candidates, so citizens who vote for such parties may have a representative who, through their vote, they have authorized to represent them.

But what is the nature of authorization in the case of the nonvoters who, in the United States, typically account for around half of the eligible electorate? Here the argument for authorization must rely on an even more abstract concept: the nonvoter's implicit acceptance of his or her national citizenship, which presumably carries with it an obligation to comply with the rules of the political game that govern the selection of representatives and provide an authorization for him to act. Finally, groups or individuals external to the constituency (i.e., they are neither residents nor eligible voters) have no explicit or implicit role in authorizing the representative to act and have no means to hold him accountable for his actions—that is, no way to require him to explain himself and no way to dismiss him should these explanations be unsatisfactory. Yet, as examined below, in some circumstances representatives view people in this category as part of their constituency.[8]

WHAT DO THE PRINCIPALS WANT?

One major problem then with applying principal-agent theory to the representative relationship is that it is difficult to understand with any precision who the principals are—that is, to whose views and interests the representative must attend, who has authorized him to act as their representative and through what mechanism, to whom the representative is accountable and how such accountability is enforced. But even if the representative clearly understands who his principals are (for example, all the voters living in his congressional district), he may well have difficulty discovering what it is that they want him to do. Our sports agent knows exactly who her client is—who has authorized her to act and to whom she must account for her actions—and she can get on the telephone to find out what her principal wants her to do in a particular situation. But our political agent has a much more challenging task if he wishes to find out what his multiple principals want him to do. Does he use public opinion polls, does he count up the letters and e-mails that arrive in his office, or does he rely on the views of those citizens whom he meets and talks with in the daily performance of

his duties or on his visits back to the constituency? Which subset of principals does he listen to: the average voters on the street, a narrow majority as
revealed in the results of an opinion survey, the leaders of the community,
or the interest groups inside and outside of his constituency that are attentive to his actions and crucial to his reelection?

One problem for the representative who attempts to discern the opinions
of his constituents is that most citizens know very little about the policy
options that confront the legislator and how the choices will affect their
lives, the welfare of his constituency, or the welfare of the nation as a
whole. In general, voters are more interested in and have more information
about policy ends than about the possible means to get to those ends.[9] For
example, they may wish to have a system that guarantees health care to all
who need it, and they will say so in response to a pollster's question. But
they are likely to have very little information and no real opinion on the
various paths to achieve that end, and they are unlikely to understand the
costs and benefits associated with each approach. They will not know the
difference between a single-payer system and the various more complex
proposals that envision a central role for insurance companies and that
have sometimes inscrutable ways of determining coverage.

Although voters usually have opinions that they are willing to express
when a pollster asks them a question, it is far from certain, even when it
comes to the goals of policies, that these opinions are based on any hard
or relevant information on the issue at hand. Citizens may have a significant amount of information on a high profile issue—the war in Iraq, for
example—but they will have much less information about mass transit subsidies, student loan programs, and regulations governing the credit card
industry. It is much more likely that the opinions they reveal when polled
on these issues are "manufactured opinions"—opinions created by the
polling question itself that forces the respondent to choose between an
"agree" or a "disagree" response and that implicitly discourages a "no opinion" or "don't know" response. And it is not always clear that the respondent has ever thought about the issue before being asked, or that when
asked the same question at a different time and perhaps in slightly different
words he will answer it in the same way.

A more reasonable view, but one that complicates the issue further, is
that voters have genuine, even informed opinions on a very few issues—
presumably those issues that affect them personally or that for one reason
or another they feel strongly about (e.g., abortion rights). Although most
voters will not know much about mass transit subsidies, big city mayors
and those who use public transportation are likely to know more. One
challenge therefore for the representative, should he wish to know where
his constituents stand, is to distinguish between those issues characterized

by manufactured opinions and those about which citizens truly care and about which they have informed and relatively stable opinions.

A second challenge is to determine whether what he is hearing accurately indicates his constituency's view. In the case of letter writers, there is ample evidence that although they may feel passionately about an issue, the opinions that they convey seldom reflect the views of the constituency as a whole. Letter writers tend to be more educated and more ideologically extreme than the average constituent, and they are more likely to ask their representative to oppose rather than to support something. Representatives know this, but they attend to these letters nonetheless because they are written by people for whom the issue at hand is important and who are very likely to remember the representative's position at the next election.

Like letter writers, at least some individuals who respond to survey questionnaires are both knowledgeable about the issue and intensely committed to their position. For example, say 55 percent of voters favor one position on a particular issue and 45 percent favor the opposite position. However, most of those who comprise the 55 percent majority do not really care that much about the issue while most of the 45 percent minority are intensely worried and concerned about how the issue is resolved. What should the representative do? Should he go with the apathetic majority, most of whom at the end of the day will neither know nor care how he voted or what the outcome of the vote was, or should he act based on the views of the intense minority, who care very much about the outcome and will know and remember how he voted? And what if that intense minority is even smaller than 45 percent? For example, public opinion polls consistently indicate that nearly 80 percent of the American public favors gun control legislation. But the 20 percent who are opposed care intensely about the issue, much more so than the anti-gun constituents. Although it does violence to the democratic and representative ideal that majorities should rule, a strong argument can be made that in such circumstances the representative may have a greater obligation to the intense minority than to the apathetic majority.

Even if a survey provides an accurate reading of constituency opinion, it will not always reveal the majority view and it may provide the representative with few voting cues. If the issue is complex, if there are more than two options, it may be impossible to determine what the majority view of the constituency might be.[10] And as the question of intensity suggests, it is not even clear that if the majority view can be detected, it is the one that should control the representative's actions. Perhaps the views of a smaller group of attentive constituents—those who know and care about the issues—should exert a greater influence on the actions of the representative. Because local business, labor, and political leaders may have a better understanding of the issues, one could make the plausible argument that the legislator should pay the greatest attention to these elite opinions and views.

The point is that measures of constituency opinion are inherently "soft," always incomplete, frequently conflicting and difficult to interpret, and often unstable in the sense that they can shift from week to week or according to how a question is worded. Moreover, constituent responses can be based on very little information about politics or government. As the best research on what American citizens know (and do not know) about politics concludes, "Political knowledge levels are in many instances depressingly low," and poorly informed citizens "hold fewer, less stable, and less consistent positions."[11] In sum, the representative who understands his role in terms of the principal-agent theory and therefore aims to do what his constituents want him to do often will have two huge problems to overcome: figuring out exactly who his constituents are and exactly what it is that they want him to do.

OPINIONS AND INTERESTS

Even if the representative is able to identify his principals and even if he can detect among them a stable and informed opinion on a particular issue, what does he do if in his view their preferred policy option is not in their best interests? *Opinion* refers to what citizens wish to happen, and *interest* means what would be best for the citizen independent of his opinions. Democratic theory has a great deal invested in the inherent wisdom of the individual citizen and her ability to decide what is best for herself and for her nation. On the other hand, the general lack of citizen information provides ample reason to pause before embracing the assumption that individuals are the best judges of their own interests.

It does not take too much imagination to identify situations in which the opinions of citizens really do conflict with their interests. For example, voters may not wish to pay more for an automobile that has equipment that reduces toxic emissions and therefore ameliorates the problems of air pollution and global warming, but doing so is clearly in their interests as well as the interests of their children and grandchildren. Should the representative respond to the opinions or to the interests of the represented when deciding how to vote on legislation that would require automobile manufacturers to install such equipment? Or citizens may not wish to pay higher taxes, but what should the representative do if higher taxes are the only way to pay for various services that these same constituents expect their government to provide, such as health care, quality public education, a strong national defense, veterans benefits, and social security?

The distinction between opinion and interest is particularly important when discussing the influence that his election campaign should have on the representative's actions. It is assumed that when a representative makes policy promises to his constituents during a campaign, he should work to fulfill those promises if elected. In such instances, representatives should interpret their elections as mandates from their principals to do as they said they would do. But this "mandate" view of elections ignores the possibility that there can be instances when a candidate once in office decides not to do as he promised because the facts he discovers after the election are inconsistent with the facts as he understood them prior to election day. "Had I known then what I know now," he might say, "I would not have made those promises." These new facts may mean that doing as he had promised would not be in the best interests of the voters.

For example, a sincere promise to cut taxes made during the election may prove to be unfeasible given the true budget situation that the representative discovers when he arrives in Congress. In such an instance, being responsive to the opinions of voters by attempting to carry out a perceived electoral mandate may conflict with being responsive to the interests of the voters. Which option should the legislator select if he wishes to be true to his responsibilities as a representative?[12] Arguably, legislators who do not live up to their election promises are not necessarily failing to discharge their responsibilities as representatives if their policy switches are in the public interest, especially if they publicly acknowledge and account for these reversals after the fact. On the other hand, one of the frequent criticisms leveled at representative government is that politicians fail to live up to the promises they make during election campaigns.[13]

This dichotomy between acting as your constituents want you to act—as their delegate—and acting in what you believe to be their best interests—as their trustee—has been a recurrent theme in both theoretical and empirical studies of representation,[14] although as noted in chapter 5, neither perspective fully describes the approach that representatives take as they make public policy decisions. A related and equally challenging problem is presented when the opinions and interests of the represented coincide but in the view of the representative they are contrary to the interests of the nation as a whole. For example, sugarcane growers in a constituency will support trade barriers that restrict imports of cheaper sugar from overseas. Although this is clearly in their economic interest, these trade barriers are certain to cause higher sugar prices for all consumers and may impoverish and perhaps contribute to instability in other nations whose economies may depend on their ability to export sugar. Such a result is presumably not in the interests of the constituency (more of whom are sugar consumers than sugar producers) or to our sugar consuming nation as a whole. What should the representative do in such a case?

The views of Edmund Burke and James Madison—two legislators who also were political theorists—were clear on this point: in such a situation, the representative's first obligation is to the nation as a whole. Madison and his colleagues at the Constitutional Convention sought representatives who displayed what they called civic virtue—the ability to place the interests of the nation ahead of the narrow interests of their constituents or their own personal interests. "The aim of every political constitution," said Madison, "ought to be, first, to obtain for rulers men who possess the most wisdom to discern, and the most virtue to pursue the common good of the society."[15] He believed that "the public voice, pronounced by the representatives of the people, will be more consonant with the public good than if pronounced by the people themselves."[16] In Burke's case, when his constituents, the electors of Bristol, asked his views on the extent to which their opinions and interests should govern his actions, he responded that he owed them his "intelligence, diligence, and judgment" and that he would betray them if he sacrificed his considered judgment to their more transitory and less-informed opinions. He went on to say that the first obligation of the representative was to the nation, that "Parliament is not a congress of ambassadors from different and hostile interests . . . but a deliberative assembly of one nation, with one interest, that of the whole; where not local purposes, not local prejudices, ought to guide, but the general good, resulting from the general reason of the whole."[17]

What determines whether the representative opts for the interests of the nation or of the constituency, or whether he relies on the judgment of his constituents or uses his own judgment about the best public policy to pursue? The principal-agent model argues that a representative relies on the judgment of his constituents because it is they whom he must "make present again," they who have authorized him, and it is to them that he must account. Clearly, the representative who opposes sugar quotas that might benefit an important segment of his constituency, or the representative who supports tax increases to pay for health care and other popular and essential services, must be able to offer a compelling explanation, phrased in terms of either the interests of his constituents or the "general good" of the nation as a whole, for his deviance from the opinions and perhaps from the narrow interests of those whom he represents. If his efforts to account for his actions fall short, he may well be replaced by his constituents at the next election. As examined below, representatives are frequently confronted with the choice of voting in accord with the wishes of their constituents, and therefore avoiding difficult questions of accountability, or voting against their wishes and thereby endangering their political futures. Representatives opting for the latter choice, though often praised by historians and journalists for their courage, should remember that shortly after Burke's speech declaring his primary obligation to act in the interests of the nation as a whole, the electors of Bristol decided to dispense with his services as their representative.

On the other hand, representatives are not necessarily motivated entirely by the desire for reelection. They may follow the wishes of their constituents or pursue constituents' interests over the interests of the nation not because it is politically expedient but because they believe it is the right thing to do. Or, as Burke did, they may act as trustees, relying on their own judgment of what is good for the district or good for the nation because they believe it is their obligation to act in that way. The point is that reelection may not be what motivates some representatives; they may think of themselves as more accountable to their own principles and beliefs about what their responsibilities should be and how they should act.[18]

ACCOUNTABILITY

This last caveat notwithstanding, accountability assumes that representatives will be called upon to explain (or account for) their actions on a consistent basis. Effective accountability depends on a number of factors: constituents having sufficient information to determine their interests in a particular policy area; their ability to monitor the behavior of their representatives to determine the extent to which representatives' actions conform with constituent interests; and the availability and utility of effective means to sanction representatives whose actions are perceived to be at odds with constituent interests.[19] Our athlete eventually will discover that he did not get the salary and perks to which he believes himself entitled, but will our citizen principals—no matter how they are defined—always know what their political agent has done or failed to do on their behalf? Will they notice that their public services have deteriorated and trace that back to their representative's resistance to higher taxes, for example? And will they recall and use this information when the next election is held?

As we have noted, citizens lack information and expertise on public policy issues. The arguments for representative rather than direct democracy turn in part on the principle of division of labor, which suggests that representatives should attend to public policy issues while citizens attend to the challenges of their own nonpolitical lives. But if it is unrealistic to expect citizens to know or to understand policy issues to a degree that would allow them to participate in decisions, is it not equally unrealistic to expect them to know if their representative has acted in concert with their opinions, or if he has protected their interests, or alternatively if he has sacrificed one or the other to the interests of the nation as a whole or, worse, to his own personal interest? One summary of the research in the United States on this subject concludes that "a generous estimate is that just under one third of the constituents and one half of the voters have the minimum knowledge that is a prerequisite for judging incumbents' policies. They know who their incumbent is and roughly what his or her policies have been."[20] The professional athlete will certainly know when it is time to fire his agent for not acting in his interests; it is far less certain that most citizen principals will know if and when the time has come to "fire" their representative.

Finally, even in an ideal situation in which all citizens have opinions and all know how their representatives vote on each issue, it is not clear that the legislator's reelection or defeat truly can be interpreted as an exercise in accountability. At least in the United States, many citizens do not vote, so the majority view of the voters may be quite different from the majority view of the entire constituency. Factors having little to do with policy, such as the personality and character of the candidate or the party allegiances of the voters, also may be important. And if there are several issues before the voters, it is not clear if or how a particular policy position can be detected from the results of a vote, even if one makes the assumption that all citizens know the issues, know the policy stances of the representative, and determine their vote entirely on the basis of these issues.

RESPONSIVENESS, CONSTRAINT, AND THE ALLOCATION OF TIME

The paradox of the representative relationship is that on the one hand representatives pay a great deal of attention to their constituents, but on the other, they face ambiguity about the identity of the constituency, lack of information on the part of the constituents, often conflicting and confusing information about what constituents want, and the potential conflict between constituency opinions and constituency interest. Some have turned to the term "responsiveness" as a theoretical way to incorporate these uncertainties and contradictions. Hanna Pitkin offers the classic formulation of this view in her seminal treatise on representation:

> Representing here means acting in the interest of the represented, in a manner responsive to them. The representative must act independently; his action must involve discretion and judgment; he must be the one who acts. . . . He must not be found persistently at odds with the wishes of the represented without good reason in terms of their interests, without a good explanation of why their wishes are not in accord with their interest.[21]

Pitkin's formulation cures some of the defects of the simple constituency control model upon which the principal-agent approach rests. It honors, as Burke does, the independence of the representative by recognizing that he must use his discretion and judgment when he acts. It recognizes as well that at various times the representative's position may differ from the wishes of his constituents and that in such instances he must be prepared to account for his actions. However, he must do so in terms that make clear that although he may be acting against their opinions, he is acting in their interest. Left open is how that interest should be defined: in terms of the specific interests of the constituency or the general national interests. Clearly the representative's "good explanation" might be phrased in terms of either. Also left open is how frequently the representative may wander from the wishes of his constituency; Pitkin says that he must not be found to be "persistently at odds" with his constituents, but how many instances does it take to turn "occasional" into "persistent"? Finally, because it is not always obvious what or who the representative views as his constituency, the question of exactly with whom he should avoid being persistently at odds is also left open. For example, is the representative "at odds" with his constituency if his position agrees with only 40 percent of all the voters in his district but with the views of 60 percent of those who voted for him?

Perhaps the most accurate way to describe the impact of constituency opinion and interests is to conceive of these factors as *constraints* on the behavior of the legislator. The constituency is always a threshold concern for the legislator—the first thing that the legislator considers—as he decides what action to take on a policy proposal or on the tasks to which he allocates his time and resources. This perspective provides a more nuanced view of constituency control, a view that accepts that a simplistic application of the principal-agent model is untenable but at the same time maintains that the representative (at least the representative who is interested in being reelected) always needs to consider the potential reaction of his constituency to what he says and how he votes and that he needs to be prepared to account to his constituents for his actions.[22] The strength of this constraint is likely to vary from issue to issue. A senator from Kansas, for example, will view his constituency as a significant constraint on his actions in regard to a farm bill but as a less significant constraint on his actions in regard to oil drilling on the north slope of Alaska.

There is evidence as well that representatives allocate more of their time to those issues that arouse intense constituency interest.[23] On those issues they draft legislation and offer amendments, make speeches, spend time negotiating with their colleagues and bureaucrats, and devote the time of their staff members. Similarly, legislators in the United States and in most other countries report that they spend a great deal of time responding to problems that individual constituents have encountered with government agencies. Citizens may experience difficulties navigating the government bureaucracy—a senior citizen is having trouble registering for social security benefits, the Veterans Administration has denied services to someone who thinks she deserves them, or a local mayor believes that the Department of Housing and Urban Development is applying its grant allocation rules in a manner that is unfair to his municipality. In none of these instances is a public policy response required; that is, no new law has to be passed, and no roll call vote needs to be cast. Rather, the legislator is being asked by his constituents to use his good offices and his position of political power to influence the discretionary authority that resides in every nation's bureaucracy.

This sort of service responsiveness comports with the principal-agent model—there is one principal (the constituent making the request), she knows what she wants, she has asked the legislator to respond, she will know if the legislator has helped, and presumably she will hold the legislator accountable for what he does or fails to do. And even if the representative is unable to get a favorable response, the constituent may be satisfied simply by the willingness of the legislator or a member of his staff to listen to her problems and try to help. These characteristics of the principal-agent model seldom apply to major public policy issues, where the identity and wishes of the constituency are ambiguous and where the mechanisms of accountability do not work well.

A similar aspect of responsiveness involves the representative's efforts to bring resources to the constituency. Governments spend money on roads, public buildings, schools, airports, dams, parks, and military equipment, among other things, and legislators work to ensure that a portion of these funds is spent in their constituencies. Their efforts can take a number of forms. When the language in legislation does not expressly direct funds to a specific project, it is up to the bureaucrats charged with administering the legislation to decide which towns, companies, and universities will receive government funds or contracts to produce research (on global warming), goods (tanks and airplanes), and services (computer maintenance) that the government requires. Another approach is to insert specific language into legislation that requires that particular projects in the constituency be funded by the agency.

These legislative provisions, called "earmarks" in the United States, became more controversial when, for example, in 2005 Senator Ted Stevens of Alaska tucked $230 million into an appropriations bill to build a bridge between Ketchikan, a city on the Alaskan mainland, and Gravina Island, a piece of real estate with a population of approximately fifty people. The so-called "bridge to nowhere" came to be viewed as an archetypal example of wasteful government spending and led to calls for reducing the number of earmarks and for stricter procedures governing their enactment. The work that legislators do in this connection will be more fully explored in chapter 4.

Political scientists refer to this sort of representational activity by the bulky term "allocational responsiveness," but the less attractive term "pork barrel" funding is more commonly used. Like constituent demands for individual services (which also has the less appealing name "errand running"), these activities conform to the requirements of the principal-agent model.[24] Requests for these allocations typically come from attentive citizens—local officeholders or leaders of constituency-based corporations and nonprofit organizations such as universities and hospitals—who will know and remember what their agent/representative was able to accomplish on these matters and will hold him accountable for his successes and failures.

Representatives report that they work diligently to meet these expectations. A record of effectiveness in securing funding for local projects and helping citizens with their problems can provide the representative with a degree of electoral security that in turn may increase his freedom to be "at odds" with his constituents on issues the meaning of which may be more ambiguous or less important to them than a new post office in the middle of town, a sizable government contract for the largest factory in the district, or help in getting a social security check to grandma. Representatives go to great lengths to take public credit for all government expenditures in their districts and they often design public policies with an eye toward increasing their opportunities to obtain these funds.[25]

ALTERNATIVE MODELS OF REPRESENTATION

Although the principal-agent model seems appropriate for understanding the service and allocational activities of representatives, it is less helpful for understanding the decisions that representatives make on major policy issues. In addition to its failure in the face of multiple principals, lack of information on the part of the principal, the difficulty in knowing the principals' views, and the uncertainty of accountability, the model also oversimplifies the relationship between representatives and their constituents.

For example, the principal-agent model assumes a one-way flow of information from the constituency to the representative. But empirical research on representation as well as common sense suggests that representatives play a significant role in *shaping the views of their constituents*. Richard Fenno's accounts of his travels with several members of the United States House of Representatives as they visited their congressional districts reveal the considerable effort that representatives make to educate their constituents by explaining to them what is going on in Washington.[26] On his visits home, for example, a representative from New Jersey, a state that depends upon rail transit, may tell his constituents that the administration is threatening to cut funds for Amtrak, and that such cuts would have a significant negative effect on the economy of the state and would cause great inconvenience and even hardship to many citizens. Such information might provoke constituents who had not previously paid much attention to Amtrak's funding problems to develop opinions on the issue. If and when their views are solicited by a pollster, they are likely to say that they are in favor of full funding for Amtrak. Rather than their views shaping the actions of the representative, in truth the representative's activities in the constituency and the information he has provided shaped the views of the constituents.

Advocates of what is called *anticipatory representation* build upon this educative function.[27] From this perspective, the actions of representatives are motivated less by the desire to respond to the wishes of the constituency and more by a desire to influence voters in future elections. Rather than construing what a representative does in the legislature as a response to constituency opinion, his efforts can be better interpreted as developing and articulating a set of positions for the next election. Although anticipatory representation shares with principal-agent theory an emphasis on the importance of the representative's connection with the views of his constituents, this approach, like the educative perspective, reverses the causal arrow in the relationship. Rather than the representative responding to constituency demands, the representative's efforts determine to a great extent the issues that the constituency will hear about. Legislators attempt to shape those opinions through a strategy of "crafted talk," by which they "track public opinion not to make policy but rather to determine how to craft their public presentations and win public support for the policies they and their supporters favor."[28] It is now quite common for campaigns to pretest the statements that their candidates will make with small focus groups to see how they will respond to particular phrases, ideas, or catchwords. The results of these tests help them to state their positions in terms that will appeal to the most voters and offend the fewest. Of course, experienced politicians may well be able to figure out how to do this without the aid of focus groups. No matter the means they use to "craft" their presentations, the result will be that the policy goals of the representative will shape the opinions of the constituents; in that case, what might appear to be the representative responding to constituency opinion is in reality constituency responsiveness to the representative's opinion.

A slightly different way of looking at the anticipatory approach is to suggest that rather than constituents having meaningful opinions on an issue at the time when the representative acts, they may have "potential preferences"[29] that will come to the fore after the policy is enacted and its effects are felt. Or these preferences may become manifest after the representative's opponent in the next election calls the constituency's attention to the policy in question and connects it with the incumbent's actions. The failure to anticipate the reaction of their constituents caused problems for some Republican legislators who voted for President Bush's Medicare Part D drug program in 2005, only to discover that many of their constituents were dissatisfied with the program's complexity and unpleasantly surprised by its cost. From this perspective, the concern that representatives have about constituency opinion—despite their nearly certain knowledge that most of their constituents knew nothing about the issue or the representative's position at the time the vote was cast—makes a great deal of sense. The key question that they ask themselves is not a prospective one—"What do my constituents want me to do?"—but rather a retrospective one—"How will my constituents react to what I have done?"

Such calculations set the stage for an election cycle during which legislators running for reelection as well as their opponents spend a great deal of time and money on speeches and advertisements designed to manipulate the views of the voters or, put more benignly, to educate them about what the representative is doing. In fact, there is some evidence that voters' opinions on specific issues derive more from their candidate preferences than the other way around. That is, voters may decide for non-policy-related reasons—the services that the representative has provided for them or for the constituency, his engaging personality, his appearance at a local event, or his partisan affiliation—that they prefer a particular candidate and then adopt that candidate's policy positions as their own.

More realistically, then, the relationship between representatives and constituents is one of *mutual communication*—that is, the flow of communication goes two ways, with representatives hearing from their constituents and constituents hearing from their representatives. Information from constituents enables the alert representative to categorize policies on the basis of how many voters know and care about the issue and how intensely they care, and to distinguish those issues about which his constituents may be educable from those issues about which the constituency seems to have clear, stable, and presumably immovable views. The representative in turn will craft his communications with his constituents in a manner that reinforces the positions on which they agree, that endeavors to shape opinions in those areas where constituency views are ambiguous or malleable, and that sells himself, his services, and his experience in an attempt to minimize the impact of the inevitable remaining policy disagreements.

Of course, misrepresentation is an aspect of the educative function and needs to be acknowledged. As U.S. representatives go home to their constituencies, their explanations for what they have done or what has occurred in Washington are often self-serving, misleading, and designed to deflect blame, as in "I wasn't able to do as you wished because the other party controls the agenda and would not let my bill out of committee," or "I opposed funding a program that would provide medical care for children because it would have led to government controlled socialized medicine." The point is that judgments and policy views of citizens as well as the votes they cast at the accountability moments that we call elections are certainly subject to manipulation by those who are being judged and held to account.

TRUST

How citizens perceive the personal characteristics of their representative may be a more important factor in determining how they evaluate his performance than the compatibility of their policy views with his actions and views. Some scholars suggest that citizens engage in *expressive voting*, defined as a voting decision that is determined primarily by the character, competency, and personality of the candidate.[30] Such an approach is given voice by those citizens who proudly proclaim that they vote "for the man, not the party"; it is given substance by those representatives who, though frequently "at odds" with the views of their constituents, are nonetheless reelected by voters who claim a level of personal affinity and trust toward them.

William Bianco defines the concept of trust in terms of retrospective evaluations. "Trust is said to exist when constituents evaluate (or are prepared to evaluate) their representative's vote favorably, regardless of whether they believe that the vote is consistent with their interests. . . . In contrast, trust is said to be absent under conditions where constituents issue (or are prepared to issue) a favorable evaluation only if the representative complies with their demands."[31] Trust may develop in a number of ways. It may be engendered by the representative's success in providing services and allocational benefits to constituents. Or it may come from a long history of personal connections that the representative has with his constituency, or it may be based on the fact that the representative is in harmony with the views of his constituents on those few issues that they feel most strongly about. Whatever the sources of trust, its existence and magnitude can provide the representative with leeway should he need to vote contrary to the views of those whom he represents.

For representation theory, the full import of the concept of trust is to reduce, though not eliminate, the role of voter self-interest in voting decisions and therefore in the representative relationship. Trust may not be entirely devoid of policy content; rather, knowledge of the representative's past positions on certain salient issues could well be a factor in the voters' assessment of the candidate's character and therefore on their level of trust in his ability to make the correct decisions, quite apart from his stance on current issues. The point is that the principal-agent model of representation and even the anticipatory representation model argue that the policy opinions of voters can alter or determine the actions of their representatives. In contrast, in expressive or, to use Jane Mansbridge's term, "gyroscopic," representation, the voter influences policy decisions through the selection of a representative with whom she feels comfortable, based on her understanding of the candidate's character and personality as well as the candidate's political position and values. Such a perspective can explain why a representative may be regularly returned to office even though on a number of issues his opinions and actions may vary from constituency opinion.[32]

DESCRIPTIVE REPRESENTATION

The idea of expressive representation also makes theoretical room for descriptive representation, a concept that emphasizes the shared demographic characteristics of the representative and the represented as a contributing factor to shared policy positions. Some argue that demographic congruence leads to more effective policy representation—that is, African-American voters will have their opinions and interests more accurately reflected by an African-American than by a white representative, and women will be better represented by females than by males. In ethnically divided nations, the parallel point is that major groups should be represented by members of that group in accordance with their numbers in the population. In India, this has meant that attention is paid to the equitable representation of Muslims in the parliament; and in Iraq that the three major groups in that country—Kurds, Sunnis, and Shiites—each have parliamentary representation that approximates their percentage of the population.

Although it is not obvious that ethnic groups can receive effective representation only from someone who is a member of that group, or that men cannot be effective representatives of the interests of women, it does seem clear that if trust, based on some combination of character, personality, competence, and policy views, is indeed a key aspect of the representative relationship, then the ability to connect with constituents on the basis of a shared demographic background and presumably some level of shared life experience can be an important factor. In nations where ethnic distinctions are potent political factors, a representative body whose membership generally reflects the divisions within the population can enhance the level of citizen trust not just in their representatives but in the political system and thereby reduce the likelihood of civic disorder.

Advocates of the point of view that representative bodies should faithfully reflect the demographic diversity of a nation have had to deal with a number of criticisms. First, they have been accused of essentialism, meaning that they seem to assume that all groups that one would wish to have represented are homogeneous in their views and interests. In reality, there is great heterogeneity within groups; not all women have the same interests or opinions on every issue, even those that are most relevant to them as women, such as the issue of reproductive freedom. Members of the same racial and ethnic group may have different views on particular issues, views that may be dictated more by their social class than by their shared demography.

On the other hand, Melissa Williams argues that although members of marginalized groups may well have different policy views, they share "a history of state-supported discrimination against the group," they experience "the continuance of contemporary patterns of social, economic, and political inequality along group lines," and they have "a shared memory of that discrimination." The common identity derived from these factors "creates an identifiable group interest which group members can claim to represent more effectively than nonmembers."[33] Jane Mansbridge adds that some group interests are "uncrystallized" in the sense that they have not been formulated as issues that are prominent on the political agenda. These uncrystallized interests are more likely to be recognized by a member of the group. She cites the example of former Senator Carol Moseley Braun of Illinois, at one time the only African-American member of the Senate, who objected to a routine amendment offered by Senator Jesse Helms of North Carolina renewing the design patent of the United Daughters of the Confederacy, a design that prominently featured the Confederate flag. Ultimately, Moseley Braun succeeded in gaining enough support to defeat the amendment. Mansbridge suggests that this issue was unlikely to have been recognized as significant by even the most progressive white senator, and indeed it was not so recognized until Moseley Braun raised it. Similarly, issues such as identifying rape in the context of marriage as a crime are more likely to be raised or recognized by a female than a male representative.[34]

Those who are skeptical about the need for descriptive representation also argue that what is most important is competent and effective representation, and the ability to be an effective representative may have less to do with the similarity between the representative and those whom he represents and more to do with political and governmental skills. Would women be better represented by an experienced male politician with an impeccable record of support for feminist policies and goals or by a woman with the same philosophical and political commitments but little in the way of political experience? Or would African-American voters in Massachusetts have been better served if Senator Ted Kennedy were replaced with an African-American senator, despite Senator Kennedy's forty years of experience in the Senate and his unflagging commitment to racial and social justice?

This objection misses the point that for marginalized groups such as women and people of color, some distrust is likely to exist between them and members of the dominant group, no matter how sympathetic the latter may be to the needs and concerns of the former. Williams argues that shared voice, trust, and memory between representatives and the members of marginalized groups provide substantively better and certainly more just representation. "Because it is their distinctive experience of policies and practices that sets marginalized groups apart from relatively privileged groups, legislative responsiveness to marginalized group concerns is most likely when that experience can be fully expressed and thoughtfully considered," something which is unlikely to take place if the representative is not a member of the marginalized group.[35] Not even the most feminist male has had to deal with an unwanted pregnancy, and no white person, no matter how committed he is to racial justice, has been subject to racial profiling. Richard Fenno concludes his discussion of what he saw and heard as he accompanied four African-American representatives on trips to their districts with the observation that in each case the representative "met with, talked to, and connected with ordinary black constituents in ways that no white Representative could have duplicated."[36]

The argument for descriptive representation implicitly accepts the point that a representative's behavior will not and cannot be completely controlled by her constituents and their opinions. There will be and should be deliberations and negotiations within the legislature, the outcome of which may well separate the representative from the opinions of those whom she descriptively represents. But precisely for that reason it is important that a member of the marginalized group serve as its representative. As she enters into the deliberative process, she does so based on the history and experiences that she shares with those whom she represents, and that fact diminishes the likelihood that the interests of the constituency will be betrayed in the final policy decisions.[37] Further, if members of such groups are to participate effectively in the deliberative process, more than token representation is required. Such groups need to be represented in numbers that approximate their presence in the population because representatives of disadvantaged groups "may need a critical mass for their own members to become willing to enunciate minority positions" as well as "to convince others—particularly members of dominant groups."[38]

A third objection to descriptive representation comes from those who argue that by constructing representative schemes that guarantee representation to particular demographic groups, a nation perpetuates group identity to the detriment of national identity. From this point of view, national unity (or political integration) requires that demographic differences among a nation's population be deemphasized in favor of a broader, more encompassing, national identity. In response, it can be said that a nation's identity changes as the demographics of its population change and that only by recognizing differences and seeking to incorporate such differences into a more fluid definition of national identity will true political integration be achieved.[39] National unity will be encouraged if all citizens trust their political system and view it as legitimate. The degree to which members of historically marginalized groups will confer legitimacy on their nation's political institutions is likely to rise as their representation in the councils of government increases.

But if a multiethnic society such as the United States were to commit to descriptive representation, it would face the challenge of deciding which groups to represent—just African-Americans, or Latinos, Asian-Americans, women, Irish-Americans, the poor—all groups that can make a plausible claim of past or current discrimination and marginalization. Leaving aside the formidable logistical challenges that would be involved in designing an electoral system that would generate the representation of multiple groups in an equitable manner, what rule should a society employ for deciding which groups deserve guaranteed representation? Finally, as examined in the next chapter, there may be no way to achieve descriptive representation that does not involve imposing some restrictions on voter choice or in some instances sorting voters by race or ethnicity. From the point of view of democratic theory, it can be argued that people should get to vote for whomever they wish, no matter what their race or gender, and that women who feel more comfortable with a particular male representative should get to vote for him. For those committed to a more just society where people are judged on their merits rather than on the basis of their skin color, gender, or ethnicity, sorting candidates and voters on the basis of those demographic characteristics seems instinctively to be a bad idea.

VIRTUAL REPRESENTATION

Groups also can be represented in the legislature, descriptively as well as substantively, by people whom they have not chosen. For example, in the United States Senate at this writing, there are three Latino senators: Robert Menendez of New Jersey, Ken Salazar of Colorado, and Mel Martinez of Florida. Each, whether they are conscious of it or not, speaks not just for the interests of their states but for the interests of Latinos around the nation. Each, for example, played an active role in the heated immigration debate during the 110th Congress and, although they took somewhat different positions on the specific issues, each spoke in their own way on behalf of Latinos nationally. Similarly, the single African-American in the Senate, Barack Obama of Illinois, is seen by many African-Americans throughout the country as their representative and not simply the representative of the people of Illinois. This category of representation cannot be accommodated within the principal-agent paradigm because the principals in question have not authorized the representative to act for them and they have no way to hold him accountable. Jane Mansbridge uses the term "surrogate representation" to refer to the representation of interests that are not formally part of one's constituency.[40] Edmund Burke referred to "virtual representation," by which he meant "a communion of interests and sympathy in feelings and desires between those who act in the name of any description of the people and the people in whose name they act" even though they are not chosen by them.[41] Although in these instances there is no electoral connection between the representative and the represented and therefore no mechanism of accountability, the fact that this sort of representation does take place provides a partial answer to the earlier question of how those who have voted for a losing candidate in their own constituency receive representation. Ideally, the argument goes, all citizens have someone in the legislature who represents their view on each issue, although not necessarily someone whom they have selected and can hold accountable.

REPRESENTATION AND DELIBERATION

Shifting the focus away from the notion of constituency control of the representative and toward the representative as an independent actor suggests a more complex set of interactions between representatives and those whom they represent than is implied by the simple principal-agent model. The representative role that emerges is more akin to that of an *entrepreneur* than to an agent. As an entrepreneur, the representative "sells" the services that he provides and his own personal qualities to his different, multiple constituencies. These services may consist of some combination of policy positions, help with individual problems, success in bringing resources to the constituency, or the ability to articulate the interests of the constituency to various audiences. The entrepreneur's appearances in the constituency and the way in which he markets himself to his constituents will do much to determine his success.[42] Most importantly, the successful entrepreneur will raise the level of trust that his constituents have in him. He will develop the equivalent of a "brand name" and therefore acquire the benefit of a doubt as citizens assess his behavior and review his explanations for why his actions or the actions of the legislature as a whole have deviated from their wishes or interests. A high level of trust relaxes the constraints that constituency opinion imposes on the activities of the representative and increases his autonomy. Of course, when trust is too high (think of the term "blind trust") and accountability becomes no more than a formality, then citizen control may diminish and the distance between the representative system and democratic principles will widen.

With that important caveat, however, thinking of the representative as both intimately involved with his constituents and loosely constrained by their opinions allows us to consider the role of deliberation in a legislature. The principal-agent model depicts each legislator as primarily interested in advancing the opinions and protecting the interests of his constituents and minimizes (or fails to deal with) the importance of legislators meeting collectively to deliberate on policy alternatives, to decide which might be more effective, and to identify the option that might be best for the nation as a whole. By turning the focus from the constituency to the representative, one endows the representative with the capacity to make independent decisions, to "sell" these decisions to his constituents, and to gain their support retrospectively rather than prospectively, as the principal-agent model would suggest. In selling these decisions, especially those that may be less popular, he draws on the reservoir of trust that he has accumulated based on the policy positions he has taken in the past, his extant record of action and activities on behalf of the constituency, and his reputation and character as it is perceived by those whom he represents.

As we move toward this perspective, we get closer to what a collective gathering of representatives, or a legislature, is all about. In John Stuart Mill's phrase, the legislature is the nation's "Congress of Opinions—an arena in which not only the general opinion of the nation but that of every section of it, and as far as possible of every eminent individual whom it contains, can produce itself in full light and challenge discussion; where every person in the country may count upon finding somebody who speaks his mind as well or better than he could speak it himself." And the purpose of such discussion is that "statesmen can assure themselves, far more certainly than by any other signs, what elements of opinion and power are growing, and what declining, are enabled to shape their measures with some regard not solely to present exigencies, but to tendencies in progress."[43]

Mill's conception of the role of the legislature turns us away from the *form* of representation and toward the *purposes* of representation. The first purpose of representation is to provide citizens with a voice in government, and the second is to make certain that all voices are heard during the policymaking process. In order to achieve those purposes, it is important to have an electoral system that will produce representation in the legislature for all politically relevant groups. Although their numbers need not necessarily be in exact proportion to their presence in the population, the representation should be sufficient in size to ensure that the particular point of view will be heard. Even if each individual representative does not always reflect the views of his constituents, the legislature as a whole may still reflect the collective views of the population. That is, the views of all citizens are represented by someone, if not by the representative in whose district they vote.[44]

Ideally, this means that policy decisions will be made only after all relevant interests are articulated. That process presumably results in better informed public policies, because all views have been taken into account, as well as policies that are responsive to the wishes and concerns of a larger number of people than would be the case without adequate representation. In addition, the policies adopted are likely to be viewed by larger publics as legitimate, not because they necessarily agree with the policy outcomes (all views are unlikely to be reflected in the final policy adopted) but because they believe that they, through their representatives, have been involved in the decision and that their views have been heard.

REPRESENTATION AS A SYSTEM

This discussion suggests the systemic context within which the relationship between the representative and the represented takes place. Although there are generic qualities to the representational relationship that are common to all political systems, the precise nature of the relationship in a specific nation is influenced by factors peculiar to that country. At the simplest level, it is clear that representation in a closed hegemonic one-party state such as China will take a different form than representation in a wide-open multiparty system such as Italy. The nature of the party system, not to mention the norms governing dissent, constrain Chinese representatives in ways that do not apply to members of the Italian Chamber of Deputies. Even in more open societies, representation will take different forms depending on the nature of the political party system, the type of electoral system that is used to select representatives, how the term constituency is understood, and the representational activities of organized interests that, like legislators and political parties, also seek to link citizens with government decision-making. What this means is that each nation has a *system of representation* not just composed of elected representatives and those who elect them but one that also includes other institutions and practices that, taken as a whole, define how its citizens are linked to their leaders.

Elections are the central institution for any representative system and a key factor that makes such systems a proxy for democratic politics. Presumably, the democratic aspect of representative government is ensured by the fact that those who make decisions have been selected by the people whom they are supposed to represent. Elections are the occasion for citizens to authorize a representative to act on their behalf and are also the primary mechanism for citizens to hold their representatives accountable for their actions. The threat that reelection may be denied is the key factor that encourages representatives to attend to the opinions and interests of those whom they represent.

There are several different electoral systems functioning in the modern world. As a first cut, however, these systems can be grouped into two broad categories. The first is the single-member district system in which one representative is elected to represent a geographically defined constituency. The representative is typically chosen in a "first past the post" process, which means that the candidate who receives the most votes (a plurality, not necessarily a majority) becomes the representative from that constituency. Australia uses an alternative vote process to ensure that the person elected has a majority rather than a plurality of the votes. Under that system, the voter lists a first and second choice on his or her ballot; if no candidate receives a majority of the votes, the candidate with the fewest votes is eliminated and that candidate's second choice votes are distributed to the other candidates. The process continues until one candidate receives a majority of the votes. France uses a two-ballot system, which means that if in a particular constituency no candidate receives a majority of the votes, a run-off election is held between the top two vote-getters on the first ballot.

The main alternative to single-member district systems is proportional representation. Under such arrangements, each constituency is represented by several members, the candidates run for election on party slates, and seats in the legislature are distributed to the political parties in proportion to the total number of votes that each receives. Variants of proportional representation provide the voter with an opportunity to indicate a preference for specific candidates on the party's list (usually called an "open list system") as opposed to the closed list system where the vote is cast for a party list and the order is determined by party leaders, with those candidates at the top of the list gaining the seats to which the party is entitled. There are several different mathematical formulae for translating votes into seat allocations for each party. Mixed systems also exist; Germans elect some of their representatives from single-member districts and others from a proportional representation list, with the latter compensating for any disproportionality produced by the single-member results.[45] In 1994, the Italians replaced their proportional representation system with a mixed system in which about 75 percent of the deputies were elected from single-member districts with the remainder elected under proportional representation, but in 2005 they returned to a closed list, proportional representation system.

The crucial point of distinction between single-member district and proportional representation systems is that in the former those who vote for candidates and parties that do not achieve a plurality are denied any representation from their district, but in the latter candidates from parties with smaller numbers of votes still have a chance to elect a representative. Exactly how many seats smaller parties can win depends on a number of factors, but the most important is the number of representatives per constituency (the larger the number, the more likely that smaller parties will be represented). Other factors include the specific mathematical formula used to allocate seats, the number of political parties contesting for seats, and the minimum threshold to receive seats. Nations with proportional representation systems usually establish a minimum percentage of the vote—say 5 percent; if a party's vote falls below that figure, they are not awarded seats.[46] Because proportional representation provides seats in the legislature to smaller political parties while single-member district systems generally shut out such parties, the former are more likely to reflect the ideological complexion and complexity of a nation than the latter.

Proportional representation systems are typically associated with strong political parties. Because the party decides which candidates will appear on its list and, in closed list systems, where exactly on the list each candidate will appear, the representative owes his election as much or perhaps more to the political party than he does to the voters. In this context, the representative may think of his constituency in partisan rather than geographical terms. Single-member district systems vary in regard to party strength. In the United States, legislative elections tend to be candidate-centered, and the role of the political party has been relatively weak. Although candidates do receive some financial support from their political parties and the voting choice of many voters is determined by party affiliation (their own and that of the candidate), still a substantial portion of the resources needed for election are raised by the candidate himself and a significant number of voters say that they vote for the person rather than the party. Additional evidence of the weakness of American political parties comes from the growing number of citizens (now a plurality) who classify themselves as independents rather than as adherents of one of the two major parties.

Britain and Canada, as well as most other nations influenced by the British Westminster model, use the single-member plurality system, but political parties tend to be stronger in these countries than they are in the United States, and a much larger percentage of the electorate views its vote in partisan terms. Nonetheless, because party activists at the constituency level often have a role in deciding who the party's nominee will be and candidates raise at least a portion of their campaign funds on their own, the personal ties that a representative is able to establish with his constituents explain at least some of the votes that he receives. However, representatives in such systems are accountable not just to their constituents (as is the case in the United States) but also to their party leaders, and as a result they have less freedom of action in regard to policy representation than their American counterparts enjoy. Although a member of the United States Congress is quite free to vote against his party leaders if he believes his constituency's interests require him to do so or if he simply disagrees with the leadership position on an issue, a member of the British Parliament faced with the same choice is very likely to opt to stay with his party. In his case, a persistent record of voting against the party can have significant and unpleasant political consequences up to and including expulsion from the party.

In general, the stronger the political party, the more it constrains the activities of the individual legislator and the more likely it is that the legislator will see his or her role as a deputy of the party rather than an agent of the constituency. However, single-member district systems also constrain the party to some extent because the representative is very much the face of the party in the constituency. The electoral success of the party in the district may rise or fall with the representative's success in meeting the expectations of the constituency, with the general perception that constituents have of the representative's diligence, and with the level of trust that his efforts have engendered.

Single-member district systems establish clear representational responsibilities. With one representative per constituency, there should be no question in the voter's mind about who his or her representative is, who to go to with problems, and who to hold accountable. Proportional representation systems create some degree of uncertainty because there are several representatives from the same constituency and voters may not be clear about exactly who their representative is. If four members are elected from a particular constituency, should constituents view all four as their representatives or just those of the party that they voted for in the past election? Or if the representatives come from different parts of the constituency, should people view the member who lives closest to them as their representative regardless of his party affiliation? One study of the travel records of members of the Colombian Senate, all of whom were elected at large, suggests that representatives may tacitly cooperate with one another by visiting their own bailiwick—defined by where they received the largest percentage of the vote—and avoiding the strongholds of their colleagues. This phenomenon may be attributed to the weak political party system in Colombia, and there might well be a different pattern in multimember systems characterized by stronger political parties.[47]

In addition to constraining the activities of representatives, the political party itself can be a representational agent. That is, citizens may view the party rather than the individual representative as the preferred mechanism for translating their opinions and interests into public policy. Strong political parties develop platforms incorporating positions on a variety of public issues. Voters who wish to have a say about the shape of public policy can accomplish that by voting for the political party that best reflects their views. And in political systems where a governing political party can assume complete responsibility for the conduct of government, the vote for the party may prove to be an extremely effective way for citizens to have their public policy views represented.

Party organizations can perform other representational roles for citizens. Local party leaders may be just as capable as elected representatives at playing the role of liaison between aggrieved constituents and government offices. A governing party may be just as effective in responding to the expectations of its supporters for the allocation of public funds as an individual legislator will be. And because the party has a long-term interest in competing for and gaining political power, they have strong and continuing incentives to be in touch with the interests and moods of the electorate. Thus, parties themselves provide representational links between citizens and their government, and the activities of legislators in this respect may best be conceived as part of a collective party effort rather than the efforts of individual representatives that are characteristic of the U.S. political system.

A final institutional component of the representational system is the interest group, which refers to an organization of like-minded citizens who use their collective resources to press for public policy that responds to the common interests of the group's members. The leaders of these groups can be seen as representatives of the interests and opinions of their members, and although these leaders may not have an official say in the design of public policy, they are often in a position to influence the views of those who do have an official say. How that influence is exerted has a great deal to do with the nature of the political party system. If political parties are the dominant force in a political system, interest groups and their members will direct their efforts at influencing party leaders both inside and outside the legislature. If, on the other hand, political parties are weak, then interest groups may seek to press their case directly with legislators and with government leaders.

SUMMARY

The principal-agent model of representation, with its bias toward constituency control of the representative, makes great sense if one wishes to argue that representative systems are proxies for democracy. Constituency control in that case becomes a surrogate means to achieve the goal of popular sovereignty in a system where the people do not rule directly. However, although the idea of constituency control seems realistic when the representative is responding to requests from individual constituents for assistance or when he is lobbying for the allocation of public resources to the constituency, it seems much less realistic when the discussion turns to decisions on public policy. Multiple and diverse constituents with ambiguous, typically uninformed and often contradictory opinions of various levels of

intensity make it difficult for the representative to know what his constituents want him to do. The need for the representative to distinguish among
the opinions of his constituents, their best interests, and the national interest makes the idea of constituency control even more problematic.

Rather than thinking strictly in terms of constituency control, our discussion has addressed views of representation that emphasize a more interac-
tive relationship between representatives and their constituents, one in
which the representative is certainly sensitive to the opinions and interests
of his constituents but also plays a role in shaping those opinions and identifying those interests. Rather than simply responding to the wishes of their
constituents, representatives work to anticipate how their constituents will
respond to what they do, and they tailor their communications with their
constituents in such a way as to evoke a favorable response. Representatives
also work diligently to establish a level of trust with their constituents, trust
that may be based on the services they perform, the resources they generate
for constituents, their personal history and relationships within their constituency, and in some instances the demographic characteristics that they
may share with those whom they represent. This level of trust provides the
representative with substantial latitude as he deliberates with his colleagues
on the various policy options before the legislature, hears and considers the
views of experts as well as advocates of different approaches to the problem,
enters into coalitions and agrees to compromises, and then decides what
the best course of action should be either for his constituents, for the
nation, or for both.

Finally, although the issue of representation raises a number of questions
that apply to representatives wherever they are, the representative relationship also varies across nations. Specifically, different electoral and party systems, as well as the various practices that organized interests adopt, provide
a context for the relationship between constituents and their representatives
and have a significant impact on the way in which representatives view and
enact their roles.

3

Constituencies and Interests

As examined in chapter 2, although the term "constituency" has a number of meanings for a representative, formally it refers to a defined territory whose resident voters select a person or persons to represent them in the councils of government. The association of constituency with geography implies a connection between interest and place. It assumes that the citizens of a particular constituency have a set of opinions and interests that derive at least in part from the place where they reside. The ability of the representative to identify these opinions and interests is affected by the constituency's physical size, the size of its population, and its demographic and economic heterogeneity. It will be relatively easy for a representative to determine the interests and opinions of a geographically small community with little in the way of economic, social, or ethnic diversity. But if a constituency includes a great deal of territory, a large number of people, a heterogeneous economy and class structure, or an ethnically or racially diverse population, it may be more difficult to discern its interests and opinions.

CONSTITUENCY SIZE

When representative institutions first emerged in England, constituencies were geographically small and relatively homogeneous. Most citizens lived in towns and villages that, given the primitive modes of transportation, were quite isolated from each other. Because few of the inhabitants of these communities were permitted to participate in the political process—the right to vote was restricted to a small number of well-off males—it was relatively easy for a representative to stay in touch and quite likely that he would know the views and interests of at least the politically active component of his constituency. In most instances, the representative viewed himself as an advocate for those community interests, as suggested by the practice of referring to members of Parliament (MP) as the member *from* Bristol or *from* Sheffield. These towns and villages continued to be the key political units of the British nation through the end of the nineteenth century, and even today MPs are still identified by the towns and cities of their constituency.

The situation in the American colonies prior to independence was similar. Although there were some relatively large cities in the colonial period—Philadelphia, New York, and Boston—most people lived in the small towns and sparsely populated counties that formed the basis for representation in the prerevolutionary colonial assemblies.[1] In 1700, the thirty members of the South Carolina colonial assembly each represented approximately twenty-one adult white males eligible to vote; by the eve of the Revolution, the size of the assembly had been expanded to fifty-one, with each member representing 192 white males. In New York State, the figure in 1700 was one legislator for every 168 eligible voters; by 1770, it was one legislator for every 1,065.[2]

Given the small constituencies and limited franchise at the time of the Revolution, a representative easily could consult with those whom he represented, determine their opinions and interests, and share with them information about the proceedings at the seat of government as well as his own views on current issues. But as constituencies grew in physical and demographic size, this process of consultation became more difficult. In the case of the national Congress established under the new Constitution, constituencies of necessity were larger than they were in the state assemblies. For example, in the congressional elections of 1792, 4,516 people voted to select Delaware's single member of the House of Representatives. Voter turnout in the eight congressional districts in the state of Pennsylvania ranged from a low of 1,517 to a high of 6,709.[3]

In Pennsylvania, as in the other states that elected more than one member of the House, counties were typically the building blocks of the congressional districts. Although there was little concern at the time about creating districts of equal population size, there were practical limits on the size of legislative institutions—that is, on how many members there would be in the House of Representatives or in the state assemblies. Therefore, as the population grew, the number of people living in each constituency would naturally increase, and counties, cities, and towns, often some distance apart, would need to be combined into one legislative district.

The greater the geographic breadth of a constituency, the more heterogeneous the district's population was likely to be and the less likely it would be that all members of the constituency would have the same political opinions and interests. For example, at the time of the first congressional elections, the city of Norfolk, Virginia, did not have enough people to constitute a congressional district, and more rural areas surrounding the city were included. Farmers living miles from Norfolk in counties such as Princess Anne and Isle of Wight would be unlikely to have the same interests as residents of one of the largest seaports in the new nation. Nonetheless, in the 3rd Congress (1793–94), all of these various areas were included in the 11th Congressional District of Virginia, with a population of more than 40,000 covering nearly 1,400 square miles—about the area of the state of Rhode Island.[4]

Size, in other words, eroded the connection between territory and interest and also made it more difficult for representatives to remain in contact with their constituents. And, of course, districts kept growing in size as the general population increased, as more people were enfranchised, and as the size of the legislature stabilized. By the end of the nineteenth century, the largest congressional district in Virginia had 187,467 people, and in Pennsylvania the figure was 309,986. Today in the United States, all districts within a state are required to have the same number of people. Although some interstate variation exists, the average population of a congressional district today is almost 700,000 people. In 1929, Congress capped the size of the House of Representatives at 435, so the number of people in each district is certain to rise each year as the population of the nation increases.

Although there is little variation in district population, the geographic size of districts varies significantly. For example, the 2nd District in California, represented in the 110th Congress by Wally Herger, extends over 21,758 square miles of northern California—about the same landmass as Massachusetts, Vermont, Connecticut, and Rhode Island combined. In contrast, the 33rd District, represented in 2007–2008 by Diane Watson, contains the same number of people as the 2nd District in an area of forty-eight square miles located in the heart of Los Angeles. Representative Herger certainly faces a more daunting task as he attempts to keep in touch with his constituents than Representative Watson faces.

Among the American state legislatures, although all districts within the same state need to have the same number of people, constituency size varies greatly because each state has a different number of seats in its legislature. Thus, according to the 2000 census, the 40 members of the California State Senate each represent nearly 850,000 citizens. The 150 members of the Vermont House of Representatives each represent around 4,100 voters, while the 400 members of the New Hampshire House represent about 3,100 voters each.[5]

THE U.S. SENATE

In the case of the United States Senate, the number of members is determined by the constitutional provision allocating two senators for each state

no matter what the population of the state might be. The Senate membership expands only when a new state enters the Union. The decision of the
Constitutional Convention to have each state equally represented in the
Senate was necessary if the new Constitution was to gain the support of
small as well as large states. That story is a familiar one: small states were
concerned that their influence in the new national government would be
limited and their interests and views ignored if the number of legislators to
which each state was entitled was determined solely by population. That
would be the case in the proposed House of Representatives, where population would determine representation and the larger states would dominate.
The price for gaining the agreement of smaller states to the Constitution
was a second chamber, the Senate, in which all states would be represented
equally. That body also would have some additional powers, including the
right to approve presidential appointees to administrative and judicial positions and the power to ratify treaties negotiated by the president.

The implication that senators were supposed to represent the interests of
their state is further suggested by the fact that the original constitutional
plan called for senators to be selected by their state legislatures rather than
by the voters of the state. As such, they could be seen as representatives of
the political leadership of each state rather than representatives of the people of the state. Members of the Continental Congress of Revolutionary
times and the Congress under the Articles of Confederation also were
thought of as representatives of the leadership of their states. The selection
process acknowledged the importance of the state assemblies during the
colonial period and reflected the idea that the states and the interests of
their leaders were the true constitutive elements of the new national government more so than "we the people of the United States." And because
the new Constitution proposed to remove significant powers from the state
legislatures, particularly economic powers in regard to contracts, currency,
commerce, and taxation, and place these in the hands of the new federal
government, it was important to reassure the states that there would be
one chamber of the national legislature where their interests would be
protected.

The decision to represent the states in the Senate also reflected a perceived congruence between geography and interest. Great variation across
the states in their laws, customs, and practices resulted from the substantial
autonomy that each of the former colonies enjoyed under the Articles of
Confederation. Economic interests differed according to geography—
tobacco growing in Virginia and North Carolina, shipping in Massachusetts
and South Carolina, a slave-based plantation economy in the South, and
so forth. In the beginning, then, representing states could be considered
equivalent to representing genuine political and policy interests, especially

in an environment with great uncertainty about the extent to which the newly created federal government would respect states' rights.

Today, suspicion of the national government and a desire to protect states' rights and interests persists, and the Senate continues as the nation's institutional commitment to a federal structure. But senators are now directly elected by the people, and many states are so large in population and so economically and demographically diverse that the idea of a community of interest uniting all citizens of a state is tenuous. Although one could perhaps point to the health of the agricultural sector of the economy as a uniting factor for all people living in South Dakota or Iowa, in most other policy areas in these states it is difficult to make such a leap. Massachusetts at the end of the eighteenth century, with a population of just over 375,000, might well have had a set of political interests shared by all or most of its citizens; discovering such a shared interest today would be unrealistic for a state with a population of nearly 6.4 million. Needless to say, a shared state-based interest among the 36 million Californians represented by Senators Boxer and Feinstein is almost unimaginable. Nonetheless, senators today continue to say both in the Congress and on the stump that they serve as advocates for the interests of their home state and as their state's defender against encroachments from other states or the national government. As will be analyzed in chapter 4, this is most readily apparent in the steps that senators take to ensure that their states receive a fair share (and often more than what is fair) of the funds that the national government spends.

DEMOCRATIZATION

As noted, many of the Founders were unenthusiastic about democratic practices, and the system they designed kept the people at some distance from the government. They did not fully anticipate the process of democratization of the electorate and of the electoral processes that took place during the nineteenth and twentieth centuries. Early in the nineteenth century, state legislatures began to eliminate property qualifications for voting, and by 1832 most of the states had committed to suffrage for all white males. Women's suffrage followed, in some states by the middle of the nineteenth century, and then as a nationwide right with the passage of the Nineteenth Amendment in 1920. The Fifteenth Amendment to the Constitution, ratified in 1870, formally extended the franchise to African-Americans, but their full right to vote, particularly in the South, did not become a reality until nearly a century later with the passage of the Voting Rights Act of 1965. It was also during the mid-twentieth century that practices such as the poll tax and unfairly administered literacy tests were discarded, opening the franchise not just to African-Americans but to poor whites and new immigrant populations that had previously been discouraged from voting.

Institutionally, several steps toward democratization that the Founders did not anticipate took place. Beginning in the first half of the nineteenth century, state legislatures gave up their right to select the members of the Electoral College that would select the president and instituted direct election of the electors. At about the same time, the political parties organized slates of electors pledged to vote for the party's candidate, thereby creating the functional equivalent of the direct election of the president that exists today. Late in the nineteenth century, state legislators also began to abandon their right to select members of the United States Senate, moving first to the election of slates of state legislators pledged to vote for particular Senate candidates and then to direct election, which was formalized in the Seventeenth Amendment to the Constitution ratified in 1913.

In sum, the original sense of a constituency composed of a small number of active citizens bound together by a common residence and a common set of interests collapsed under the weight of population increases, a dramatic expansion of the franchise, and therefore much larger and more diverse constituencies in terms of both population size and area. Nowhere was this more apparent than in the Senate. Whereas under the original constitutional design senators represented and presumably would stay in touch with a small number of state legislators, they now have their entire state populations as their constituencies.

ONE PERSON, ONE VOTE

Over the course of the nineteenth and twentieth centuries, as more citizens were afforded the right to vote and more offices were subject to direct election by citizens, representative systems became more democratic. However, large disparities in the population of constituencies raised the question of whether some people's votes counted more than others, thus violating the democratic principle of political equality. In Great Britain, the term "rotten borough" was used to refer to small-population constituencies that nonetheless retained representation—often through the intervention of an aristocratic patron whose family controlled both the seat and its occupant. In the first third of the nineteenth century, it was estimated that more than 140 of Parliament's 658 seats could be classified as rotten boroughs, with around fifty having fewer than fifty eligible voters.[6] The Reform Acts of 1832 and 1867 did away with the most egregious cases by extending voting rights to the middle class and urban working class and redistributing parliamentary seats to better reflect the population shifts that had taken place from rural areas to the cities.[7] Nonetheless, disparities in the size of British constituencies remain today.

In the United States, disparities in district populations became more pronounced in the late nineteenth and early twentieth centuries, also as a result of population growth and the decline in the number of people living in rural areas. The responsibility for drawing the lines of legislative districts both for seats in Congress and for seats in the state legislatures resided in the state legislatures themselves. Legislators from rural areas where population was decreasing (or at least not increasing to the degree that urban populations were increasing) were loath to enlarge districts or expand the size of the legislature so that more representatives could be allotted to the growing urban areas. As a result, the population of urban districts kept growing and the gap between the largest and smallest districts increased. In Illinois, for example, after the 1940 census congressional districts in the rural, southern part of the state had as few as 112,000 citizens while some Chicago districts included as many as 900,000 citizens.

In 1946, the Supreme Court was asked to consider the Illinois situation and the constitutionality of such wide disparities in district population. The plaintiffs from the state's larger urban districts claimed that their right to equal protection under the law was being denied because they were allotted fewer representatives than their numbers would suggest compared with their fellow citizens in the less populated rural districts. In the case of *Colegrove v. Green*,[8] the Court decided that these population disparities across legislative districts in the same state, while lamentable, did not constitute a violation of the equal protection clause of the Fourteenth Amendment. The remedy for the aggrieved citizens who had brought the suit, they said, was to convince the state legislature to rectify the situation. The Supreme Court seemed not to consider how unlikely it would be for legislators from overrepresented rural areas to voluntarily give up their privileged situation.

In 1963, however, the Supreme Court reconsidered and reversed the *Colegrove* decision and mandated that legislative districts within the same state be equal in population. In its landmark decision, *Baker v. Carr*,[9] dealing with the state legislature of Tennessee, the Court concluded that malapportionment in fact did constitute a violation of the equal protection clause of the Fourteenth Amendment. Then, a year later in the case of *Wesberry v. Sanders*,[10] the Court extended its mandate for legislative districts of equal size at the state legislative level to congressional districts within the same state. In subsequent decisions over the years, the Supreme Court strengthened the rule of equal populations in legislative districts, striking down districting schemes that in some cases had only fractional differences in constituency size. In doing so, the justices rejected the argument that historically recognized units such as counties or towns needed to have their own representatives, as they did in colonial times. They also rejected state arrangements that would have one chamber whose members came from districts of equal size and a second chamber in which seats would be distributed on a county basis, an arrangement that would be similar to the bicameral structure of the U.S. Congress. In the case of *Reynolds v. Sims*,[11] decided in 1964, the Court said that the Senate was a unique part of the original constitutional arrangement and that it set no precedent for state legislative bodies.

With the exception of the Senate, the Court's view was that representatives represented people, not places. Representing people required that the democratic principle of political equality be respected with districts of equal size. But representing people further attenuated the tie between the geographical district and constituency interests. This series of cases resulted in congressional and state legislative districts that incorporated many counties, in some instances over vast geographical expanses, or divided heavily populated counties and cities among several legislative districts.

This idea that legislators represent people, not places, and therefore each constituency needs to be equal in size is not universally shared. For example, the Canadian Supreme Court explicitly rejected the U.S. Supreme Court's egalitarian, one person, one vote formula, arguing that the purpose of the right to vote was to provide "effective representation," which meant that factors such as geography, community history and interests, and minority representation could be taken into consideration and could supersede numerical parity across districts. Although specific numerical guidelines were not established, the Canadian court endorsed (but did not really define) "relative parity"; variations in the size of constituencies (or "ridings," as they are called in Canada) of plus or minus 25 percent became the informal point where parity became a concern. The commissions responsible for demarcating ridings in Canada have preferred more equally sized districts, with variations among districts in most jurisdictions falling within the 10 percent or less category,[12] a figure that would not pass muster with the U.S. Supreme Court.

In the United Kingdom, the commissions in charge of "constituency redistributions" are supposed to strive for districts of equal size, but borough and county lines need to be respected as well and can be ignored only if absolutely necessary to avoid extreme disparities in district population. But there is a clear and primary commitment to the representation of places rather than citizens if these two criteria come into conflict.[13] This process produces constituencies within the same county that have some variation in population size and also some greater disparities across districts nationwide. For example, within the county of Berkshire, the latest report from the commission recommended eight constituencies, with the largest, Bracknell, having a population of 81,831 and the smallest, Maidenhead, having a population of 63,821, a variance in excess of 22 percent. On the other hand, the Isle of Wight has one constituency with 107,790 people, and Wirral South, in another part of the country, has a population of 56,665, a variance in excess of 47 percent.[14]

The situation in England is more typical of countries around the world than is the current American arrangement for the House of Representatives. In Chile, the Santiago and Valparaiso metropolitan areas together encompass 50 percent of the country's voting population but elect only 37 percent of the Chamber of Deputies. In Ecuador, the two largest districts hold 45 percent of the population but have only 23 percent of the seats in the Parliament.[15] In India, Article 81 of the Constitution indicates that the number of seats in Parliament allotted to each state "shall be divided into territorial constituencies in such manner that the ratio between the population of each constituency and the number of seats allotted to it is, so far as practicable, the same throughout the state." Originally, these allocations were to be made according to the results of the 1971 census, and a Delimitation Commission was established to mark the boundaries of each constituency. However, the commission is instructed that "Constituencies shall, as far as practicable, be geographically compact areas, and in delimiting them regard shall be had to physical features, existing boundaries of administrative units, facilities of communication and public convenience." Obviously, these instructions, along with the "so far as practicable" clause, allow significant deviations from the one person, one vote principle. Perhaps a desire not to reopen the issue explains why the demarcations established on the basis of the 1971 census are still in force despite the availability of more current census data.[16]

Political scientists David Samuels and Richard Snyder studied seventy-eight nations in the most comprehensive attempt to measure the extent to which the allocation of seats in national legislatures reflects the distribution of the nation's population.[17] Perfect apportionment, according to their measure, would be one in which, for example, a district that had 5 percent of the nation's population would have 5 percent of the seats in the legislature. Under such a measure, perfect apportionment occurs only in countries such as Israel and the Netherlands where there are no districts and all legislators are elected at large. Their measure of malapportionment in that case would be zero. The most malapportioned lower house in their study, Tanzania, has a score of .262, indicating that more than 26 percent of the seats in that chamber are allocated to areas that do not deserve the seats by virtue of their percentage of the population. In fifteen countries the scores were higher than 10 percent; in twenty-two they were between 5 and 10 percent; and in the remaining forty-one the figure was under 5 percent. The total picture, then, for lower houses reflects a general though not particularly egregious pattern of malapportionment.

The figure for the United States House of Representatives is 1.4 percent, which ranks it as the thirteenth most fairly apportioned lower house among the seventy-eight nations included in the study. This score is attributable almost entirely to the Supreme Court's one-man, one vote decision; the fact that the score is not lower is explained by the constitutional requirement that each state must have at least one representative in the House. The most sparsely populated states, such as Alaska and Wyoming, have one representative each but fewer voters statewide than exist in the average district in the more populous states. Nonetheless, the U.S. record is notable because, comparatively, single-member district systems are normally associated with the highest levels of malapportionment. Canada and the United Kingdom both had scores higher than the United States, and seven of the ten most malapportioned lower chambers in the Samuels-Snyder study used single-member district systems. Unlike in the United States, in most countries the judiciary has neither the power nor the status to alter systems of malapportionment, so it is left to the incumbent legislators, who benefit from the current arrangements, to make the decisions that would change it.

The U.S. Senate is a quite different story. Upper houses in general tend to be more malapportioned than lower houses because, as was the case with the United States, they are often created in federal systems to provide representation to the federating states in ways that recognize their autonomy and equality and balance the more population-based distributions that are characteristic of lower houses. The highest index number for the twenty-five upper houses included in the Samuels-Snyder study is 48.5 percent in Argentina; eleven of the fourteen most malapportioned upper houses, including Argentina, are in nations with federal systems. Of the twenty-five chambers, eleven score above 25 percent, ten below, and four have scores of zero because of their at-large election systems. The figure for the United States Senate is 36.4 percent, ranking it as the fifth most malapportioned upper house in the study. The reasons for that are clear. Each state, from the smallest to the largest, has two senators; on the basis of the 2000 census, 17.8 percent of the country's population live in the twenty-six smallest states, whose senators account for 52 percent of the senators as compared with the six senators (or 6 percent of the Senate) from California, Texas, and New York, the three largest states, which account for more than 26 percent of country's population.[18]

NONTERRITORIAL BASES
FOR REPRESENTATION

When representation is based on territory, as it almost always is, there are at least two dangers which to some extent are in tension with each other.

One is malapportionment; if a constituency with relatively few people has the same representation as a constituency with a larger population, the principle of political equality is violated. The second is that the process of creating constituencies of equal population may result in geographically large districts, meaning that territory is less likely to be coincidental with interests and opinions than it was when representative institutions first emerged.

To the extent therefore that nations strive for fair apportionment, they may well sacrifice communities of interest by joining areas together that have little in common. Malapportionment is sometimes justified (as it is in Canada) by the desire to represent entities such as communities or groups that have a common interest. In the United States, meeting the one person, one vote criterion often results in such geographically large and diverse constituencies that one would be hard pressed to discover a coherent constituency interest. If there are many instances in which territory and interest no longer coincide, then viewing territory as the basis of constituency must turn more on factors of tradition and convenience than on an argument for effective representation. In that case, would nongeographic alternatives to the definition of constituency reunite it with the concept of interest?

Although in a legal sense a representative's constituency may be a geographically defined territory, he also may view himself as a representative of a constituency that transcends geographic borders. Thus, legislators who favor the reproductive rights of women may think of the nation's entire pro-choice population as their constituency. Or a constituency may be based on demographic characteristics: African-American members of Congress may view African-Americans, no matter where they reside, as their constituents. This is what was referred to previously as virtual representation, which means that the representative serves as an advocate for a group that is not defined territorially and has not authorized him via election to be its representative. Rather, he has taken it upon himself to represent the interests of this nonterritorially defined group, many of whose members may welcome his efforts but to which he has no formal obligation and therefore no formal means to be held accountable.

There is also the possibility that representatives from territorially defined constituencies may have more formal, and to them more important, connections with or allegiances to nonconstituency groups. In one study, representatives from Belgium, Italy, and Switzerland were asked how they defined their constituency. About half of these deputies regarded "organized groups such as labor unions and political parties as their constituents" rather than the citizens living in the geographical area from which they were elected.[19] In ethnically divided states such as Belgium, Lebanon, or Iraq, legislators from one ethnic group may view that entire group as their constituency even if they have been elected by only a small territorial slice of that group.

Virtual representation is for the most part driven by a legislator's personal commitment to the interests of those on whose behalf he believes himself to be acting and speaking. But in some instances, he may have a more concrete reason for being an advocate for these nonconstituency-based interests. At one time in the United States, most of the money to finance congressional campaigns came from the local constituency. Today, however, legislators receive campaign money from interest groups and individual donors nationwide based, one would suppose, at least in part on a policy or interest affinity between donor and candidate. National political parties also receive campaign contributions from across the country that they channel to their congressional candidates. Campaign finance practices are examined in more detail in chapter 6. The point here is that representatives quite understandably think of their donors and the interests of these donors, no matter where they might be located, as part of their constituency. More generally, thinking of the constituency only in geographic terms will miss this as well as other aspects of the representational relationship.

There have been and still are examples of nonterritorially based constituencies with which a representative does have a formal relationship and can be held to account. The Estates General that existed in France prior to the Revolution represented the nobles, the clergy, and the bourgeois in separate bodies on the assumption that each of these classes had different political interests. Similar forms of "interest" representation existed in other European countries during the eighteenth and nineteenth centuries.[20] More recently, the Yugoslav Parliament following World War II contained several "second" chambers representing various sectors of the society, including the Economic Chamber, the Educational-Cultural Chamber, and the Socio-Health Chamber.[21] In India, special seats are reserved for members of the lower castes, and representatives who hold these seats are accountable to members of the caste, no matter where they may live.

Another approach to reserving legislative seats for particular ethnic groups is to require that voters register by ethnicity. This was the system used in Cyprus to guarantee an appropriate number of seats to the minority Turkish population. The problem with this approach is to decide in a multiethnic society exactly which groups will be guaranteed representation and how to determine to which ethnic group each voter should be assigned. In many countries there will be understandable resistance to any legislation that requires people to identify themselves with a demographic group as a prerequisite for participating in the election process, either as a candidate or a voter. In New Zealand, ethnic Maoris had the option to register on a Maori roll and to vote only for a Maori representative or to retain their registration on the general electoral rolls. In Lebanon during the 1970s, seats in multimember, multiethnic districts were reserved for members of different ethnic groups. Although voters did not have to register by ethnicity, their voting choices were constrained so that they would need to vote for a certain number of Maronites, Druze, and Shias.[22]

All of this suggests that in order to reunite the concept of constituency with the concept of interest, there are instances in which demography rather than geography should be the basis for defining constituency. In various countries, demographic groups defined on the basis of gender, race, religion, and ethnicity have argued that if their representative institutions are to be responsive to their interests, members of their group must have a presence in the legislature. Proponents of "descriptive representation" go a step further, arguing that the membership of the legislature must accurately reflect the diversity of the nation's population. From that perspective, women should have equal representation with men, and the relevant racial, religious, and ethnic groups should be represented in proportion to their presence in the population. Such a definition of "constituency" implies that the constituents of these representatives are members of that demographic group no matter where they happen to reside.

GENDER AND RACE

Nations vary significantly in their interest in and success at achieving some level of descriptive representation. Although women comprise about 50 percent of every nation's population and although the number of women in national legislatures has increased in recent years, representative bodies are still largely male-dominated. As of November 2006, only 17 percent of the seats in national legislatures the world over were held by women. In the Scandinavian countries of Europe, the figure was 40.8 percent, and in Arab nations, the figure was 8.5 percent.[23]

In the case of the United States Congress, while neither the House nor (especially) the Senate reflects the demographic diversity of the American population, significant movement in that direction has occurred, with the number of women in the House tripling over a twenty-year period and the number of African-Americans and Latinos nearly doubling (see table 3.1). Still, women comprise less than 20 percent of the United States House of Representatives and only 16 percent of the Senate.

Undoubtedly, the failure of most legislatures to reflect the demographic diversity of their nations is at least in part the result of discrimination, stereotyping, and economic inequities, but it is also important to note the significant challenges to designing an electoral system that will guarantee demographic representation. Assuming that all members of a particular demographic group wish to be represented by someone who is "like" them

Table 3.1.   **Demographic Representation in the U.S. Congress**

	Women		African-Americans		Latinos	
	House	*Senate*	*House*	*Senate*	*House*	*Senate*
2007	74	16	42	1	27	3
1997	51	9	37	1	17	0
1987	23	2	22	0	11	0

(a questionable assumption, as the discussion in chapter 2 suggested), single-member district electoral systems will generate representation for that group only if their residences are geographically concentrated so that they can dominate the voting in the district. Drawing a district in New York City's Harlem that will elect an African-American to Congress is not at all difficult. Similarly, in Belgium the key ethnic division is between the Flemish population that speaks Dutch and the French-speaking Walloons. Because these populations live in geographically distinct areas, constituencies are drawn to provide five districts for each language group and one district for the capital, Brussels, which is officially bilingual. Except for Brussels, Francophone parties compete against each other in the Walloon districts and Flemish parties compete against each other in Flanders. Only in Brussels do voters have a choice between Francophone and Flemish parties. This system is reinforced by separate parliaments in the two language regions that attend to local and regional issues.[24]

But if members of a group are evenly dispersed across a state or a nation, it is very difficult to draw districts in which they constitute a dominant majority. Because the populations of most legislative districts are divided equally between men and women, single-member districts are not effective at enhancing the representation of females in the legislature. Similarly, there can be no districts dominated by members of scheduled castes in India and no districts dominated by non-Catholics in Ireland. One reason why there is about the same percentage of black members of the United States House of Representatives as there are black citizens is because the unfortunate reality of racially segregated housing patterns has ensured that black voters, with certain exceptions, are geographically concentrated. Representation for Asian-Americans is more difficult to achieve because members of that community tend to be more geographically dispersed, a result of fewer restraints on their residential choices.

MAJORITY-MINORITY DISTRICTING
IN THE UNITED STATES

The most visible example in the United States of an attempt to square single-member district systems with the representation of demographic groups arises in regard to African-American and Latino representation in the House of Representatives and in state legislatures. Efforts to provide these groups with the opportunity to elect "one of their own" to Congress have involved the creation of districts where the targeted demographic group accounts for a majority of the voters. This race-conscious approach to designing legislative districts has engendered a high level of ethical and legal controversy.

This issue first arose when Congress passed the Voting Rights Act of 1965, a landmark piece of legislation aimed at dismantling the barriers to political participation by African-Americans that were erected in most southern states in the years after the Civil War and persisted nearly a century later. In addition to reaffirming the right to vote and doing away with various formal and informal practices that had been used to suppress voting by African-Americans, the act required states that had a history of restricting access to the polls to clear any changes in electoral laws with the Department of Justice so that it could be determined if those changes would have the effect of discouraging the participation of African-Americans. When the Voting Rights Act was amended in 1982, Congress included a provision that indicated that the extent to which members of a protected class (e.g., African-Americans, Latinos) were elected to office was a factor that could be considered by the Department of Justice as it determined whether or not the electoral process was truly open to all.

Although the 1982 amendments specifically disavowed proportional representation as a goal—that is, a state would not be required to have the same percentage of African-American legislators as it had African-American voters—the provision allowing Justice to consider the number of members of the protected class that were elected was taken as an invitation and by some as a mandate to design legislative districts that would increase the likelihood of minority electoral success. In that way, the specified minorities would have representation that would begin to approximate their numbers in the population. This could be accomplished if, utilizing detailed census data, the district boundaries were drawn to create "majority-minority" districts (e.g., a district in which African-Americans constituted a majority of the citizens); in that case, the voters in that district were almost certain to elect an African-American to Congress.

Those charged with drawing state and federal legislative district boundaries decided that the creation of these majority-minority districts was the best and easiest way for their maps to pass the scrutiny of the Justice Department or the federal courts. Thus, as a result of the redistricting that occurred in 1992, the number of majority-minority districts increased significantly, and the number of African-Americans and Latinos elected to the House and to state legislatures increased as well. Although there were many instances in which majority-minority districts could be created easily, given the residential patterns of the groups in question, there also were a number of regions in which doing so required the creation of oddly-shaped congressional districts, the boundaries of which could be explained only by the desire to combine dispersed areas where minority voters lived. The odd shape was mandated by the congressionally imposed requirement that districts be "compact and contiguous." Although it was difficult to define "compact" with any precision, the meaning of "contiguous" was clear: one needed to be able to travel, at least on a map, from one part of the district to any other part of the district without crossing into another district.

One example of what this process can produce is the 4th Congressional District in Illinois, designed to provide representation for Chicago's Latino community. The problem facing the designers of the district was that there were two large concentrations of Latino voters in Chicago—on the near Northwest Side of the city and in parts of the South Side. In between was the predominantly African-American West Side. The solution was the district shown in figure 3.1, a district shaped like the letter "c" with a thin piece (actually the width of an interstate highway) connecting the northern part of the district with the southern part in order to make the district "contiguous."

A similar challenge confronted the legislators in North Carolina as they attempted to design a second African-American district in their state. One district had been easily constructed in the eastern part of the state, an area with a high concentration of African-American citizens. But because several other African-American communities were located near geographically dispersed large cities such as Durham, Greensboro, Winston-Salem, and Charlotte, a long thin district, shown in figure 3.2, was created that connected and incorporated African-American sections of these cities.

This district, the North Carolina 12th, has been the subject of numerous legal challenges, with opponents arguing that the only explanation for its shape and length was the desire to group voters on the basis of race. The U.S. Supreme Court has issued a number of decisions on these matters, weighing on the one hand the language and intent of the Voting Rights Act and its amendments, which encourage the creation of majority-minority districts and, on the other, the equal protection clause of the Fourteenth Amendment, which suggests that allocating citizens to legislative districts based on race, which is essentially what happens when majority-minority districts are created, is unconstitutional. As Justice Sandra Day O'Connor, writing for the majority in the case of *Shaw v. Reno*, said, such districting plans bear "an uncomfortable resemblance to political apartheid. It reinforces the perception that members of the same racial group . . . think alike, share the same political interests, and will prefer the same candidates at the polls."[25]

In contrast, the Supreme Court has refused to take a role when districts shaped almost as oddly as the North Carolina 12th were created for partisan reasons. Gerrymandering—the term for drawing a district so that one

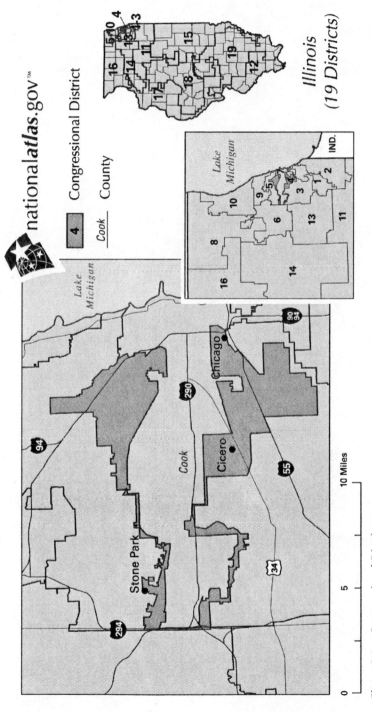

Figure 3.1. Congressional District 4

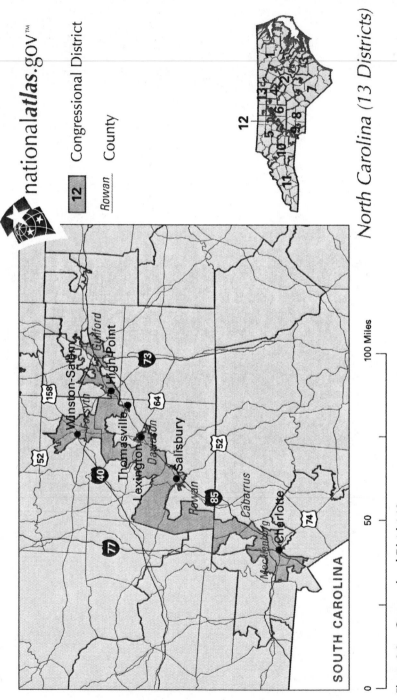

12 Congressional District

Rowan County

North Carolina (13 Districts)

Figure 3.2.   Congressional District 12

party or the other would be advantaged—is a practice as old as the Republic. As noted earlier, all the Supreme Court has insisted upon is that the number of people in each district within a state be equal. When presented with instances where equally populated but oddly shaped legislative districts have been created so that one party benefits at the expense of the other, the Court has not raised any questions, viewing the issue as a political rather than a legal one. Although in the 1986 case of *Davis v. Bandemer*[26] the Court seemed to indicate that partisan gerrymandering might conceivably raise issues that the justices would need to consider, at this writing the Court has not found a case that would justify its intervention.

Interestingly, the justices' reluctance to interfere with partisan gerrymandering has provided it with a way to accept racial gerrymandering, because the creation of majority-minority districts, especially for African-Americans, has been as much a partisan as a racial issue. For the last seventy years African-Americans have exhibited a consistent pattern of Democratic voting habits. By the end of the twentieth century, they were the most solidly Democratic voting group, regularly casting upwards of 90 percent of their votes for Democratic candidates. Because of this, the creation of majority-minority districts in the South was, in many instances, the product of a tacit agreement between southern Republicans and southern blacks. By placing large numbers of African-Americans into majority-minority districts (the districting term of art here is "packing"), the Democratic percentage of the vote in the districts from which African-Americans were removed was diminished and the chances for a Republican victory in those districts therefore increased. At the same time, the majority-minority districts reliably elected black Democratic legislators, thus satisfying the representational demands of African-Americans as well as the concerns of the Department of Justice. The losers in these arrangements were white Democratic legislators who, because there were fewer black Democratic voters in their districts, began to lose elections to conservative Republicans whose views were more congruent with the majority of the white voters left in these districts.[27] Given these facts, what might be viewed as racial gerrymandering could just as reasonably be viewed as partisan gerrymandering, and that allowed the Supreme Court to be more receptive to majority-minority districts as long as it could be shown that race correlates with political behavior and that "racial considerations did not predominate" in the drawing of the district boundaries.[28]

The point of this discussion is not to wade into the complexities of American election law or to parse the Supreme Court decisions that have interpreted these laws and their constitutionality, but rather to demonstrate that the process of identifying the piece of geography that will constitute a constituency is contested partisan terrain and, at least in the United States, contested legal terrain. It is extraordinarily difficult for a nation with an electoral system committed to single-member districts of equal population to provide any level of descriptive representation to marginalized racial or ethnic groups, sometimes even when those groups are concentrated in the same area (they may be too small in number to constitute a majority) and especially when the members of these groups are dispersed over a larger area. However, if a nation is not committed to districts of equal population size, then achieving minority representation may be easier. In Canada, the judicial idea of "effective representation" as a guideline for the drawing of riding boundaries made specific accommodation for minority representation. Thus, districts much smaller in population than the average were created in New Brunswick to accommodate Acadian and African-Canadian communities with long historical roots in the province.[29] If the one person, one vote principle did not govern legislative districts in the United States, constituencies could more easily be defined to represent historically important groups of varying sizes. Of course, the price for such descriptive representation would be the erosion of the democratic principle of equal representation.

PROPORTIONAL REPRESENTATION

Advocates of the point of view that legislatures should reflect the demographic makeup of the nation usually have been proponents of proportional representation electoral systems. John Stuart Mill argued for the Hare system of proportional representation as "among the greatest improvements yet made in the theory and practice of government" because it "secures a representation, in proportion to numbers, of every division of the electoral body" including "every minority in the whole nation consisting of a sufficiently large number to be, on principles of equal justice, entitled to a representative."[30]

Although Mill's concern was with political minorities, his reasoning also was applicable to demographic minorities. It is well established that western systems that use proportional representation tend to have higher percentages of women in parliament than nations that use single-member district systems.[31] In Germany, which elects some legislators from single-member districts and some through proportional representation, many more women are elected through the proportional process than from the districts. And in Australia and Japan, where members of the lower house are elected from single-member districts and members of the upper house via proportional representation, the percentage of women in the upper house is several times greater than in the lower house.[32]

In less developed countries, proportional representation is also an important factor in increasing the representation of women, but so, apparently, are other variables. One study of the representation of women in twenty-eight sub-Saharan African national parliaments finds that although proportional representation does increase the number of women in the legislature, an even more important variable is the presence of legal or party requirements reserving seats for women. For example, at the time of that research, Tanzania required that 17.5 percent of the seats in its legislature be held by women, and the ruling party in South Africa, the African National Congress, required that of its seats in the legislature, one-third be held by women.[33] In Taiwan, women are guaranteed a certain number of seats in each multimember constituency, with the result that women generally have about 10 percent of the seats in the legislature.[34] The problem with these guarantees is that minimum representation may turn into maximum representation; that is, women have a difficult time exceeding their number of guaranteed seats.

One limitation of proportional representation as a mechanism for achieving effective representation for demographic groups stems from the fact that proportional systems are typically associated with strong political parties that play the key role in nominating and electing candidates for office. Party leaders have the power to decide where a candidate will be placed on the party's electoral list and, especially in closed list systems, that decision can virtually determine the candidate's chances for election. A high position on the list ensures election, a low one guarantees defeat, and a position in the middle can make for a long election night. Because of this, party leaders have a primary claim on the loyalty of the representative that may well restrict the representative's capacity to act on behalf of the demographic group to which she belongs. The irony of the proportional representation system, then, may be that although it creates a more demographically representative legislature, its members may not have the necessary autonomy to be effective advocates for their demographic group.

Although some European countries have gone back and forth between single-member and proportional systems (e.g., France and Italy), there is little likelihood that nations such as the United States and the various Westminster countries that have used the single-member district system for centuries will move to proportional representation. Nor is there much chance that even more novel voting formats designed to enhance the representation of particular demographic groups will be implemented—systems such as reserved seats, separate electorates, cumulative voting,[35] or limited voting,[36] all of which potentially can achieve the goals of descriptive representation without sorting voters at least implicitly by race or creating odd looking district designs. But at least in the United States, there has been little receptivity to such reform discussions outside the halls of academe.

Rather than overhauling electoral systems, the political scientist Jane Mansbridge argues for institutionalizing "fluid forms of descriptive representation" that can be easily altered, given her view that the benefits of descriptive representation vary according to context. The creation of majority-minority districts is less fluid than decisions by political parties to nominate candidates that more fully represent the demographic characteristics of the population; even more fluid and in the long run more effective would be "enabling devices" such as public funding of nomination campaigns, establishing formal search committees within political parties to identify and nominate candidates from disadvantaged groups, and other affirmative actions that increase the pool of candidates from such groups.[37]

Issues of history and culture also account for some of the failures to create demographically representative legislatures. In many Muslim nations, an active political role for women is considered to be religiously inappropriate, and in some of these nations women are not even allowed to vote let alone hold seats in Parliament. Even in non-Muslim nations, gender stereotypes that classify politics as "men's work" and relegate women to caring for children and working in the home have disadvantaged women who have sought to become representatives. These factors taken together may be more important than a nation's electoral system in explaining the under-representation of women in the legislature.

Women are not the only demographic group that has been disadvantaged in seeking seats in legislatures. In most nations, members of newly arrived immigrant groups and other ethnic and racial minorities face an uphill battle. Despite the presence of approximately 3 million Muslims in the United States, it was not until 2006 that the first Muslim member of the United States House of Representatives, Keith Ellison of the Fifth District of Minnesota, was elected. Similarly, nonwhites from the Caribbean and from South Asia constitute about 10 percent of the population of the United Kingdom but hold only 15 (2.3 percent) of the 646 seats in the House of Commons. In France, where nonwhites constitute anywhere from 5–10 percent of the population, there are only ten nonwhite members of the National Assembly, all representing overseas constituencies.

DOES DESCRIPTIVE REPRESENTATION MAKE A SUBSTANTIVE DIFFERENCE?

The large number of academic and popular studies decrying the underrepresentation of women and other marginalized groups in legislatures would lead one to assume that descriptive representation makes a difference—that representatives who share the demographic characteristics of those whom they represent are more likely to be responsive to the opinions and interests of the represented than those who do not. Interestingly, the jury is still out on that issue.

In 2006, the primary for the Democratic nomination for the House of Representatives in a heavily African-American district in Memphis, Tennessee, was won by a white candidate, Steve Cohen, who had a distinguished record as an effective member of the Tennessee state legislature and a very strong record of support for the interests of African-Americans. Cohen won the primary with a plurality of the vote because he had some support in the African-American community based on his state legislative record and because several African-American candidates in the race divided the votes of those who would have preferred an African-American representative. There was significant discontent among black voters with the outcome of the primary. Many noted the effort that had gone into the creation of this majority-minority district and felt it was wrong to turn its representation over to a white person, no matter how supportive he might be of black issues. This sentiment led to a write-in campaign for Jake Ford, a person with no political experience but the cousin of the incumbent from that district, Harold Ford, who had vacated the seat to run for the Senate. Cohen ultimately won the race (and after his election joined the Black Caucus in the House) but many remained convinced that the district would be better represented by an African-American. At this writing, black leaders in Memphis are preparing to field a challenger to Cohen in the 2008 Democratic primary.

The question raised by this episode is whether it makes a difference if an African-American community is represented by an African-American. Some research indicates that by some measures whites are as capable of representing black interests as are African-Americans.[38] Evidence also indicates that political party is the most important variable in explaining voting behavior in Congress. To get a better sense of whether the race of the representative matters, the votes and legislative activities of Representative Cohen during his first nine months in office were compared with the votes and activities of Representative John Lewis, an African-American representative from Atlanta—like Memphis, a southern urban constituency. From the beginning of the 110th Congress in January, 2007, through September, 2007, Representatives Cohen and Lewis both participated on 891 recorded votes. They differed from each other on thirty-four occasions, or less than 4 percent of the time, mostly on budget and defense issues, none of which explicitly related to African-American interests.

It has been argued that the difference between African-American and white representatives may be one of policy emphasis rather than voting behavior. Judging not just by how these representatives vote but by the totality of their work in the legislature, the interests of the African-American community may be a higher priority to representatives of the same race. For example, one study found that blacks are "disproportionately represented on committees that address black interests, their speeches touch on racial issues more frequently than do those of whites, and a far greater proportion of the bills they sponsor and cosponsor had racial content."[39] Although their voting record might not differ from that of their white liberal colleagues, these African-American legislators took leadership roles on civil rights and economic issues of concern to the black community.[40]

In the 110th Congress, Representative Lewis served on the House Ways and Means Committee, chaired the Subcommittee on Oversight, and was a member of the Subcommittee on Income Security and Family Support. Representative Cohen served on the Judiciary Committee and the Transportation and Infrastructure Committee. On the former, he served on three subcommittees on the Constitution, including the Subcommittee on Civil Rights, and Civil Liberties. On the latter, he served on the Subcommittee on Economic Development, Public Buildings and Emergency Management, and the Subcommittee on Aviation, and Highways and Transit. Both members, in other words, had some committee assignments that addressed issues that were particularly relevant to their African-American constituents: income security and family support for Mr. Lewis and civil rights and civil liberties for Mr. Cohen.

Both representatives introduced and worked on legislation dealing with a variety of issues, but each also introduced legislation of symbolic importance to African-Americans. Among the bills and resolutions introduced by Representative Cohen was a resolution recognizing the contributions of the Negro baseball leagues and their players, a resolution apologizing for the enslavement and racial segregation of African-Americans, and two bills naming public buildings in the Memphis area after prominent African-Americans. Representative Lewis proposed a resolution encouraging Americans to observe the birthday of Dr. Martin Luther King, Jr. and a resolution calling for the investigation of several unsolved civil rights crimes. He introduced bills to require the Secretary of the Treasury to mint coins in commemoration of the passage of the Civil Rights Act of 1964 and to establish a congressional commission on the abolition of modern-day slavery.

In various floor speeches, Representative Cohen on several occasions spoke in support of the hate crimes bill, offered congratulations to the Southern Christian Leadership Conference on the occasion of its fiftieth anniversary, spoke on behalf of an amendment that would increase funding to historically black colleges, and called his colleagues' attention to Juneteenth, an important day in the African-American community commemorating the emancipation of slaves in Texas. For his part, Representative Lewis spoke on behalf of equal pay for women, noting that the adverse impact of pay discrimination was greater for African-American than white women; he urged the passage of legislation that would force the reopening of the notorious Emmett Till case, and spoke in favor of increased federal funding for kidney care, noting that African-Americans faced higher levels of kidney disease than whites.

As one looks then at the overall records of these two Democratic representatives from different southern cities, one would be hard pressed to find marked differences in the content of their legislative activities as they related to the interests of their African-American constituents. Their voting records were nearly identical, they both introduced resolutions and bills and spoke out on issues of symbol and substance to the African-American community, and they both had committee assignments that provided them with opportunities to address the needs of their constituents.

One must be careful about generalizing the Lewis-Cohen comparison. Cohen was not a typical white Democrat from the South; rather, he was a first-year Democrat elected almost by accident in a heavily African-American constituency. Most other white Democrats from the South represent districts with white majorities, and although they depend on African-American votes and will be sympathetic to many of the concerns of the African-American community, they tend to be less aggressive on these issues because they want to avoid offending the white voters whom they also need if they are to win. Cohen's reelection prospects have little to do with white voters, who account for only 30 percent of his district's population, and so his strenuous efforts to establish his credentials with his black constituents are to some extent atypical. Finally, Lewis was likely a more effective representative than Cohen, but because of his seniority rather than his race; Representative Lewis is now in his eleventh term in the House, is a subcommittee chair, and serves as Senior Chief Deputy Whip in the Democratic Party leadership.

Although the behavior of representatives may not differ significantly based on their race, from the perspective of the constituent, members of a marginalized group may feel more comfortable and at ease with the representative who is "like" them because they assume that he will have a better, more instinctive understanding of their opinions and interests than someone who is not a member of the group. Thus, African-American constituents consistently express higher levels of satisfaction with their representative in Washington when that representative is black, even when controlling for a variety of other factors such as the representative's political party.[41] This may have more to do with symbol and style than with substance. African-Americans take pride in the presence of black representatives in Congress. When African-American representatives speak to their black constituents, they invoke "a sense of group identity and a sense of group progress toward inclusion in American political life."[42]

African-Americans as well as whites are more likely to contact representatives belonging to the same race—white voters even more so than black voters. Some argue as well that such demographic representation also increases the integration and involvement of racial minorities in their political system.[43] In New Zealand, for example, members of the Maori minority who were represented by a Maori member of Parliament displayed higher levels of electoral participation and were more positive in their evaluations of governmental responsiveness than Maoris who were represented by a white.[44] On the other hand, there is no evidence that the presence of an African-American representative increases the level of political engagement among African-American citizens.[45]

The comparison of Representatives Lewis and Cohen notwithstanding, it may well be that as a general rule the concerns of the African-American community will get more consistent and sympathetic attention from an African-American than from a white representative, particularly if the district has a white majority. But, ironically, there is also some evidence that the creation of majority-minority districts, which has done so much to increase the number of African-American members in Congress, may have decreased the responsiveness of the institution as a whole to African-American concerns. As noted, in many instances these districts have been created by moving reliably Democratic African-American voters out of constituencies represented by white Democrats. This has meant a decrease in the Democratic vote in those districts, in many cases resulting in the defeat of moderate white Democrats and their replacement by much more conservative white Republicans. Because party affiliation explains much more of the variance in the voting behavior of representatives than race, the total effect may be to reduce the number of members of the Congress who are ideologically disposed to support the interests of African-Americans. And even if the Democrat in this "whiter" district is able to win reelection, because he will have fewer black constituents to whom he must account, he may have less of an electoral incentive to be responsive to the interests of African-American constituents.[46]

The findings on the behavior of female legislators are similar to the findings in regard to African-Americans. Attempts to identify systematic differences in policy positions and in voting behavior between male and female legislators generally have failed. For example, one study found that women in the United States Congress were more likely than their male colleagues to support abortion rights and policies promoting women's health, but on other issues, any distinction between male and female legislators was overwhelmed by factors such as party, constituency, and ideology.[47] Indeed, one recent study of the United States Congress concludes that, as is the case with race, a representative's party is a much more important variable than gender in explaining the behavior of the representative, and that the policy preferences of women are more accurately represented by the voting behavior of male Democrats than by female Republicans.[48] Cross-nationally, there is reason to believe that the total number of women in a parliament may be less important in advancing issues of importance to women than a strong governing party of the left that has a commitment to women's issues and the presence in the country of an active women's movement.[49]

When voting behavior and policy advocacy among female legislators in the United Kingdom, Australia, and South Africa were analyzed, the differences between males and females were found to be more rhetorical than real.[50] On the other hand, a study of the attitudes (though not the voting behavior) of members of five Nordic legislatures found that "women are more 'leftist' than men," that they are less favorably disposed toward pornography, and more favorably disposed toward policies such as shorter working days, prohibiting cars in the inner city, and steps that would increase the number of women in higher office. These distinctions persist across countries and even when party affiliation is controlled. But whether or not these attitudes have a policy impact in these party-dominated legislative bodies is an open question.

As was the case with African-American legislators, female legislators are distinguished from their male colleagues less by their voting behavior and more by their priorities and by how they view their responsibilities. Women are much more likely than their male counterparts to view the representation of women as important, they are more likely than males to express pride in what they have been able to accomplish on behalf of women and children, and their legislative priorities are more likely than those of men to focus on issues concerning women. As the legislative presence of women increases, so too does the level of energy that they invest in women's issues.[51] In Canada, both male and female MPs spoke and acted in support of women's issues in the House of Commons, but female legislators were more involved and concerned with those issues than their male counterparts.[52]

One small example of the effect that the presence of women in decision-making positions has on the shape of public policy comes from a study of the adoption of childcare coverage in Norwegian municipalities. As the level of female representation on town councils increased over a twenty-year period, so too did the expansion of childcare coverage.[53] In the same vein, a set of interviews with newly elected female Labor MPs in Great Britain indicated that they felt their presence in Parliament had raised the prominence of a feminist policy agenda in parliamentary debate and in select committees. At the constituency level, their presence facilitated the access of women and women's organizations to government and made it easier to voice the concerns of women.[54]

However, the evidence on whether women voters feel better about being represented by women is mixed. Women who are represented by women tend to offer more positive evaluations of their members of Congress, but one study concludes that after controlling for party congruence between the representative and the represented, there is little evidence of the symbolic effects that are often ascribed to the presence of women in Congress and that are found in the attitudes of African-American voters toward the presence of black representatives. Simply put, women who identified as Republicans did not feel better about being represented by a Democratic woman.[55]

On the other hand, in the Nordic countries, there seems to be a stronger connection between gender and policy congruence. The attitudes of male MPs are consistently closer to the attitudes of male citizens than are the attitudes of female MPs. The converse is also true: the attitudes of female MPs are more congruent than those of male MPs with the attitudes of female voters. However, in the case of women, there tends to be some variation across issues, with female representatives more closely reflecting the views of female voters on issues such as pornography and the length of the work day; this relationship was less pronounced on basic left-right issues dealing with the economy.[56]

To summarize, the data from the United States and other Western nations suggests that if one looks solely at the most visible form of legislative activity—how a representative votes—there is little payoff for demographic representation alone. Knowing the gender or race of a member will be much less helpful in predicting how that member will vote than knowing the member's political party affiliation. This is explained in part by the fact that representatives engage in a deliberative process within the legislature, a process that requires them to take into account and in some ways accommodate the views of others. On the other hand, it does seem clear that the gender and race of a member will help to explain the policy interests and priorities of the legislator. If on many, or perhaps most, issues, a representative must discern the attitudes and interests of his constituents with little in the way of substantive input from them, it is reasonable to believe that under those circumstances a member of a particular demographic group with the same life experiences will come to a more accurate assessment than someone who is not a member of that group. Therefore, as the number of female representatives or the number of African-American representatives increases, it is likely that the priorities of these demographic groups will be reflected in the issues that make it onto the institution's agenda and in the positions taken by political party leaders. In other words, the real payoff for demographic representation may be seen less in how members vote than in what they are voting on.

ETHNICITY, PARTY AND CLASS

These conclusions about the effect of descriptive representation may not apply to nations characterized by deep ethnic divisions of long historical lineage. There is little doubt that the stability of Cyprus, for example, depends in large measure on the appropriate representation of people of Turkish and Greek descent in the councils of government. For many years, Lebanon has been held together by a carefully constructed power-sharing arrangement among Christians, Druze, and Shiites. Although strong empirical data are not available, it nonetheless seems clear that in these nations, demographic representation does make a difference. But there will be situations in which ethnic tensions are so strong that they cannot be contained by representational arrangements. After the death of Tito, Yugoslavia, with much bloodshed, disintegrated into its ethnically based and, sadly, ethnically cleansed republics.

Another dimension of descriptive representation is the extent to which the legislature reflects the partisan and ideological divisions within the country. Single-member district systems, for example, tend to award the political party that wins the most votes nationwide a larger percentage of legislative seats than their percentage of the popular vote merits. They also provide losing parties with fewer seats than they deserve and marginalize the smallest parties, often depriving them of any representation in the legislature. Although proportional representation systems also exaggerate the number of seats that the party with the most votes receives, they do so to a lesser degree than single-member district systems while also providing minority parties with significant representation. In this way, legislatures selected via proportional representation are much more likely to reflect the ideological makeup of the nation than legislatures elected through single-member district arrangements.[57]

Finally, it can be argued that the most important aspect of a legislature's failure to reflect the demography of a nation lies in the socioeconomic status of its members. Legislatures the world over are composed of a nation's elite, defined in terms of income, education, and class. Those at the lower end of the socioeconomic scale are seldom represented by people who are "like" them in terms of class, with the only exception being the legislative assemblies in Marxist states. In the former Soviet Union, people who were defined as laborers typically accounted for 50 percent of the membership of the Supreme Soviet, and in Poland in the late 1960s, the figure was 32 percent. Of course, most of those people were party apparatchiks and no longer workers by the time that they got to be representatives. In Western democracies, the figure is more typically around 10 percent or less.[58] Early in the twentieth century, 88 percent of the Labor Party MPs in the United Kingdom had only an elementary school education; in the second half of the century, that figure was 16 percent. Laborers are now represented in the House of Commons by union leaders, not by active workers, and these MPs are most likely to be lawyers or teachers.[59]

The poor in the United States are represented by people who may have been raised in similar circumstances but are now successful professionals. Certainly such people should more readily understand the plight of the poor than those who have never known poverty, but just as certainly there are people raised in more privileged surroundings who are passionate and articulate advocates for the poor. However, neither alternative is equivalent to having the voice of the poor themselves heard directly. As Iris Young observed, "Policy issues are often defined by the assumptions and priorities of the privileged. Specific representation for oppressed groups interrupts this process, because it gives voice to the assumptions and priorities of other groups." Young goes on to say that differently positioned people in society have different "experiences, history, and social knowledge derived from that positioning" that, taken together, provide them with a unique social perspective from which they interpret political events and policy priorities.[60]

It is difficult to argue, of course, that less educated citizens should be public policymakers; one of the key arguments for representative rather than direct democracy is that policymaking is now so complex that it requires people who devote themselves full-time to that enterprise and who are equipped to understand the issues involved. Nonetheless, democratic theory relies on the equality of everyone's voice, and it is not uncommon for elites to underestimate the intelligence and abilities of mass publics. The common complaint of a society's disadvantaged is that election results do not make much difference to their lives, no matter who is elected. Certainly, the failure in most representative democracies to adequately address issues of economic inequality must be attributed at least in part to the fact that those making the policy either are not themselves experiencing any privations or have romanticized their long-past privations by suggesting that they succeeded by virtue of their own hard work with little or no help from the government. It is that perspective that formed the context for Karl Marx's famous remark that parliamentary elections provide the slaves with the periodic opportunity to select their masters.

4

Earmarks and Errands

Legislators around the world and at every level of government report that they devote substantial time to errand-running and pork-barrel activities on behalf of individuals or specific groups of constituents.[1] Most representatives view these efforts as important to their reelection, but many also believe that responding to these individual requests for assistance is simply a part of their job. Some representatives complain that such work is tedious and distracts them from what they view to be more important policymaking duties, but others report that they derive genuine satisfaction from being of service to individuals or helping to provide specific benefits to their constituency.

ERRANDS

The requests for assistance that representatives receive and the corresponding activities that these requests provoke can be grouped into two broad categories: assisting individual citizens with problems that they may be having with the government (often called "errand running" or "casework") and working to direct government funds or projects to the constituency (often called "pork barreling" or "project work.") Errand running, perhaps the more common of these two activities, places the representative in the role of ombudsman, or intermediary, between individual citizens and the government. In some instances, the representative is asked simply to provide information—how to apply for benefits from a government program, or how a newly approved set of regulations affects the constituent's business—but

more typical are requests that ask the representative to help resolve a problem that the constituent has encountered with the bureaucracy.

As the role of governments expanded during the twentieth century, the
decisions of government officials came to affect the lives of individuals in
countless ways. Government commitments to provide for the financial
security of its senior citizens, for the health care of its veterans, or for the
economic security of family farmers, to cite three examples, are implemented by large bureaucracies that must deal with a multitude of individual cases. Incidents of denial of service, lengthy and unexplained delays, or
the adverse application of the rules to a particular case, either through error,
malfeasance, or discretionary actions by administrators, are inevitable.
Because no formal means may exist to appeal such decisions, or because
the appeal process is too complex and difficult for ordinary people to use,
aggrieved citizens will seek out powerful people to intervene on their behalf
as they seek to benefit from government programs or as they attempt to
cope with the various laws and rules that regulate their behavior.

Members of the United States Congress report that a large portion of the
cases they deal with involve Social Security benefits, health services for veterans, and immigration issues. A broader range of topics are reported by
French deputies—social security and pensions, military and civilian post-
ings and promotions, help in securing government positions, and intervention in judicial matters.[2] These types of requests are not restricted to nations
that we ordinarily view as democratic. Even in more authoritarian political
systems where individual legislators have little if any say about public policy issues, there is evidence that citizens expect their representatives to deal
with similar issues and that the leaders of these nations support such efforts
on the part of legislators. Several studies of the former Soviet Union conducted during the 1950s and 1960s report that hearing and responding to
citizen grievances had become a major responsibility of members of the
Supreme Soviet, perhaps their only responsibility given their negligible role
compared with that of the Communist Party hierarchy in designing and
deciding upon public policy. The party leaders apparently viewed these
activities as important enough that they required bureaucrats to respond to
requests from deputies within a specified time period. In Singapore's one
party system, representatives were required to attend regular "meet the people" sessions and were reprimanded by party leaders if they failed to do so.[3]

In some countries, these requests for assistance go beyond what might be
considered the normal responsibilities of government officials to include
favors of a more personal nature. For example, in the Indian Parliament,
requests from constituents for help finding employment accounted for
the largest number of communications to legislators.[4] In Costa Rica, deputies have been asked to use their influence with the Ministry of Education
to help constituents get teaching positions and to help the children of

constituents get into better schools.[5] Members of the legislature in India and Thailand report that they are regularly asked to lend or give money to their constituents, and Thai legislators have been asked to intervene in court cases and to bail people out of jail.[6] Japanese legislators have even been asked to help arrange marriages.[7]

PORK

A second category of requests seeks the assistance of the representative in securing government funds for the constituency. Most of every nation's annual budget is spent within the country, and where the money is spent and for what purposes can have a significant effect on the economic condition of the locality. Infrastructure improvements such as roads, bridges, airports, dams, and sanitation systems can make a big difference to the quality of life in a community and, if financed from the national treasury, such projects will not place a strain on the budgets of local government entities. Money to subsidize mass transit, health facilities, public housing, or law enforcement can improve the quality of local services at no cost to local taxpayers. In poorer nations, or in poorer sections of richer nations, where local or private resources are limited, such projects can make a huge difference to the lives of citizens. Not surprisingly, then, representatives are expected to do all that they can to ensure that a portion of these funds (the more the better) finds its way to their constituencies.

WHY? THE ELECTORAL CONNECTION

The people who can deliver these services to individual constituents or to the constituency at large do not necessarily need to be legislators—party leaders, presidents, or even lobbyists and lawyers also can and sometimes do play this role—but the representative is an obvious choice. The services that he might provide come at no cost to the individual, and the fact that the representative was elected by the voters creates an implicit understanding that he should be open to and responsive toward these sorts of requests. In some instances, this understanding is more explicit, virtually a cultural imperative that has been called "clientelism." This concept, also referred to as a "patron-client relationship," depicts leaders and their supporters as linked by a set of mutual obligations. Clientelism originates in the feudal notion that those who lived on the land of the property owner owed him their loyalty, and he in turn was obligated to provide them with a fundamental level of support and protection. In a more modern and directly political sense, clients (constituents) provide something of value (votes) to their patrons (representatives), and the representative is expected to use the power that he has attained through the support of constituents to provide services in return.

The patron-client system reverses the principal-agent model. In the latter, authority is assumed to be in the hands of the constituent, who directs the representative to do his bidding; in the former, the patron is assumed to have the power. The clients do not have the option of withdrawing their support, but the patron's power carries with it a set of obligations to respond to the needs of his supporters. In Latin America, the Philippines, France, and Italy, such relationships are long-established components of the culture and explain a great deal about the relationship between the represented and the representative. In the United States, the relationship that existed in the late nineteenth and early twentieth centuries between political bosses and newly arrived immigrants in large urban areas such as Boston, Chicago, and New York also was a form of clientelism. Party leaders, rather than the government, provided a range of social services, including jobs, housing, and food, and in return the recipients of these services and their families were expected to provide political support to the party organization. The clientelism perspective suggests why in some instances the requests for assistance that representatives receive are more personal than political. The patron is viewed as someone who has a general responsibility for the welfare of his "clients," a responsibility that does not always recognize the distinction between the public and the private. One French deputy referred to the perception of the parliamentarian among rural voters as simply *"le pouvoir fait homme"*(power in human form).[8]

Even when not a cultural imperative, representatives believe that their efforts on behalf of their constituents will enable them to secure voters' favor and trust and therefore help them to stay in office. In the United States, members of Congress say that they work diligently to respond to these individual requests from their constituents because doing so is essential to reelection. In the Philippines, "being of service" and "doing personal favors" were cited by legislators as among the primary reasons for their electoral success, and a majority cited their ability to bring public works and other benefits to the district as the main reason why they won their previous election.[9] As one scholar has noted, service and pork-barrel activities are ways for representatives to make friends without making enemies, whereas a representative's positions on more general public policy issues can well make enemies for him, especially in heterogeneous constituencies where opinion on most issues is likely to be divided.[10]

WHY? PART OF THE JOB

Even if there is no direct electoral payoff, legislators still may view providing service to their constituents as an obligation of their office. This is the conclusion reached by one study that found that legislators in Norway and Sweden who, given the nature of their electoral systems and the strength of their political parties, were very unlikely to gain personal electoral benefits from constituency work; nonetheless they did it because they saw it as "simply a part of the job to assist persons who seek their help."[11] A significant number of Turkish deputies also described interceding with officials on behalf of their constituents as an important part of their job.[12] One group of French MPs used terms such as "social worker," "solicitor," "servant," and "valet" to describe the role in which they were cast by their constituents, and many indicated that these activities were more satisfying and rewarding than the limited policymaking role that their party leaders allowed them to play.[13]

When members of the United States House of Representatives were asked their views on the work that was expected of them, 87 percent mentioned being a "legislator" but 79 percent mentioned the role of "constituency servant." When members also were asked how they spent their time, 68 percent said that they spent a "great deal" of their time meeting with citizens in their states or districts. This was the only part of the job on which a majority of respondents said that they spent a "great deal" of time. The next highest "great deal" response was 48 percent for attending committee meetings.[14] In one study of Kenya, Korea, and Turkey, most MPs defined their role primarily in terms of activities directly related to the constituency such as obtaining government projects for the district and interceding with the bureaucracy to help constituents.[15] Several studies drawing on interviews with members of state legislatures in India found that representatives, when asked to describe their jobs, most frequently mentioned "intervening" on behalf of constituents, "helping" individual constituents, and otherwise "serving" constituents. In Mexico, two-thirds of a relatively small sample of representatives said that acting as an advocate for their constituents was either the first or second most important aspect of their jobs.[16]

The U.S. CONGRESS

Members of the United States House of Representatives who seek reelection are nearly always successful, with reelection rates generally 95 percent or higher. For these representatives as well as their Senate colleagues, it is an article of faith that dealing with constituent requests in a timely, effective, and respectful manner and seeing to it that one's constituency receives federal dollars in support of local programs and projects is a necessary and often sufficient requirement for reelection. Although, as we shall see, the empirical data to support the connection between constituency service and reelection is mixed, at a minimum doing these sorts of things well builds trust between the representative and his constituents and, as discussed in chapter 2, trust can help the representative overcome the electoral consequences of actions that he might take that diverge from the opinions or wishes of his constituents.

Members of the United States Congress advertise their willingness to perform these services to their constituents, provide themselves with the resources to do these things well, and structure the legislature itself to facilitate their ability to deliver these services. In meetings with local officials, business leaders, and civic groups, representatives usually ask what they can do to help them in Washington. In their newsletters, mass mailings, and particularly on their web sites, they invite citizens to bring problems and concerns to them or to the staff members who run their local offices. The web sites of most House members will show a link to "constituent service," often listing specific areas such as student financial aid, grants and federal assistance, social security requests, veterans affairs requests, and tax issues. Instructions on how to contact the representative are also included, and many provide an online form for those requesting help. It may well be that the workload of representatives in regard to constituency service would be lower if they did not work so hard to solicit business. The fact that they do attests to the importance that they attach to this aspect of their responsibilities.

The committee and subcommittee organization of Congress, designed to make the work of the Congress more efficient by providing for expertise and division of labor, also fosters close relationships between representatives and bureaucrats. Government officials know that the Congress through its committee system authorizes, funds, and oversees their programs, and that is usually enough to guarantee a favorable or at least prompt response to a representative who brings a constituent problem to them. Federal agencies are so aware of the importance of good relations with Congress that each has a congressional liaison office that has as one of its chief functions assisting representatives in responding to the special requests and needs of their constituents. It has been argued that this close continuing relationship between career bureaucrats and long-serving members of Congress explains a great deal of the electoral success of representatives.[17]

Finally, members of Congress provide themselves with the resources they need to respond to their constituents. These include funds to hire staff members, many of whom devote most of their time to constituency service. Money is also provided to open and staff offices in the legislator's district that have the handling of constituent requests as their primary purpose. Members of the House allocate about half of their personal staff to their district offices and senators about one-third of their staff.[18] Members have postage budgets that they use to advertise their services and their accomplishments to their constituents and generous travel allowances that enable them to return to their districts as frequently as they wish. The Congress usually avoids conducting business or holding votes from Thursday afternoon through late Tuesday morning so members can travel home to their constituencies for four-day weekends. And every year, Congress takes several one- or two-week recesses that most members use for extended visits to their constituencies. These recesses are now referred to as "constituency work periods," lest the voters think that these breaks constitute congressional vacations from their formal responsibilities.

Representatives devote this much attention and resources to service activities because their constituents expect their help. When samples of American and British voters were asked how their representative would respond if they had a problem that they brought to his attention, about 25 percent said they thought their representative would be "very helpful," and only about 10 percent said they expected their representative would not be helpful.[19] In the above-mentioned comparative study of attitudes in Korea, Kenya, and Turkey, citizens were asked about their expectations of their legislators. The most common response was that they expected their representatives to tell the government what the people in the district think, but the second most frequent response was that they expected the representative to work to obtain projects and benefits for the district; third was to help constituents who had personal problems with the government.[20] In the United States, scholars and pundits alike have puzzled over the fact that although citizens generally have little confidence in the job performance of Congress, they hold their individual representative and the work that he is doing in higher regard. This finding is often attributed to the constituency-related activities that representatives perform, and it is one of the most commonly offered reasons for why, despite traditionally low public approval ratings of the Congress, nearly all members who seek reelection succeed.[21]

In contrast to the general absence of information that most citizens have about the position that their representative has taken on major public policy issues, those who make these more particularized requests to their representatives will be quite aware of what he has accomplished or failed to accomplish. Even if the representative has not been able to resolve the problem or deliver the funds, citizens are made aware of and appreciate the efforts that the member or his staff has made on their behalf. On occasion this process takes on elements of an elaborate dance involving the representative, the agency, and the citizen. The representative (or more likely a staff member) hears the concern of a constituent, communicates it to a bureaucrat who, even if she cannot resolve the problem, nonetheless writes a letter to the representative offering sympathy while explaining why she was unable to help. The member in turn writes to the constituent indicating that he tried his best; he will cite the letter from the bureaucrat as the reason for not being able to help (and perhaps even criticize the bureaucracy for its nonresponsiveness) and vow to keep trying in the future. The success of this strategy is suggested by one survey in which 61 percent of those who had asked their representative for assistance said they were satisfied while 16 percent said they were not; of those who had asked for information, 64 percent reported themselves satisfied compared with 8 percent who were dissatisfied.[22]

United States senators, particularly those from large states, may find it more difficult to deal effectively with requests for individual assistance or for help in gaining project funds. Senators from smaller states are more likely to have direct contact with their constituents than their colleagues from larger states, and that contact is just as likely to involve requests for personal assistance as an exchange of views on more general policy issues. But for senators from larger states, policy issues tend to dominate these interactions. It is not surprising that a senator from Rhode Island, with a population of just over one million, would be able to have personal contact with a significant percentage of voters and provide service representation for many of them; it would be quite surprising if a senator from California, with a population of 36 million, were able to have that same level of contact and provide the same level of services as her colleague from Rhode Island. This reasoning, as well as the importance to constituents of such services, may be why senators from smaller states tend to be more favorably evaluated by their constituents than their colleagues from larger states.[23]

SHOW THEM THE MONEY!

Representatives use a variety of methods to direct federal funds to their congressional districts or to their states. The legislation authorizing most distributive programs contains a formula that determines how dollars will be allocated among the states and how much will go directly to local units of government. These programs tend to be characterized by what political scientists call "universalism," meaning that virtually everyone gets a piece of the pie. Typically, formulas are written so that each state, regardless of population and often regardless of need, is guaranteed a minimum of one-half of one percent of the total funds appropriated in the legislation.[24]

Shortly after the September 11, 2001, attacks, when Congress authorized funds for the new Department of Homeland Security, the legislation included a provision requiring that nearly 40 percent of the money for first responders be shared equally among the states, with most of the balance distributed on the basis of population. Although some extra funding was provided for high-risk cities such as Washington and New York, because of the formula, significant dollars went to places where there was very little likelihood of a terrorist attack. Through June 2003, Homeland Security allocated a total of $2.2 billion to police and fire departments around the country. New York received $125.4 million—the third largest sum behind California and Texas; however, Wyoming received $23 million. One would be hard pressed to identify terrorist targets in that state that would warrant 20 percent of what New York receives.[25] Attempts in the House to revise the formula so that smaller states would still receive a guaranteed minimum but not as much as the current formula provides have been resisted in the Senate, where the equal representation of each state gives disproportionate power to smaller states that have an interest in keeping the minimum payment as high as possible.[26]

Although the bulk of federal funds are distributed on a formula basis, some funds are directed to support specific projects. These provisions, inserted into legislation by members of Congress who wish to support projects in their districts or states, are called "earmarks." An example of how the earmark process works is found in this *New York Times* account:

> St. Vincent College, a small Benedictine college southeast of Pittsburgh, wanted to realign a two-lane state road serving the campus. But the state transportation department did not have the money. So St. Vincent tried Washington instead. The college hired a professional lobbyist in 2004 and, later that year, two paragraphs were tucked into federal appropriations bills with the help of Representative John P. Murtha, Democrat of Pennsylvania, awarding $4 million solely for that project.[27]

Similarly, the legislation authorizing and appropriating the $12–$20 billion a year that the Army Corps of Engineers spends on various flood control projects typically specifies exactly what levees to build, harbors to dredge, dams to construct, and beaches and ecosystems to restore.[28] Certainly, the bill needn't look like that. The Corps could simply be given a lump sum of money and told to fund only those projects that, based on scientific and engineering criteria, were of the highest priority. Or if there were a concern that needy projects in some areas might be shortchanged, money could be allocated by region, with the agency deciding on the basis of merit exactly which projects in each region to fund. Although either of these approaches might be wiser from a policy standpoint, neither would be as politically attractive to representatives as a specific provision funding a specific district project.

Congress also may authorize and appropriate federal money to support a particular policy goal but require that those who wish to access the money meet certain criteria embedded in the legislation. Although the legislation leaves it to the bureaucracy to decide how and where dollars should be

spent, or which firm should receive government contracts, local leaders—
mayors, governors, businesses, heads of educational institutions—will ask
the legislator to use his influence to gain preferential treatment for their
applications for these funds. In some instances, the discretion of the agency
can be undermined by the practice of placing earmarks in committee
reports rather than in the law itself. In that case, these "soft earmarks"
become strong suggestions to the administration that they can of course
ignore, rather than statutory requirements to which they must adhere.[29]
However, ignoring either the suggestions contained in committee reports
or more informal communications from representatives after the legislation
is passed is risky considering that the budgets under which these bureaucrats operate are controlled by Congress. According to John Solomon and
Jeffrey Birnbaum of the *Washington Post*, representatives hold "hearings
meant to cajole or pressure executive branch officials into providing money
for their pet projects—even when those agencies already have rejected the
requests." Sometimes the pressure comes less publicly. In February 2007,
nineteen Illinois representatives signed a letter to the Department of Energy
expressing "strong support" for funding for a bioenergy project at the University of Illinois. In addition to signing that letter, Representative Rahm
Emanuel from Chicago sent a separate letter to the department seeking
"support and assistance" in securing $500,000 for Children's Memorial
Hospital and $750,000 for the Illinois Institute of Technology, both Chi-
cago institutions.[30]

The White House Office of Management and Budget (OMB), which is
responsible for supervising federal expenditures, takes a dim view of this
practice of representatives seeking to influence the decisions of administrators concerning the distribution of funds. In the winter of 2007, shortly
after the Democrats gained control of the Congress, Rob Portman, the
Director of OMB (and himself a former member of the House) sent a
memo to all federal agencies indicating that "while the administration wel-
comes input to help make informed decisions, no oral or written communication concerning earmarks shall supersede statutory criteria, competitive
awards, or merit-based decision-making." The memorandum was not well
received by members of Congress from both parties, who warned that
administrators dependent on the Congress for their funding would ignore
legislative advice on how these funds should be spent at their peril.[31]

Finally, legislation may be written so that a seemingly general provision
will apply to and benefit only one recipient and therefore become a *de facto*
earmark. In July 2007, the House of Representatives approved an extension
and expansion of the State Children's Health Insurance Program along with
several changes in the Medicare program. The bill also included several provisions that would change the formulas used to calculate Medicare reimbursements for at least twenty-seven hospitals, all but one of which was

located in districts represented by Democrats, including several senior members of the two committees that jointly wrote the bill, the Energy and Commerce and Ways and Means Committees. One such provision, in the words of the statute, was designed to benefit a hospital "located in a State that as of December 31, 2006, had only one center under section 15.414 of the Public Health Service Act that has been designated by the National Cancer Institute as a comprehensive center currently serving all 21 counties in the most densely populated State in the nation . . . serving more than 70,000 patient visits annually." The only hospital in the nation that fit that description was the Cancer Institute of New Jersey, located in the district represented by Frank Pallone Jr., chairman of the Energy and Commerce Subcommittee on Health.

Another provision in the bill instructed federal officials to assume that "any hospital that is co-located in Marinette, Wisconsin and Menominee, Michigan" be deemed located in Chicago (!) for the purposes of calculating Medicare reimbursements. (Hospitals in large urban areas such as Chicago, where costs are higher, receive higher Medicare reimbursements than hospitals located in rural areas.) Only one hospital fit that description: the Bay Area Medical Center, located more than 200 miles north of Chicago on the Wisconsin/Michigan border. The provision was sponsored by Representative Bart Stupak who lives in Menominee and represents the district.[32]

Republicans, although the minority party in 2007, also participated in this process. One provision of the bill reassigned an unnamed hospital in Burlington County, New Jersey, to the New York City metropolitan area. The provision was written for the Deborah Heart and Lung Center in Pemberton Township, New Jersey, more than sixty miles from New York City in what the hospital's brochure describes as a "bucolic countryside surrounded by farms and pine forests." The provision, sponsored by Representative H. James Saxton, the Republican representative from the district, would increase Medicare payments to Deborah by between $3 million and $5 million a year.[33]

Members of both chambers and members from each political party have used all of these techniques to try to channel funds to their constituencies. Although senators also use earmarks, they pay a great deal of attention to formulas to make certain that they will work to the advantage (or at least not to the disadvantage) of their states. In comparison, members of the House of Representatives are more likely to focus on earmarks that are directed to specific projects in their districts.[34]

This inter-chamber difference is explained by what David Mayhew called "credit claiming."[35] If one assumes that bringing resources to the constituency, by whatever means, is important for a representative's reelection prospects, then it is also important that there be a means for the representative to claim the credit for the successful delivery of these resources. Those who actually receive the resources should know who is responsible, of course, but that will not help the representative much if the rest of his constituents are unaware of his efforts. To serve this credit claiming need, it is often the practice of an agency to allow the representative himself to announce that funds have been awarded to a project in his district, even in those instances when the representative may not have had much to do with the award. Credit, albeit somewhat deceptively, is claimed. During the Bush Adminis- tration, and in previous administrations as well, the White House has seen to it that representatives from the president's party who face tough reelec- tion races had the opportunity to announce any grant that came to the dis- trict.[36] Even without the assistance of the administration, representatives find ways to advertise their successes. Representative Jesse Jackson Jr. of the 2nd District of Illinois has a link on his web site labeled "What I've Done for You," where he lists nearly $450 million in grant awards that he claims to have secured since 2005.

However, in a large state, it is more difficult for a senator to reap much in the way of political benefits for a specific project that may affect only a small group of people in one small area of the state. It is much more effi- cient for them to take credit for the share of federal resources that they are able to gain for their states as a whole ("over the last six years, I have secured x billion dollars in federal grants and contracts"), and they guaran- tee that they get a share worth boasting about by supporting the appro- priate formula. One senator from a small state told an interviewer, in terms that the Founders would have recognized, that the "Senate brings with it the responsibility to represent the state governments. You must represent the state's interest in the major formula programs. . . . They [senators] are there to give states an active policymaking role in federal policy. That is one of the purposes of the Senate envisioned from the beginning."[37]

In contrast, it is difficult for House members to claim credit for funds going to the state through a formula, especially when it may not be possible to identify exactly how much money went to the representative's district and on what it was spent. However, they can gain political advantage from specific projects—a building constructed, a main road widened, a new bridge built—and all with a photo op of a ribbon being cut or ground being broken. Earmarks rather than formulas produce such projects and the photo ops that go with them. In such instances, the total value of the ear- marks that a representative can take credit for may be less important than the number of earmarks secured. Ten earmarks of $100,000 each to ten dif- ferent projects spread throughout the district may reap greater electoral rewards than one earmark of $1,000,000 for one project in the district.

Representative Nancy Boyda of Kansas is a case in point. She was elected as a Democrat to the House of Representatives in 2006, unseating a five- term Republican in one of the major political upsets of that election.

Usually members of Congress take credit for the earmarks that they are successful in obtaining, but Representative Boyda, during her first year in the
House, took the unusual step of listing on her web site sixty-four earmark
projects that she had asked the various committees to consider during the
budget process. These requests ranged from $47 million to rehabilitate the
Amelia Earhart Bridge on Route 59 in her district to $25,000 to support
the Children's Identification and Location Database in the Miami County
Sheriff's office.[38]

Representative Boyda may have been taking a chance listing these
requests because if only a small proportion were funded, she would leave
herself vulnerable to the charge of being an ineffective member of the
House. On the other hand, she argued that she was doing it this way so that
her efforts would be transparent given the concerns that some had been
raising about corruption in the earmark process (see below). To her fiscally
conservative constituents, she made the further argument that earmarks do
not increase federal expenditures and that by working to secure them, all
she was doing was making sure that her constituents got their share of what
was being spent. Better she said for representatives to be deciding what
projects should be supported "instead of someone sitting on the 4th floor
in an office building in DC deciding where federal funds go."[39]

Once the earmarks started to come in, Representative Boyda was not shy
about taking credit for them and defending them. On July 27, 2007, she
announced on her website that she had been able to secure $3.2 million in
earmarks in the Departments of Transportation and Housing and Urban
Development Appropriations Act of 2008 to support roads and transportation projects in her district including :

- $1,000,000 for runway improvements at the Manhattan Airport
- $1,000,000 for Interstate 70 viaduct realignment
- $300,000 for bus replacement for the Topeka Transit Authority
- $250,000 for work on highway US 69
- $250,000 for work on highway K-20
- $200,000 for the Ottawa Industrial Park
- $100,000 for streetscape improvements in Fredonia
- $100,000 for public access to park land adjacent to Great Overland
  Station.[40]

Another earmark that Representative Boyda secured in a separate bill was
$100,000 for a prison museum at Ft. Leavenworth, Kansas. When the ear-
mark was challenged on the House floor, she rose to defend these funds as
well as her district. She boasted that Leavenworth County had more prisons
than any other county in America—prisons that had housed such "nota-
bles" as Machine Gun Kelly and the Birdman of Alcatraz (obviously, before
he was sent to Alcatraz). "The local residents are proud of their heritage,

and rightly so."[41] Representative Rahm Emanuel also took public pride in his work in regard to earmarks for Chicago. In an op-ed piece in the *New York Times*, he defended earmarks and said that the ones that he had pushed provided "money for after-school programs, computers for police patrol cars, master teacher training programs and a children's hospital research facility. I make no apologies for these earmarks, which serve important public purposes—and might even save a life."[42]

Whatever their motivation or their merits, there is little doubt that the number of earmarks contained in congressional legislation has increased exponentially over the past fifty years. In the case of highway funding, prior to 1970 these bills allowed state highway commissioners to determine how the funds allocated to their state would be spent. The 1970 highway bill marked a small departure from this practice, earmarking funds for three projects. In subsequent years, a small number of earmarked projects were included in each highway bill, usually less than ten. In 1987, however, 155 projects specifically were included in the bill. The 1998 bill contained 1,859 earmarks at a total cost of $9.5 billion, and the 2005 bill included 6,731 earmarks at a cost of $23 billion. Of all the earmarks contained in all highway bills over the past fifty years, 92 percent were inserted into the three bills approved between 1995 and 2006 when the Republican Party controlled the House.[43] Nor is this trend restricted to highway funds. Earmarks appear in bills funding veterans programs, housing bills, NASA, the Environmental Protection Agency, and the Department of Health and Human Services. In 2005, there were 13,997 earmarks at a total cost of $27.3 billion compared with 892 earmarks in 1992 at a cost of $2.6 billion.[44]

When there were a very small number of earmarks, they were viewed as special cases that reflected the political muscle of a powerful senior member of Congress or were a reward to a member for a particularly important or difficult vote in support of the leadership or the president. The explosion in earmarks meant that such provisions would now benefit a much larger number of congressional districts with virtually everyone getting something. Indeed, some defenders of the earmark process argue that the increase reflects a much needed democratization of the process, with the benefits of the process more broadly distributed beyond a small number of congressional leaders.

Figuring out which districts get what is a bit complex. There are informal understandings in both houses that members of the majority party get around 60 percent of the earmarks with the minority party getting the rest, an arrangement that ensures bipartisan support for the system. The way in which earmarks are distributed also has a great deal to do with committee power in the Congress. In July 2007, when the appropriations bill for the Department of Health and Human Services was approved by the House of Representatives, it contained approximately $282 million in earmarks for schools, hospitals, and other programs. Of that figure, about one-third went to districts represented by the sixty-six members of the Appropriations Committee, including $4.1 million to the district of Appropriations Committee chair David Obey of Wisconsin. When earmarks in all appropriations bills approved by the House in 2007 are totaled, those sponsored by Obey came to more than $93 million. Obey, however, was only fourth on the list of the most successful earmarkers. At the top of the list was Representative John Murtha, chair of the Defense Appropriations Subcommittee, whose total was $179.8 million. Bill Young of Florida and Jerry Lewis of California—the top two Republicans on the Appropriations Committee—came next, with $126.5 million and $109.6 million respectively.[45]

In September 2007, when the Senate approved the Water Resource Development Act funding Army Corps of Engineers projects around the country, the bill included $23 billion in earmarked provisions, including $1.8 billion (8 percent of the earmarked funds) for flood control on the Santa Ana River in California. The chair of the Senate's Environment and Public Works Committee that reported the bill is Barbara Boxer of California.[46] However, plenty of money was left for others, including Republicans, because when President Bush vetoed the final bill in November 2007, saying that it had too many earmarks in it and exceeded his budget targets, the veto was overridden by large bipartisan votes in both chambers, the only one of President Bush's vetoes up to that date to be overridden.

As the number of earmarks expanded, efforts were made by both parties to supply extra funds to members in electorally vulnerable seats. In the 2007 Health and Human Services appropriations bill, Republican Representative James Walsh from Syracuse, the ranking minority member of the subcommittee that handled the bill, received the highest figure in earmarks ($3.25 million), presumably something that he thought would be helpful to him in the 2008 election given his very narrow margin of victory in 2006.[47] Democratic representatives from competitive districts averaged about twice as much in earmarks as members from safer seats. For example, Democratic Representative Ron Klein, who unseated Republican E. Clay Shaw Jr. in Florida's 22nd District with 51 percent of the vote in the 2006 election, received $825,000 in earmarks, including $325,000 for the South Florida Science Museum. This led to some complaints that poorer minority districts that were safely Democratic were being shortchanged in favor of more competitive and richer districts. The median income in Representative Klein's district was $51,200; in contrast, the Los Angeles district represented by Representative Xavier Becerra, the fourth poorest House district as measured by median household income, received $400,000 in earmarks in the bill, half of what Representative Klein's district received.[48] This pattern seemed to be repeated across all House-passed appropriations bills for the 2008 fiscal year. Districts represented by white Democrats received on average almost twice as much in the way of earmarked money ($12 million) as districts represented by African-Americans ($6.1 million) and Latinos ($5.6 million), in large measure because the latter districts were safe Democratic seats while the most competitive Democratic seats in the House were held by whites.[49]

DOES IT MATTER?

Clearly the increase in the number of earmarks suggests that representatives and their party leaders are convinced that such measures have an electoral benefit. Anecdotal evidence, the behavior of legislators, as well as simple common sense argues that they are correct, but it has been difficult to find convincing empirical evidence of a connection between constituency service and electoral success. For the most part, the research has noted that both the increase in incumbent reelection rates and the decrease in the number of House members who win reelection by narrow margins have coincided with an increase in the resources that House members devote to constituency service. But the comfortable electoral margins experienced by members from relatively safe districts do not seem to be explainable in terms of the earmarks that they receive (as we have just seen, safe Democrats seem to get less than vulnerable Democrats), and the electoral security of incumbents became apparent well before earmarks came into extensive usage. This suggests the possibility of a more nuanced relationship between constituency service and project funds, on the one hand, and members' reelection success on the other.

One explanation already mentioned for weak correlations between the number and size of the earmarks and electoral margin is the strategic decision to channel more earmarks to more competitive districts in order to help reelect the party's more vulnerable members. That approach means that large reelection margins would be associated with lower earmark funding while narrow or even losing reelection margins would be associated with higher earmark funding. Another explanation is that representatives may act in a politically strategic manner by making special efforts to direct federal funds to those areas of their district that will provide them with the greatest return in terms of votes.[50] In other words, it may not be the amount of the award but exactly where it is spent that pays electoral dividends. Finally, these efforts may reap greater political rewards in some districts than in others. One study found that a representative's success at generating pork barrel projects only produced electoral benefits for Democratic members.[51] This finding suggests that the link between pork barrel success and electoral success may depend on whether the representative has a reputation as a fiscal liberal or conservative. In districts receiving substantial allocations, fiscally liberal incumbents perform better electorally than fiscal conservatives, but in those districts receiving little in the way of federal allocations, fiscal conservatives perform better.[52]

It is possible then that all constituents are not equally enthusiastic about bringing federal dollars to the constituency, particularly those constituencies dominated by voters who view such expenditures as examples of government extravagance with taxpayer dollars. Because of those sentiments, all members of Congress may not have the same commitment to seeking funds for their districts. Those who are skeptical about federal spending may as a matter of principle (theirs and their constituents') avoid such efforts. *Congressional Quarterly* lists eight representatives, all Republicans, who were neither sponsors nor cosponsors of earmarks during 2007.[53] One of these representatives said in an interview that he does not ask for earmarks and politely refuses requests from constituents that he pursue such projects on their behalf. He regularly wins reelection by comfortable margins because, he believes, his constituents understand and support his commitment to fiscal conservatism. That said, other members on one day will decry the high cost of government and on the next do all they can to bring dollars home. The fiscally conservative members of Congress from Louisiana and Mississippi, for example, seemed to have had no problem asking for huge amounts of money for their districts after Hurricane Katrina and were among the Republicans who voted to override President Bush's veto of the water projects bill. Simply, if somewhat cynically put, for some it may not be pork if it is spent at home.

It does seem to be the case that those representatives who are most vulnerable to electoral defeat are the most likely to seek increases in awards made to projects in their districts.[54] This may explain Representative Boyda's decision to publicize her earmark requests and her successes. As a Democrat elected from a district that had regularly sent Republicans to Congress, she was sure to face a tough reelection campaign in 2008. But what is not clear is how many constituents will know about or be impressed by her earmark successes. Awareness may be restricted to certain subgroups of constituents, particularly those who have been helped directly by a project; these constituents who benefit are more likely to reward the member with more favorable evaluations than constituents who do not benefit.[55] The efforts that Representative Boyda and her colleagues make to publicize their earmark successes are designed to expand the electoral impact of their accomplishments beyond that circle of direct beneficiaries.

Representatives also can win friends at home through legislative achievements that do not bring funds to the district. In 2006, in Connecticut's 2nd Congressional District, Joe Courtney, a Democrat, defeated incumbent Republican Representative Rob Simmons by eighty-three votes, the closest election in the country that year. In 2007, Representative Courtney was the sponsor of the Eightmile Wild and Scenic River Act (HR 986), which passed 253–172. The bill added parts of the Eightmile River in Connecticut to the National Wild and Scenic Rivers System, a designation that would ban dams on the river and set in place other conservation measures. The bill had strong bipartisan support within the state and the district, and Courtney's leading role in sponsoring the bill (obviously facilitated by the Democratic leadership in the House) surely will help him in what is likely to be a very competitive reelection campaign in 2008.[56]

On the other hand, a particular project may have an adverse impact on the electoral fortunes of a representative. One former member of the House told me that he had worked hard to secure funds to build a large federal prison in an economically depressed county in his district. Although many benefited from the jobs and money that came to the area because of the prison, some opposed building a prison in the county, arguing that such an institution would attract undesirable people to their rural area. In the subsequent election, he lost that county for the first time in his career because the opponents of the prison, a minority to be sure, were intense and did not forget the issue, but those who had benefited had moved on to other issues and concerns. So the caution here, in addition to the fact that fiscally conservative voters may view such projects as examples of government waste, is that a member cannot provide a project for everyone and that some projects may make you as many enemies as friends.

Survey data suggests that few votes can be explained directly by constituency service. In one study, 22 percent of respondents who reported that they had asked for help did not even vote in the next election, and 42 percent who reported that someone in their family had asked for service also did not vote. Given the relatively small number (compared with the total number of voters in the district) of service requests that members deal with, these data do not allow for many votes from grateful recipients of legislative assistance. Similarly, when district attentiveness as measured by trips home and the allocation of staff resources to the home district is used as an independent variable to explain reelection rates, they do not appear to account for many votes.[57]

Research on congressional elections has identified several alternative explanations for the high reelection rates of House members. These include the overwhelming advantage that incumbents have in raising funds to finance their reelection, the fact that they usually run against underfinanced and relatively unknown challengers, and the increasingly refined art and science of gerrymandering. One scholar has concluded that the personal incumbency advantage that accrued from district attentiveness and the various resources that representatives have allotted to themselves for this purpose has been eroding in recent years. The more homogeneous and more partisan districts produced in recent years through sophisticated computer assisted gerrymandering linking census data with survey data has done much more to ensure the reelection of a member than the individual services that he may perform for his constituents.[58]

However, it would be wrong to conclude from these analyses that district service really does not matter or that its effects are marginal. A more reasonable view is that members take public credit for their work on behalf of the constituency in mailings, in campaign speeches, and on their web sites; public credit, along with their persistent solicitations asking constituents to contact them or their office if they are having problems, creates the general impression among voters that the representative is hard at work on behalf of the constituency, even among the vast majority of voters who never have and likely never will contact the representative or ask for help. It is this impression rather than the work itself that generates voter support.[59] That reputation for diligence on behalf of the constituency makes the biggest difference for members who represent districts with large numbers of voters who are more favorably disposed toward the opposition party.[60] Work of this sort is among the factors that increase an incumbent's visibility among his constituents, which in turn makes it easier for him to attract campaign funds. In summary, although it may be difficult to discern a direct payoff for constituency attentiveness, there can be severe consequences for not doing it, much the same way as showing up on time for your job does not necessarily get you a raise, but coming in late to work every day probably gets you fired.

Representatives can also attend to the needs of their constituents by working on more general legislation that, if passed, would redound to the benefit of their districts. As an example, take the position of Representative Earl Blumenauer of Oregon on the 2007 reauthorization of the farm bill. The farm bill as it stood provided nearly all of its subsidies to growers of five crops: corn, cotton, rice, soybeans, and wheat. The main crops in Blumenauer's district are grapes for wine, fruit, and Christmas trees, none of which benefit from federal subsidies. Blumenauer argued that revising the farm bill was "critically important to my state," which he viewed as "shortchanged" by the current legislation. But larger issues in his view were also at stake. The current legislation, he said, "is not serving most states, it's not serving most farmers, it's not fiscally conservative." Changing all of this would send the message that Congress "was serious about making government work right."[61]

On the other hand, the members of the House Agriculture Committee, including its chair, Collin Peterson of Minnesota, represent constituents who benefit enormously from the current legislation. The forty-six members of that committee (10 percent of the House membership) represent districts that received 40 percent of all farm subsidies between 2003 and 2005[62] and, not surprisingly, they differ with Representative Blumenauer about what is good for the country. The same applied to the Senate. Although Senator Harkin of Iowa, the chair of the Agriculture Committee, said that he was interested in reforming the program, the final draft of the Senate bill left the subsidy program essentially unchanged. Some raised questions about how hard Senator Harkin had tried to change the program, given the fact that Iowa ranks second only to Texas in terms of farm subsidies collected over the last decade. In fact, Senator Harkin said, "It wouldn't terribly upset me and break my heart if we just had to extend the present farm bill for a couple of years."[63]

THE PROBLEM WITH EARMARKS

In 2006 and 2007, there was a growing chorus of criticism among politicians, pundits, scholars, and even some ordinary citizens concerning earmarks. Some of this was attributable to the "Bridge to Nowhere" controversy involving Senator Stevens of Alaska discussed in chapter 2, and some was attributable to scandals involving lobbyist Jack Abramoff who, among other misdeeds, traded personal favors as well as campaign contributions to representatives for earmarks for his clients. The most persistent criticism of earmarks, voiced well before these events, is that they create upward pressure on federal spending. One conservative member of Congress referred to earmarks as "the gateway drug to deficit spending." Representative Boyda's assertion that these earmarks do not increase federal expenditures but simply direct how dollars that otherwise would be appropriated should be spent needs to be taken with a large grain of salt. Certainly, as more representatives request more earmarks, pressure on the appropriators to raise the total figure so that more of their colleagues can be accommodated will be inevitable and perhaps irresistible. On the other hand, it is interesting—and to some deliciously ironic—that the number of earmarks increased most dramatically during the years when Congress was controlled by the Republican Party, a party rhetorically committed to curbing wasteful government spending.[64] One Republican member of Congress who has made it his personal mission to fight against earmarks was caustic in his criticism of his fellow party members. In an interview, he said that his party came to power in 1995 committed to reform but as time wore on their main goal appeared to shift to staying in power, as the rising emphasis on earmarks proved.

In fairness, however, it should be noted that all of the earmarks approved by the House in 2007 totaled $14.1 billion, or less than one half of 1 percent of a federal budget in excess of $3 trillion.[65] If all earmarks were eliminated, the estimated deficit for FY 2008 would have dropped from $410 billion to just under $400 billion. Of course, the most likely course of events would be that these dollars would have been allocated to federal and local agencies to spend for designated purposes, if not designated projects, with no net savings to the government. Earmarks also are a way to create legislative majorities for bills that serve important public purposes. As one observer put it, "Favoring legislators with small gifts for their districts in order to achieve great things for the nation is an act not of sin but of statesmanship." Another suggested that earmarks were simply the cost of doing business in a complex legislative body where different, often competing, interests needed to be satisfied in order to generate legislative majorities.[66]

The implications for the amount of government spending aside, a second criticism is that there is no guarantee that earmarks are funding worthy or even high priority needs. Indeed, some earmarks appear downright frivolous; one 2007 earmark was for $100,000 for "signage" in Los Angeles's fashion district, and another was for $9 million for "rural domestic preparedness" in Kentucky.[67] In the case of federal highway funds, some argue that if these dollars went to states as a lump sum with no earmarked projects, state transportation officials, drawing on their experience and expertise, would allocate these funds to their most pressing needs. During the summer of 2007, the nation was shocked when a bridge carrying Interstate Highway 35 over the Mississippi River at Minneapolis collapsed with substantial loss of life. In the wake of the disaster, a spate of newspaper stories appeared indicating that a large number of bridges had structural problems similar to the I-35 bridge. This in turn provoked demands in Congress to spend more money on infrastructure maintenance and repair. But some pointed out that a great deal of federal money already had been allocated to the states for these efforts, but that much of it was earmarked for specific projects advocated by members of Congress. Representative Jeff Flake of Arizona, an outspoken critic of earmarks, pointed out that Minnesota received 140 earmarks in the most recent highway bill totaling nearly half a billion dollars, including nearly $1.6 million for bike trails, more than $1.5 million for streetscaping, and more than $1 million for new visitor centers. He concluded that if highway officials in Minnesota had been allowed to spend the funds that they received on their priorities, they might well have chosen maintenance of the I-35 bridge, thereby avoiding the collapse.[68]

Representatives in Washington do not have the necessary expertise, and the staff members of the various committees do not have the necessary time, to do a complete analysis of every earmark proposal. The result, critics of earmarks argue, is that low priority projects in terms of need may be ignored in favor of high priority projects in terms of political considerations. And because of the lack of quality control exercised by those who approve earmarks and the disposition to defer to powerful representatives and senators, every year will see some earmarks like the Bridge to Nowhere or signage in Los Angeles that will be embarrassing to Congress and enhance its reputation as an institution that plays fast and loose with tax-payer dollars.

There are at least two problems with this critique. One is the assumption that the state officials who would receive the nonearmarked funds in a lump sum would make their expenditure decisions without taking political considerations into account. But politics does not end at the borders of Washington, D.C.; public expenditures in every state capitol are influenced by the same partisan and geographic considerations that affect congressional decisions. As the Illinois legislature struggled over that state's budget during the summer of 2007, projects for local districts were being distributed by party leaders as a way to generate support. It was estimated that "member initiatives," as earmarks in Illinois are called, accounted for $200 million in budgetary funds.[69] There is also the question of how much discretion a representative system should turn over to unelected government officials. As Representative Boyda suggested, and as exponents of the view that representative systems should provide some measure of popular sovereignty should agree, expenditure decisions, for good or for ill, should be made by the people's representatives, and if the people disapprove of what their representatives are doing, they have the option of holding them accountable at the ballot box.

Of even greater concern to some critics of earmarking is the potential for corruption with this sort of allocational representation. Although resources are brought to the constituency by such activities, it is not always clear that these resources are used to address real, generalized needs of constituents. Rather, they may serve the interests of a small number of constituents and, more to the point, may be primarily intended to address the career and personal interests of the legislator by serving the needs of those who provide reelection support, especially campaign contributions. Some members have been caught up in scandals because of their work on earmarks. In 2005, Representative Randy (Duke) Cunningham, a member of the House Armed Services Committee, was forced to resign his seat and went to prison after pleading guilty to accepting $2.4 million in bribes from defense contractors in return for his work earmarking federal contracts for them.

Of more significance than these rare cases of outright bribery is the connection between earmarks and campaign contributions. The relationship between Representative John Murtha of Pennsylvania, chair of the Appropriations Subcommittee that handles the Defense Department budget, and Concurrent Technologies, a government contractor based in Murtha's district outside of Pittsburgh, is typical. Employees of the company have contributed more than $132,000 to Murtha's election campaigns over the past ten years while Murtha has steered government contracts, mostly from the

Defense Department, to them. Concurrent also has opened offices in other areas of the country, including an office in the district of Representative Bill Young of Florida, the ranking Republican on the defense appropriations subcommittee. Young as well as the representatives from the other districts where Concurrent has offices have been equally aggressive advocates for the organization. In 2007, Murtha and four other Democratic and Republican members of the Appropriations Subcommittee proposed $18 million in earmarked contracts for the firm, including logistics analysis for the Marine Corps, pollution prevention for the Air Force, and special operations tactical systems development for the Defense Department.[70] Since 2004, Concurrent has been awarded $226 million in earmarks and Concurrent, along with other firms benefiting from earmarks secured by Murtha, gave about $437,000 to his campaign since 2005. About $110,000 of these contributions came in just before the deadline for filing earmark requests with the committee. In the same period, Representative Young received about $150,000 from firms for whom he requested earmarks.

Bad publicity on earmarks does not seem to bother Representative Murtha, who said on the floor of the House, "I don't make apologies for having earmarks." Mr. Murtha and Mr. Young argue that their efforts are aimed at helping businesses based in their districts, and that is what their constituents expect them to do. They indicate as well that they and their staff check on the merits of each earmark that they propose and that they also check with the Defense Department to make certain that the project fits its needs. Of course, it is difficult to imagine the Pentagon raising objections to a relatively small $2 *million* earmark "suggested" by the representative who chairs the subcommittee that appropriates its annual $625 *billion* budget. The cost of all of the earmarks in the FY 2008 bill approved by the subcommittee was $1.8 billion—about one-third of 1 percent of the entire Defense Department budget.[71]

Like Representative Murtha, Senator Ted Stevens of Alaska also makes no apologies for the earmarks that he has procured for his state. In the midst of a federal investigation of his activities, he gave a speech to the Anchorage Downtown Rotary Club trumpeting a list of projects he said he had helped make possible, including modernizing Alaskan native villages and fisheries restoration. He said he was proud of this work, "regardless of the slings and arrows I've faced attacking what I've tried to do for Alaskans in Alaska."[72] And he's done a great deal; thanks largely to his efforts, Alaska receives more money per capita from the federal government than any other state in the Union.[73]

In that spirit, Senator Stevens was back in the news in 2007, not for a "bridge to nowhere" but for what might be called an "airport for nowhere." He was responsible for placing $3.5 million into the Department of Transportation budget to support the building of an airport on Akutan, an island in the Aleutians with only 100 permanent residents but also the location of a large seafood processing plant operated by Trident Seafoods, Inc., of Seattle. Trident and Stevens were no strangers; the company's founder had been a longtime donor to Senator Stevens's reelection campaigns. Senator Stevens's office, in response to questions, indicated that the airport would benefit the island as much as it would Trident by providing a connection with the mainland and better emergency services. Critics, of course, indicated that if Trident needed an airport for its business, it should build it itself.[74]

At least Senator Stevens' efforts on behalf of Akutan and Trident had a constituency connection. In 2006, Senator Stevens' House colleague, Representative Don Young, also of Alaska, chair of the House Committee on Transportation and Infrastructure, was criticized for inserting a $10 million earmark into a transportation bill to fund an interchange on Interstate Highway 75 in Lee County, Florida—about as far away from Alaska as you can get and still be in North America. Representative Young's action took place only days after a local real estate developer with property adjoining the proposed interchange raised and donated $40,000 to Representative Young's reelection campaign. The earmark was a last-minute addition after the legislation had been approved by the House and Senate and was being prepared for the president's signature. Funding for the interchange had not been requested by the local community or by the congressman representing the district, and ultimately the Lee County Metropolitan Transportation Authority voted to return the money to the government with a request that they be allowed to use it for higher priority projects.[75]

Examples of this sort, along with the previously cited crimes of Representative Cunningham, diminish the reputation of the legislature, as citizens come to believe that legislators are using their position for self-enrichment or for their own political purposes. In response to these concerns, after the Democrats regained control of Congress in 2007, they enacted reforms that attempted to bring a degree of transparency to the earmark process. Legislation passed in the summer of 2007 required that members of the House and Senate seeking earmarks (or "congressionally directed spending items," as they are now called) publicize their proposals at least forty-eight hours before the chamber votes on them and declare that neither they nor their families would directly benefit financially. The bill allowed a point of order in the Senate against any earmark added to the bill during Conference Committee deliberations. In addition, the legislation also required that the representative who had requested the earmark be named in the committee report, and if a lobbyist had pressed for the earmark he or she also had to be named. More informally, the party leadership in both chambers pledged to reduce the total number of earmarks. By one count, the final appropriations bills for FY 2008 represented a 51 percent reduction in the total cost of earmarks from the FY 2006 figure.[76]

Some argued that the transparency provision could be evaded because it was left to the floor leaders and the committee chairs rather than to a neutral person such as the parliamentarian to decide whether or not an earmark had been properly reported. There also are cases in which earmarks are sponsored by more than one representative and instances when a representative sponsors an earmark as a favor to his colleague, thus obscuring who is really responsible for it. The hope that transparency would embarrass members who sought too many earmarks and create public pressures to reduce their numbers does not seem to have worked out. In 2007, despite the reduction in the cost of earmarks, 428 of the 435 members of the House successfully sponsored at least one earmark, suggesting that everyone is still getting something from the somewhat smaller overall pie.[77]

In fact, transparency may have had the perverse effect of enhancing members' incentives to seek earmarks. Because everyone can see who is receiving what, members will be under greater pressure to obtain a bigger share for their districts—"How come Representative X got twice as much for his constituency than you did?"—and as the process becomes more broadly publicized, constituents may become more aggressive in their requests to members. Representative José E. Serrano, a New York Democrat who chairs the House Appropriations Subcommittee on Financial Services put it this way: "What's happened is that the system is more open to the public, to the press and indeed to other members. Of course, when it becomes open to other members, everybody looks around and says, 'Oh, I could have gotten that for myself.'"[78]

The provision requiring the naming of the lobbyist also could have a double-edged effect. Such a record may help a political opponent or even a prosecutor to show a connection between campaign contributions and earmarks. On the other hand, it may provide a lobbyist with a means to advertise her effectiveness in gaining earmarks to potential clients. "Look what we got for these folks; we can do the same thing for you." Transparency may raise questions for members such as Representative Young, who might sponsor earmarks intended for interests outside their constituencies, or for members such as Senator Stevens, who seem to favor people who have been overly generous contributors to their election campaigns, or members such as Representative Ralph Regula of Ohio, who has sponsored earmarks for the National First Ladies' Library in Canton, Ohio, an institution founded by his wife and run by his daughter.[79] But it is unlikely to reduce the taste for earmarks. "Democracy is a contact sport," said Representative Nancy Boyda as she defended the earmarks that she had requested, "and I'm not going to be shy about asking for money for my community. My guess is that next year I'm going to be putting in more earmarks."[80]

PORK BARREL AND SERVICE
IN COMPARATIVE PERSPECTIVE

Constituency service activities are a cross-national phenomenon. In Argentina, members of the legislature report that they spend a great deal of time doing casework for their constituents and, like their American counterparts, they travel home to their districts on most weekends and meet regularly with their constituents.[81] One survey of British members of Parliament found that 91 percent, excluding ministers, held "surgeries," or meetings in their districts with individual voters who have problems or concerns with the government. By 1996, MPs reported that about 40 percent of their time during sessions and as much as 60 percent of their time during recesses was devoted to constituency work.[82] In response to another survey, approximately 70 percent of MPs said that they advertised their surgeries, either through notices in the newspaper or by sending out circulars. Some even went door to door asking if there was anything that they could do, while others wrote letters to individual constituents seeking out cases.[83]

Although all representatives do this work, there is some variation within and across nations. In countries with strong and highly disciplined political parties, individual legislators will have little to do with designing major public policies. In that case, responding to the individual concerns of their constituents may well be their primary function. During the Fifth Republic in France, with the emergence of a strong presidency and the continued strength of their political parties, individual French deputies have become much less important players in the policymaking process. Because so many deputies concurrently hold positions as local government officials, their main role appears to be seeking favors for their constituents from the central government. Deputies receive "numerous demands from local councils on matters like road maintenance, school building, water supply, or flood damage."[84]

As suggested earlier, in authoritarian systems representatives may be encouraged to concentrate on such activities as a way to convey to citizens the sense (if not always the reality) that the government cares about their problems, thereby helping to maintain popular support for the regime. But pork barrel activities involving the distribution of public funds may not be quite as big a component of their jobs because such work depends in part upon the ability of the legislator to have some impact on public policy. As we have seen, the pork barrel success of members of the United States Congress is attributable to their key role in designing and funding the programs that government agencies are responsible for implementing. If individual legislators cannot shape government policy and if party discipline guarantees their support for the policy initiatives of the executive branch, they will have little leverage with government officials if they seek to gain funds for local projects. In Russia, for example, deputies were reminded by those in power that the interests of their constituencies in terms of public works projects were secondary to the higher priority projects that had been identified by the country's leadership.[85]

In the more open political systems characterized by strong governing parties, members of the majority party may not have the ability to vote against the wishes of their leaders, but they can communicate the needs and concerns of their constituents to leaders. The party leadership may be responsive to these requests as it plans public expenditures in order to maintain intraparty harmony and solidify the party's electoral position. In Australia, pork barrel activities are "a partisan phenomenon," with "benefits disproportionately accruing to the governing party's own incumbents" and with a particular emphasis on supporting the governing party's "most vulnerable colleagues in marginal seats." The goal appears to be explicitly to help the governing party maintain its parliamentary majority, whereas in the United States, although marginal representatives seem to be favored, a large proportion of such projects also find their way to members of the minority party.[86]

Some see the resources and effort that members of Congress invest in constituency service as the product of a weak political party system in the United States. To get reelected, representatives need to rely on the goodwill of their local constituents and also are personally responsible for raising most of the large sums of money required to finance their campaigns. But as we have seen, such constituency service activities also have been reported in countries with stronger political party systems. British MPs seek redress for the problems that constituents bring to their attention in their "surgeries" by contacting responsible government ministers, who invariably respond. Although such responses do not always solve the constituent's problem, they leave the voter with the impression that the legislator has made an effort to help. An examination of the records of the House of Commons shows that during the 1994–1995 session, 87 percent of the backbenchers raised constituency concerns during floor debates in the House or during the question period when members of the government respond to questions from the opposition and from their own backbenchers. And there is evidence that in recent years the amount of time that British MPs have been putting into constituency work has been increasing.[87]

Although the conventional wisdom is that pork barrel politics is "an alien feature" to British parliamentary life, a strengthened committee system has provided MPs with a venue to "pursue inquiries and issue reports to influence government policies that affect members' constituencies." One MP reports that his position on the Defense Committee enabled him "to make contacts" which were useful in getting contracts for a company in his district.[88] Finally, in Great Britain maintaining party discipline these days is more than simply cracking the whip; it does require some degree of responsiveness on the part of party leaders to the concerns of backbench MPs, and it seems reasonable that assisting MPs with local concerns is one way for the leadership to respond.

Some argue that these trends toward more constituency based efforts are a product of a weakening party system in Great Britain and are aimed at securing a "personal vote" for the MP—that is, a constituent's vote that is not determined by the MP's party affiliation but rather as a reward for his services from constituents who may not support his political party. There is some question about the size and importance (though not the existence) of such a personal vote for members of the United States Congress, but in Great Britain researchers are not convinced that a personal vote actually exists. Nonetheless, MPs, both in Britain and in other strong party systems, do seem convinced that there are some personal votes to be had, and there is no dispute that MPs do work on behalf of individual constituents that is quite similar to that in which their American counterparts engage.[89] And given the modest staff support afforded MPs, they spend as much or perhaps even more of their own time on this work than members of the U.S. Congress. Similarly, in France "the new deputy quickly realizes that local obligations occupy a significant portion of his time and take most of his energy," and voters "show their gratitude to their deputy for services rendered to the local community" as well as "the personal services" that the deputy has provided. Like their American counterparts, French deputies advertise their success in bringing local projects home to their constituencies, and although citizens in France vote primarily for the party, one of the reasons that they do so is because of the reputation and attention of their local deputy.[90]

Thus, in strong party systems, even if constituency work yields few personal votes for representatives, it should strengthen the reputation of their political party in the constituency and in that way redound to the members' electoral benefit. In other words, the electoral connection in strong party systems may be indirect; constituency service helps the party and therefore the representatives, rather than helping the representative directly or compensating for the weakness of political parties, as is the case in the United States.

The notion that representatives engage in constituency work primarily because they wish to be reelected assumes that reelection is their major career goal. And for many representatives, reelection is indeed an important and in some instances overriding goal. But there are other ways to continue one's political career, and in some countries remaining in the good graces of party leaders is the best approach. In Costa Rica and Mexico, legislators are legally prohibited from running for immediate reelection; nonetheless, they engage in constituency service to the same extent as their reelection-obsessed counterparts in the United States. Although the individual may not be running again, the party does run, and if the voters feel well served by the legislator's activities, his party presumably will benefit. The party, in turn, will be able to provide career assistance to the legislator after his assembly term is over, perhaps through a job in a government ministry or assistance in obtaining a private-sector post.[91] In Brazil, providing funds for local projects is a major activity of representatives even though, or perhaps because, there is very high turnover among members of Congress. They leave Congress because political or bureaucratic positions at the local and state levels are more financially rewarding and of greater status than a legislative career. One close observer of Brazilian politics concludes that "expectations of short careers discourage investment in legislative expertise and encourage concentration on pork," as members seek short-term gains rather than worrying about long-term policies or, for that matter, the reputation of the Congress.[92]

In a weak party system where voters cast their ballots for the person rather than the party and where the party has fewer resources to reward individual officeholders, the same calculation may not hold. When the activities of members of U.S. state legislatures who are term limited are compared with legislators in states where term limits do not exist, the former, whose time in office is legally restricted, appear to spend significantly less time seeking projects for their districts than their non-term-limited counterparts in other states who will face the electorate again.[93]

In Chile, legislators find themselves in the unenviable position of being expected by their constituents to respond to their particularized requests for personal services or favors, or for funds to support local projects, but being unable to really deliver on these expectations because of their relatively limited policymaking role. A member of one deputy's staff estimated that 95 percent of the communications that the legislator received from constituents dealt with these sorts of requests. This expectation for local service is rooted in the role that legislators played in the democratic period prior to the 1973 military coup, a time when more than half of the legislation considered by the Congress dealt with local issues. Legislators "could support their clients either by obtaining specific legislation or more often by amending a law, such as the budget law, to earmark resources for a particular end." Private laws providing pensions and other dispensations for individuals also could be enacted.[94] However, the new constitutional provisions put in place with the reestablishment of republican government in the 1990s severely limited the ability of legislators to respond to these demands. They now have little control over spending, and their ability to amend legislation to provide support for their constituents is restricted. In essence, they are relegated to making recommendations that the government can respond to or ignore as it pleases. In the words of one scholar,

"Deputies are expected to provide pork, have incentives to provide pork, but are limited in their capacity to do so."[95]

Electoral systems also may be a factor. It would seem at first glance that such constituency service would be most likely to occur in single-member district systems, where constituents know exactly who their representative is and expect him to perform the role of patron with them as the clients. The original concept of the representative from the single-member district as an advocate for the interests and concerns of a clearly defined and relatively homogeneous constituency would support such an assumption, and some data seems to verify that conclusion. A cross-national study of representatives in Australia, New Zealand, Ireland, Canada, and the United Kingdom found that 78 percent of the representatives elected from single-member districts had a high or medium constituency focus, meaning that they ranked constituency activity as either their top focus or tied with another aspect of their work. In contrast, only 42 percent of the representatives from multimember districts ranked constituency work in that manner. Among the single-member district representatives, those who were classified as marginal from an electoral standpoint had a stronger commitment to constituency service than their colleagues from safer districts.[96] It also appears that when France moved from proportional representation under the Fourth Republic to single-member districts under the Fifth Republic, the constituency activities of representatives increased.[97]

One study comparing the constituency activity of MPs in Britain and Ireland finds that Irish legislators are more active on every dimension of constituency work than their British counterparts. Although some of this is attributable to cultural differences between Ireland and Great Britain, the most significant factor is the single transferable vote electoral system used in Ireland. Under this system, voters list second and third choices when they vote, and excess votes captured by winning candidates as well as those votes won by minor candidates are transferred to these second and third choices. This arrangement seems to motivate Irish legislators to engage in constituency service activities as a way of bolstering their reelection chances.[98]

However, such constituency activities also occur in proportional representation systems with multimember districts. This is particularly so in open list systems, where the voter is permitted to express preferences among candidates, as opposed to the closed list systems where voters can cast their ballot only for the party list. One comparative study of several Latin American nations concludes that in every instance when a system other than a closed list is used, there is an electoral incentive for candidates of the same party to differentiate themselves from each other by "building a reputation among a set of followers for being able to provide jobs, public works projects, or outright graft to their followers."[99] However, in those proportional representation systems where the national party leadership exercises control over the nomination and election process, members are more likely to concentrate on national issues and less likely to be concerned with legislation that targets their constituencies for special benefits.[100] In pre-Chavez Venezuela, there was little evidence that members devoted much effort to getting pork barrel projects for their districts or that they initiated legislation with a specific local focus. That is because voters selected political parties and had little knowledge of or attachment to individual legislators.[101]

Cross-national evidence suggests that closed list proportional representation systems reduce the national budgetary pressures that come from an emphasis on pork barrel legislation.[102] In Germany's mixed single member-proportional representation system, a survey of members found that those who were elected from single-member districts had a greater interest in pork barrel projects than those elected from party lists.[103] New Zealand also elects some members from districts and some from party lists, but the parties assign "duty electorates" to members elected from the party list to serve as the party's designated representative in that geographic constituency (usually a constituency that has elected a member of the other party) to deal with casework and other constituency concerns.[104]

In less developed countries with weaker political parties, the pork barrel system resembles the situation in the United States to the extent that its goal is to support the careers of individual parliamentarians. It differs from the American system in the sense that individual legislators have relatively little to do with the design of major public policies and therefore spend most of their time importuning government officials to fund projects in their constituencies. In sub-Saharan Africa, these undertakings run the gamut from schools, health centers, and irrigation works to feeder roads, crop and settlement schemes, and various forms of cottage industries. Despite their limited size, projects of this type have an immediate tangible effect on the lives of the rural population, are highly visible, and constitute the substance of most demands for government assistance.[105] Because sources of private capital in these nations are often limited, virtually all funds for economic development need to come from the central government, and the representative's role in procuring these funds is a key expectation of constituents and crucial for the legislator's political survival. It is so crucial, in fact, that presidents or prime ministers who cannot rely on disciplined political parties to support their agendas use their control or influence over the federal budget as a way to solidify support among members of the legislature, explicitly trading local projects for legislative support.

In Colombia, fierce competition for parliamentary seats provides a major incentive for members to focus their activities "on extracting resources to reward supporters with jobs and other private goods." Their involvement in policy issues only occurs if the policy proposal at hand "furthers their primary interest in converting public funds into private payoffs." Rather than being accountable for public policy, members of the Colombian Parliament are concerned primarily with how public policy can provide them with the opportunity to bring resources to their constituents. Colombian presidents, aware of this situation, make deals with representatives, trading support for the president's agenda for resources for the constituency.[106] These activities are designed to build the reputation of legislators, many of whom are less interested in reelection to the legislature or a long career in that body (there is a high level of turnover among members of this parliament) and more interested in lucrative, long-term positions in a regional or state office or in the federal bureaucracy.[107]

This also seems to be the case in Brazil. One member of the Brazilian Congress indicated that "a political career in Brazil is closely connected to success in bringing home material benefits. . . . Especially in the poorest regions, communities judge their deputies on what they bring home." Another deputy said the legislator's "reason for being in Brasilia [the capital of Brazil] is to bring home resources. Otherwise, he's not doing his job." A member of the upper house, the Senate, added that "both deputies and senators have an obligation to seek funds to solve the problems of their region. Those who fail to do so are remiss." Local officials, community and business leaders, and interest group leaders "depend on deputies to get federal resources," and deputies in turn depend on the electoral support of these local elites.[108] Brazilian legislators have promised work on infrastructure improvements to specific firms in return for the votes of the firm's employees. And as in Colombia, Brazilian presidents build coalitions "by coupling deputies' disinterest in broad policy with their desire for pork."[109]

These examples from Latin America have some obvious parallels to the United States. One of the classic tools that American presidents have used to gain congressional support for their proposals is promising their support for a representative's pet project. Such trades are one of the ways that things get done in Washington, both in terms of presidential-congressional relations and in terms of gaining majorities in the Congress. During the administration of George W. Bush, Republican leaders in Congress used earmarks as a way to gather support for the president's agenda among some of their more recalcitrant members. And certainly, as in Brazil, if American representatives disappoint local elites such as constituency based interest groups, major industries, or local government leaders by failing to produce resources that they need, then in many cases their electoral prospects are likely to be at risk.

SUMMARY

The influence of constituents on the behavior of their representatives is most visible and robust when the representatives play the role of intermediaries between their constituents and the government bureaucracy. In that role, they can take care of small problems that individuals may be having with the government and can work to bring government resources to individuals, business enterprises, local governments, and public and private institutions in their constituencies. Members of the United States Congress have great leverage to deliver these services because of the crucial role that they play in designing and funding the programs that government agencies administer. Although such efforts can result in inefficiencies and wasteful government spending, representatives engage in such activities because they believe that doing so is essential to reelection and because they think that it is one of their responsibilities to those whom they represent. This work raises their visibility and their level of trust among their constituents and also seems connected to the generation of the campaign funds that members need to ensure their reelection. Unfortunately, such work sometimes carries with it the appearance, and on occasion the reality, of corruption.

This role of working on behalf of the constituency, and particularly on the problems of individual constituents, seems to describe the activities of legislators around the world. But the effort that representatives put into delivering government resources to their constituents and the extent to which these efforts succeed depends on the nature of the country's electoral system and the strength of its party system. When the electoral and party systems provide few incentives for representatives to gain a personal vote based on their services, they still may perform services for individual constituents, but they are less likely to be able to influence the distribution of government resources. Weaker political parties and electoral systems that allow the voters to choose not just among political parties but among candidates create much greater incentives for representatives to engage in the full range of constituency activities. Their success in these endeavors will turn on their ability as individual representatives to affect the policy decisions that the government takes.

5

Representation and Public Policy

To this point we have assessed representation from a descriptive perspective (being "like" one's constituency) and a service perspective (providing assistance and resources to one's constituency). In this chapter, we turn to a discussion of the representative's role in the policymaking process and, more particularly, the extent to which constituency attitudes compared with other factors affect the representative's decisions concerning which policy initiatives to advocate or support.

The principal agent model suggests that the representative's policy decisions should be *determined* by constituency opinion and interest. But the greater plausibility of alternative models of representation that emphasize two-way communication between constituents and representatives suggests that these decisions are *influenced* rather than determined by constituency opinion and interest. Other influences on the representative's decision include his own beliefs and the views of his colleagues, those holding executive positions, his party leaders, and interest groups. The relative influence of these different factors will vary across countries and from issue to issue within countries.

Analyses of the role orientations of representatives (by which we mean their understanding of their job) suggest two main perspectives on what the relationship should be between constituency opinions and the policy positions that legislators take.[1] The representative who thinks of himself as a "delegate" believes that the job of the legislator is to reflect the opinions of his constituents as he makes policy decisions, regardless of his own views on the subject. If one's constituents are opposed to tax increases, the delegate representative should vote against tax increases, even if he believes that higher taxes will better serve the budgetary and revenue needs of the nation. Just as a country's delegate to the United Nations acts under the instructions of his government, the representative who views himself as a delegate acts under the instructions of his constituents. As such, the delegate view is compatible with the democratic view of representation; ideally citizens should govern themselves, but because from a practical standpoint it is impossible for them to do so in the modern nation-state, the representative is bound to carry out their wishes when he knows what those wishes are.

An alternative role orientation—that of trustee—emphasizes the responsibility of the representative to use his own judgment about what is best for his constituents when deciding which policy options to support. To understand what the term trustee means, consider the example of a minor child who has inherited a great deal of money. Usually, a court appoints a trustee who decides how to invest or spend the child's money. The trustee, of course, is unlikely to solicit the opinion of the child on these matters, but the decisions that she takes must be in the best interests of the child. In the same way, the legislator as trustee is bound always to act in the best interests of his constituents when he decides how to vote on taxes or on any other issue, but he neither seeks nor follows their instructions, and he is not required to act in accord with their opinions. The rationale for this position, which has been associated with the British parliamentarian Edmund Burke, has been explored earlier as we discussed the deficiencies of the principal-agent model. The representative should have latitude to use his own judgment because he has more information than his constituents and a better understanding of what is in their interests than they themselves have. Rather than vote as they wish, he thinks of himself as voting as they would wish him to if they had the same information and expertise as he had.

Burke also argued that if the best interests of the constituency are in conflict with the best interests of the nation as a whole, the representative should vote for what is good for the nation. This variation of the trustee orientation stands in opposition to the views of many representatives who, although they think of themselves as trustees, believe that it is their job to act first in the interests of their constituencies. Such a position makes the implicit assumption that what is good for the constituency is good for the nation. Others who view themselves as trustees reason, with Burke, that the representative's first responsibility is to the national interest.

DELEGATES OR TRUSTEES?

The delegate-trustee dichotomy provides the theoretical framework for a great deal of empirical research on the extent to which the actions of representatives reflect the opinions of their constituents. This sort of research begins with something of a paradox. On the one hand, there is overwhelming evidence that citizens do not actively monitor the behavior of their representatives, that many do not even know who their representatives are, that very few communicate with their representatives, that most know very little about the policy questions before the legislature, and that constituency opinion on most issues most of the time is either vague, not discoverable, or subject to change based on how the issue is framed. On the other hand, although members of all legislatures are well aware of these facts and in practice act for the most part as trustees, it is nonetheless the conviction of many, particularly members of the United States Congress, that the views and interests of their constituents should always be at the forefront of their deliberations and that the first thing they must do as they decide what position to take on a non-routine issue is to assess the constituency implications of their actions.[2]

One resolution of this paradox—the lack of information and attentiveness on the part of the represented juxtaposed with the acute concern that representatives have about constituency opinion—is to conceive of the representative's concern in anticipatory terms. He wants to know how his constituents will react to what he does rather than what they want him to do, as the principal-agent model would suggest. Representatives try to anticipate or predict how or whether their constituents will react to what they have done. Such predictions will depend on a number of factors: the type of issue involved; how intensely their constituents, or a group of constituents, may feel about the issue; the salience of the issue in terms of media coverage; and the importance of the issue to key interest groups, particularly those groups with a strong presence in the constituency.

Studies conducted in a number of different nations have asked questions of representatives designed to reveal whether they view themselves more as trustees or as delegates. The most common responses suggest a trustee orientation, but often the representative indicates that the importance of constituency opinion in their decisions depends on the issue. This answer is not a matter of waffling.[3] Rather, legislators operate in an environment characterized by electoral and information uncertainty. Although they may have won their previous elections, they are always concerned that a series of votes or even one specific vote with which significant numbers of their constituents, or significant interests within the constituency, disagree can spell trouble in their next election campaign. Thus, representatives "are keen to pick up the faintest signals in their political environment. Like antelope in the open field, they cock their ears and focus their full attention on the slightest sign of danger."[4]

They also listen for signals from the constituency because there is reason to believe that although they may act as trustees, the expectations of many of their constituents are oriented more toward the delegate than the trustee model. When a sample of the British electorate was asked how their MP should resolve a conflict between what the MP thinks is best and what he thinks the constituency would want, 53 percent said the MP should follow the constituency; only 11 percent said the MP should follow his own conscience, and 34 percent said it depended on the issue. When the "depends on the issue" option is not offered, 76 percent opt for the constituents' preferences as the deciding factor. When the respondents were given the hypothetical choice between the MP following the views of his party leadership or the views of the constituency, 83 percent said the constituency's views should be the determining factor.[5] Although these exact questions have not been asked of U.S. respondents, one proximate question suggests a somewhat different result. When asked to agree or disagree with the statement that "members of Congress should do what their district wants them to do even if they think it is a bad idea," 49 percent agreed and 41 percent disagreed. It is possible that the large number of disagrees is explained by the use of the strong phrase "bad idea" in the question. On the other hand, 85 percent of respondents agreed that "members of Congress should do what is best for the entire country, not just for their districts."[6] But when French citizens were asked whether their deputies should be representatives of the nation or representatives of the district, more than 50 percent said the nation, with only one-third indicating that the district should come first.[7]

It may be difficult to categorize legislators as either trustees or delegates because the wrong sort of question is being asked. Typically, the researcher wants to know how the representative will resolve a hypothetical conflict between his views and the views of his constituents. But in real life the representative is seldom confronted with that choice because most of the time he does not know the opinions of his constituents with any degree of precision. Rather, as suggested earlier, he is trying to figure out how his constituents will react *after* he has cast his vote, or in the parlance of principal-agent theory, he wants to know if and how he will be held to account for what he has done.

Nonetheless, political scientists have continued to look for linkages between constituency attitudes and the votes that representatives cast. This research agenda has been bedeviled by a number of methodological challenges. First, it is often difficult to measure constituency opinion in a reliable manner, especially when it comes to opinion at the legislative district level. National or even statewide polls seldom produce enough respondents in a particular congressional district to yield an accurate reading of constituency opinion, and district level sampling that would include a sufficient number of respondents is very expensive and seldom done.

Second, assuming that the breakdown of constituency opinion on an issue is known, what does the representative or the researcher do with that data? If 55 percent of all eligible voters in a district support President Bush on the war in Iraq and 45 percent are against, should we assume that constituency opinion favors the Bush strategy? Or should one look at the breakdown among actual voters, or among those voters who are among the representative's strongest supporters? A representative might determine that the minority on an issue includes a large percentage of his most active supporters, or that the majority contains many who are unlikely to vote in the next election. And what if more than two options exist, as is often the case on public policy issues? Is constituency opinion fairly represented by the option that receives the most support, even if that figure only constitutes a plurality rather than a majority of the respondents? Finally, there is the question of causation. If the representative's vote agrees with constituency opinion, does that mean that the representative is responding to the views of his constituents, or is he simply voting his own views which happen to be in harmony with those of his constituents? Has the representative taken steps to shape the views of his constituents so that the congruence between his views and those of a majority of his constituents is largely a product of the representative's efforts rather than the product of constituency pressure placed on the representative?

The first major empirical study of the relationship between constituency opinion and the voting behavior of representatives was conducted by Warren Miller and Donald Stokes of the University of Michigan using data collected in 1958. Miller and Stokes sought to measure four variables: the attitude of constituents on a particular issue, the attitude of the representative on the same issue, the representative's perception of the attitude of his constituents on that issue, and how the representative actually voted on that issue. Although their research encountered all of the methodological problems mentioned above (particularly estimating constituency opinion on the basis of very small samples), their findings pointed the way for more sophisticated studies. In brief, they found no direct relationship between constituency attitudes and the votes that representatives cast on foreign policy issues or on general social welfare issues, but they did detect a direct connection on civil rights issues. They found much more significant correlations between the representatives' own attitudes on all of these issues and their votes, as well as a strong correlation between their perception of their constituent's attitudes and their votes. In the case of the latter, however, there were low correlations between their perceptions of constituency attitudes and the actual attitudes that constituents conveyed to their interviewers (especially on foreign policy and social welfare issues), suggesting the possibility that although members may think they are voting in accord with their constituents' views, they may not really know where their constituents stand. There also was little support for the view that constituents elect representatives who think as they do, with low correlations between representatives' attitudes on issues and constituency attitudes.[8]

The enduring components of the Miller-Stokes findings are that the relationship between representatives and their constituents will vary depending on the salience of the issue (civil rights being more salient in 1958 than foreign policy) and that representatives seem to believe they are voting in accord with constituency attitudes, even if they are not in fact doing so. What was missing from their analysis was a sense of how representatives conceived of their constituency and, therefore, whose opinions they thought they were replicating—for example, the representative's co-partisans in the district, or segments of the constituency that felt intensely about an issue and to whom the particular policy or vote was therefore important.

Later research found a stronger relationship between the views of constituents who identified with the representative's party and the representative's votes.[9] Some research efforts focused less on the direct relationship between constituency attitudes and representative behavior and more on the connection between the representative's behavior and his perception of constituency views.[10] Given the ambiguity often associated with the views of voters and the difficulty in assessing those opinions in any precise way, subjective congruence (the representative's belief that he is voting as his constituents wish) might be more important than objective congruence (actually voting as the constituency wishes).

THE NATURE OF THE ISSUES

The impact of constituency views can depend on the complexity and visibility of the issue, with the latter influenced by how central it is to a nation's partisan divisions. Issues that divide people along party lines tend to be more visible to the public. In the United States, the Democratic position on minimum wage legislation is clear and quite different from the Republican position, whereas the Democratic position on relations with China is not very clearly differentiated from that of the Republican Party. And the minimum wage issue is certainly more salient to the public than China policy. Combining these two factors, Patricia Hurley and Kim Hill[11] present several possibilities. On issues that are highly visible, easy to understand, and central to the discourse among political parties—for example, abortion or minimum wage laws—a strong connection between the representative's views and his perception of constituency views should be found. On more complex, less visible issues that are not central to partisan cleavages, such as China policy, the connection between constituency views and legislative behavior would be a good deal more tenuous, and public opinion is unlikely to have much influence. On more complicated party-defining issues, such as social security reform, the flow of communication would more likely be from the representative to the represented; any congruence on these issues between the representative's views and his perception of constituency views would be largely a product of what the representative tells his constituents rather than what his constituents tell him.

Support for this approach comes from several studies that have detected virtually no constituency influence on foreign and defense policy issues, generally complex issues where opinion does not break along party lines. On these issues, "the predominant pattern is for senators to vote in accord with their own ideological preferences—even when that involves voting against constituency preferences." On domestic issues, the data are mixed, with voting on these issues "probably more responsive to constituency preferences than on defense and foreign policy."[12]

Constituency preferences may be more important on more visible votes. Some votes taken in Congress receive much more attention from the media than others. Except in times of war, media coverage is more likely to focus on domestic than on foreign affairs. Also, votes taken in the Senate are more visible and more likely to be subject to intensive media coverage than votes taken in the House. That is because there are fewer senators than representatives, because many senators are likely to be known nationally, and because on controversial issues the decisions of the Senate may turn on only one or two votes. For these reasons, "the media regard the actions of individual senators as inherently more newsworthy than the actions of individual House members." While House members may cast their votes in relative anonymity, for voters for whom highly publicized senatorial votes are important, information and awareness of how senators vote is quite high. For example, in the case of the Senate vote on the controversial nomination of Clarence Thomas to the Supreme Court in 1991, information levels were particularly high among African-Americans, conservative men, and liberal women. Similarly, when a representative's vote is raised during a campaign, members of groups that have displayed an interest in the issue exhibit heightened levels of information, which tend to affect their vote.[13]

In sum, when issues are publicized, either through the media or in a campaign, subsets of the public that are concerned with these issues display a great deal of information and are quite likely to be aware of how their representatives vote. This idea was first introduced by Phillip Converse, one of the pioneers of public opinion research, who suggested that researchers would do well to focus on "issue publics," by which he meant that "different controversies excite different people to the point of real opinion formation." What excites whom depends in large measure on voter self interest, which in turn will encourage members of an issue public to learn more about the issue and to be more attentive to how their political leaders act on that issue. Farmers will be particularly interested in agriculture policy, Jewish voters in issues having to do with Israel, and African-American voters in civil rights issues.[14] An illustration of this point comes from one study of the voting behavior of Southern Democrats in Congress on two pieces of civil rights legislation—the Civil Rights Act of 1990 and a relatively minor amendment dealing with employment discrimination. The higher the percentage of African-Americans in a representative's district, the more likely he was to vote for the act. But the relationship broke down on the less visible amendment. The author concludes that representatives assumed that their constituents would discover how they voted on the more salient issue but that their vote on the less visible amendment was likely to go unnoticed.[15]

ASSESSING AND REACTING
TO CONSTITUENCY OPINION

As our discussion has suggested, constituency opinion may be congruent with the opinions of representatives for any number of reasons aside from the traditional delegate view that constituents "instruct" their representatives. When people vote for a representative, their decision is at least partially influenced by the compatibility between a candidate's worldview or basic philosophy of government and their own, and it is reasonable to believe that concurrence on specific issues derives from this more diffuse level of agreement. Conservative representatives who are opposed to big government and in favor of tax cuts are elected by citizens who have similar views. Although the voter may not have an opinion or know very much about a particular tax issue before Congress, chances are that she will agree with what the representative does because of their general philosophical compatibility. Thus, agreement between the representative and those whom he represents on a specific vote may be less a product of constituent pressure on the representative to conform and more of a preexisting condition.

Citizens elect those who most strongly reflect their own view of the political world; although representatives may stray somewhat from these preferences after the election, if they do not move back in the direction of their constituents when the next election approaches they are likely to face increasingly difficult reelection campaigns.[16] The most important variable explaining the popularity of United States senators appears to be their ideological distance from their constituents. As a senator's views begin to deviate substantially from those of her constituents, her popularity tends to decline.[17] And as they get closer to their next reelection, there are often detectable shifts in their voting behavior and their issue stances as they attempt to more closely align their public positions with current constituency opinion.

As the 2008 congressional elections approached, two of the most vulnerable members of the United States Senate appeared to be Susan Collins, Republican of Maine, and Mary Landrieu, Democrat of Louisiana. Both represented states that had voted for the other party's presidential candidate in 2004. Collins would be facing an electorate that was strongly opposed to the war in Iraq and decidedly negative about President Bush. Landrieu would be facing an electorate that was more conservative than her voting record, especially given the decline in the number of African-Americans in New Orleans after Hurricane Katrina. Collins responded by shifting her position on Iraq, which previously had been supportive of the Bush Administration. She stated that she no longer supported "an open ended and unconditional commitment of U.S. troops in Iraq," and she joined with a bipartisan coalition of senators that proposed implementing the recommendations of the Iraq Study Group. She also was one of four Republican senators who voted to allow a floor vote on a proposal to withdraw troops by the spring of 2007, although she later voted against the proposal itself. For her part, Landrieu opposed her party leaders in the Senate more often than all but one other Senate Democrat. Notably, she opposed an energy tax package that she said would hurt Louisiana's oil and gas industries, and she was among the small number of Democrats to oppose a compromise immigration bill on the grounds that it would be too accommodating to undocumented immigrants.[18]

The representative's assessments of constituency opinion and predictions on how the constituency is likely to react to his policy stands draw on a number of diverse data sources. Taken together, communication from community leaders, editorials in local newspapers, public opinion polling when it is available at the constituency level, mail from constituents, and visits home can provide the legislator with a good sense of the direction and intensity of public opinion on many issues. Added to that is the general knowledge of the constituency that the representative has gathered from his time in office as well as during his pre-congressional career. Prior to taking office, the typical representative is likely to have had a lengthy period of residence in the constituency and a record of involvement in community affairs. This history with his constituents can help him to anticipate their views and their likely response to many issues and can guide him toward the best approach to educating them and shaping their opinion on the issues.

Legislators can educate their constituents in a variety of ways. Many U.S. legislators send "newsletters" to their constituents highlighting their activities in Congress and the positions they have taken. Some include questionnaires with these newsletters inviting constituents to let them know their views. Because those who return such questionnaires do not constitute a valid sample of the constituency and because such questionnaires often contain loaded questions—questions that by their wording not too subtly point the respondent in a certain direction and are therefore designed more to shape than to solicit opinion—they seldom provide the legislator with a reliable guide to constituency opinion. Rather, their real purpose is to convey to the constituents the sense that the legislator is interested in and cares about their views. Nonetheless, there is anecdotal evidence that representatives do monitor the responses to these questionnaires, reasoning that those citizens who take the trouble to fill them out and return them are likely to be among the representative's more politically active and attentive constituents. One former member of the House told me that when the results from his questionnaires were running against the policy direction that he was inclined to support, it gave him some pause, and on occasion led him to reconsider his position.

All representatives and senators now have web sites that they use as another vehicle to educate their constituents. In addition to advertising their availability to help constituents and their success in doing so, they often provide an explanation of their positions on the important issues facing Congress and the nation. For example, Democratic Representative Rahm Emanuel from Chicago has posted on his web site a side-by-side comparison of the cost of prescription drugs in the United States and the cost of the same drugs in Canada. Representative Mark Kirk, a Republican from the northern suburbs of Chicago, has a number of entries on his web site urging a tougher stance against Iran, and Representative Judy Biggert, a Republican from a district south of Chicago, has a portion of her web site devoted to "Judy on the Issues," where she explains her position on energy, health care, immigration, and tax policy. Virtually all web sites also provide an easy link that allows constituents to contact the representative to express their opinions. We have no data on how many people view or utilize these web sites, but they do provide a representative with a no-cost method of framing the issues and his positions for his constituents, and they provide at least some constituents with a quick and easy way to let their representatives know what they think.

Legislators also seek to build strong relationships with the media in their district to help them learn what is on the minds of their constituents and the opinion leaders who write editorials and make election endorsements. These relationships also provide a way for representatives to tell their constituents about themselves, their positions, and their activities. It has been estimated that about half the stories that local media run about incumbent members of the House of Representatives are initiated by the representative or his staff; such coverage encourages the perception among constituents that the legislator is hard at work on their behalf and seems to make a positive impression, especially on those constituents who do not share the legislator's party affiliation.[19]

It is difficult to overestimate the importance that members of Congress attach to "staying in touch" with their constituents, and the most effective way that they do so is by spending time in their constituency. Representatives regularly travel home on weekends and during periodic ten-day to two-week "constituency work periods." In a series of fascinating books, political scientist Richard Fenno reported on what he saw and heard as he spent several days traveling with a number of representatives through their districts.[20] When they come home, members usually have full schedules of meetings and appearances across the constituency; these are indeed "work periods." They have speaking engagements at local civic organizations, meet and greets at the private homes of supporters or at public places such as diners or shopping centers, one-on-one meetings with constituents who are having specific problems that they want the representative to help solve, and sessions with local leaders such as mayors, party leaders, state legislators, journalists, and key industry and union personnel. There is good reason to believe that these visits home are important to the voters. When asked to agree or disagree with the statement that "members of Congress come back to their districts too much," only 9 percent of the sample agreed and 78 percent disagreed.[21]

For his part, the representative has a number of things that he wishes to accomplish in these interactions. He wants to present himself to his constituents as a person who is one of them, who identifies with them and with the area, and who cares about what they think. By his presence, he advertises his availability to them to hear their problems and to participate in their rituals, such as high school graduation ceremonies or July 4 parades. He wants to listen, to hear what is on their minds, what seems of most concern to them, what they are upset about, and how they feel in general about events in Washington and in the world. These interchanges will provide the representative with crucial pieces of intelligence as he seeks to anticipate how his constituents will respond to what he does in Congress.

As they converse with their constituents, some representatives will emphasize their personal connections with the constituency, making the point that he is "one of them." Others emphasize policy in these discussions, as the representative identifies himself with issue positions that are important to and congruent with those with whom he is speaking. Most representatives adopt some combination of these approaches, depending on the culture and characteristics of the district. These efforts provide an opportunity to educate the constituency and to influence public opinion, but most importantly, they build trust for the representative. As citizens come into contact with their representative, see him connect with them as individuals, hear his views, share their opinions, and get to ask him or his staff for help with individual problems, their level of trust goes up. Trust is "the holy grail in producing positive, stable relationships between politicians and constituents."[22] It constitutes a reserve against which the representative can draw when he is back in Washington and an issue comes up that divides his constituency, if a tough no-win vote needs to be cast, or if the general public mood turns sour.

During the April 2007 spring recess, members of the House went home expecting to hear a great deal about Iraq. And by and large, they were not disappointed. One Republican, Judy Biggert of Illinois, a supporter of President Bush's war policy, said that her conversations with constituents indicated that although issues such as immigration and health care were on their minds, there was great anxiety about the war and people "were very weary of us being over there." She found her constituents worried "that we've spent so much money on a war when there are services that are needed and are not there, like health care." As representatives hear the concerns of constituents, they adopt an empathic attitude: "I feel your pain, I understand your worries, I'll do what I can." And finally, they try to educate. That means the representative will provide information to constituents about the Congress's current business, framing current issues so that her position on them will make sense, and often advocating a point of view in an attempt to move constituency opinion closer to her own. In Ms. Biggert's case, she defended her votes in support of the president and tried to provide a more positive image of progress in Iraq than the "bad news" that she said was consistently reported in the press.[23]

Staying in touch, creating trust, and fostering some level of compatibility between constituent views and the views of the representatives becomes more challenging as constituency size increases. Going home to meet with constituents is more likely to generate trust for Senator Leahy of Vermont than for Senator Boxer of California because on his trips home Senator Leahy can meet with a large percentage of Vermont's approximately 500,000 voting age citizens; Senator Boxer can meet with a tiny percentage of California's 25,000,000 potential voters. Because House districts are smaller and do not vary much in population, it is easier for representatives to stay in touch, although, as noted, some representatives' districts extend over thousands of square miles while others have districts of several city blocks.

CONSTITUENCY HETEROGENEITY

Some districts are more heterogeneous than others, and faithfully reflecting the opinions and interests of a heterogeneous constituency, assuming that a legislator is inclined to do so, will present significant challenges. The process of redrawing legislative districts in response to the decennial census tends to be affected primarily by partisan concerns, the desire to ensure the reelection of incumbents, the legal mandate that each district be equal in population, and, as noted, attempts to create majority-minority districts. The idea that districts should be drawn to reflect coherent, geographically based communities of interest and therefore a set of homogeneous views is a less important factor,[24] although there is some evidence that efforts to create safe seats may have had the effect of creating more homogeneous districts in a partisan sense.[25]

For those members of the United States Senate who represent the larger states in the Union, district heterogeneity is already a problem. Senators from states such as New York and California tend to have lower job approval ratings than senators from smaller states in part because it is difficult for them to discern a coherent state opinion or interest on many issues or to anticipate accurately how the state as a whole is likely to respond to a particular vote.[26]

Generally speaking, those who represent relatively homogeneous constituencies appear to have opinions that are more congruent with the opinions of their constituency as a whole than their colleagues who represent more heterogeneous constituencies. The problem is not that these representatives wish to be at odds with their constituents, but rather that it is difficult for them to figure out what it is that their constituents want. In that context, their most reasonable course of action may be to attend and be responsive to those whose views they do know—those who are most strongly and vocally committed on the issues and those who are among their traditional supporters.

From this perspective, representatives from heterogeneous constituencies are likely to be less interested in the opinions of the district as a whole and more interested in the opinions of the issue publics or subconstituencies mentioned earlier—identifiable subsets of the constituency with known, strong views on a subject.[27] This insight may account for the somewhat anomalous research findings on the relationship between electoral uncertainty and responsiveness to constituency wishes. One might assume that as electoral uncertainty increases—as a district becomes more competitive—a representative would become even more attentive and responsive to the opinions of his constituents, but one study of the voting behavior of United States senators found just the opposite: that the votes of senators from electorally safe states were more likely to be congruent with constituency opinion than the votes of senators from more competitive states.[28] Because competitive states are likely to be heterogeneous, their senators give up on the possibility of reflecting, or even being able to discover, a general constituency view; instead, they seek to identify and respond to the views of significant subconstituencies, particularly those that are attentive to the issues and that are among their electoral supporters.

In that context, the shifts in the positions of Senator Collins and Senator Landrieu as they approached the 2008 election made sense. Senator Collins was less interested in winning over Democrats by her shift on the Iraq war and more interested in shoring up support among the increasingly anti-war Republican moderates and independents that had long been her base. Senator Landrieu was attempting to underline her position to the right of the national Democratic Party, the place where most white Louisiana Democrats always have been most comfortable.

Subconstituencies also may explain why Republican senators worry so much about the views of the National Rifle Association or far right fundamentalist groups and Democrats are highly sensitive to the views of labor unions and other more progressive elements of their party. Although the electorate as a whole may disagree with many of the positions of these groups, in a competitive race a representative must ensure that his base of supporters is satisfied. Maintaining the excitement and commitment of supporters has a greater political payoff then attempting to figure out an average constituency opinion on an issue or attempting the even more difficult task of converting those who identify with the opposing political party to your cause. Thus, in a competitive district where voters may be divided on the issue of gun control, with a majority favoring gun control but an intense minority opposing, the representative may be well advised to deviate from the majority view and support the intense minority, particularly if the members of that minority have been a traditional part of the representative's electoral coalition. This politically wise decision will produce an empirical result that shows the legislator at odds with the (majority) view of his constituency, but it is exactly such a decision that will work to his advantage at the next election.

ISSUE UPTAKE

Constituency or subconstituency concern about an issue may be aroused by extensive media coverage, so representatives need to be particularly careful when they cast votes on high profile issues. They also worry about those issues that constituents would care a great deal about if they were called to voters' attention by the representative's political opponent in the next election. In that context, increased attentiveness and responsiveness to the policy concerns of constituents can be stimulated by the representative's previous election campaign. Legislators appear to take up the issues raised by their unsuccessful challengers in those campaigns in an attempt to strengthen their position for their next campaign. They reason that their opponent would not have raised these issues unless he perceived that the incumbent was vulnerable on these points, or unless there was some indication that the issue could be important to significant segments of the constituency. Representatives engage in "issue uptake" to address these potential vulnerabilities, sometimes by changing their voting patterns on the policy issues involved, by addressing the issue in floor speeches, or by introducing and cosponsoring legislation that deals with the issue.[29]

The issue uptake phenomenon need not necessarily result from their own previous election campaign. After several Republican senators and representatives lost their reelection campaigns in 2006 in part because of growing discontent with the war in Iraq, a number of Republicans facing reelection in 2008 began to distance themselves from President Bush and his war policies. Some, such as Senator Gordon Smith of Oregon, went as far as advocating withdrawal of troops, and others, such as Senators John Sununu of New Hampshire, John Warner of Virginia, and Pete Domenici of New Mexico, called upon the president to change his strategy. Ultimately, the latter two decided against running for reelection, although for reasons of age and health, they said, rather than fear of losing. On the House side, Republican Representative Mark Kirk, who in previous elections had sailed to easy victories in his district in the northern suburbs of Chicago, came within a few percentage points of losing his seat in 2006 to a relatively unknown and underfinanced challenger who had made a significant issue of Kirk's support for the war and President Bush. In 2007, Kirk began to move away from President Bush, joining a group of Republicans who went to the White House for a high profile visit with the president to express their concerns about the administration's Iraq policy. He also began to cast at least some votes that demonstrated his independence from the administration.

THE INFLUENCE OF CAMPAIGN TACTICS

Despite their knowledge and involvement with their constituents, representatives are never entirely certain how their constituents will react to their stand on an issue and therefore what the electoral consequences of their actions (or inaction) might be. The advent of expensive and often vicious negative advertising sometimes financed by national party committees and outside interest groups that target specific incumbents for defeat can place a particular vote, often in highly simplified and inflammatory language, under the public microscope. Representatives say that when they cast a vote on a controversial issue, they sometimes consider how that vote will appear to constituents when subjected to a nasty thirty-second attack ad. There is also evidence that in many instances, legislation and amendments are proposed that will have little chance of passage but have as their real purpose forcing the representative to cast a vote that will be grist for his opponent's television commercials in the next election. In the fall of 2007, Democrats scheduled repeated votes on their version of the State Child

Health Insurance Program, despite their knowledge that President Bush was going to veto the legislation, in part so that they could depict their Republican colleagues who supported the veto as hostile to a program aimed at providing health insurance to children. Similarly, Republicans in the House forced a vote on a proposal to permanently repeal the estate tax, hoping to get freshman Democrats from more conservative districts to cast votes that could be characterized as favoring a tax hike.[30]

Earlier, in the summer of 2007, the Democratic Congressional Campaign Committee began running ads against three Florida Republican representatives for voting against a proposal to "lower seniors' Medicare deductibles and co-payments." Not to be outdone, the Republican Congressional Campaign Committee ran radio spots accusing freshman Democratic Representative Joe Donnelly of Indiana of giving "union organizers more power to intimidate employees" and for voting "for outrageous pork-barrel spending on peanut storage and transporting tropical fish." In both instances, the votes in question were described in highly partisan and oversimplified terms (what else can one do in thirty seconds?) and were cast on larger and more complex pieces of legislation of which these provisions were a relatively small part. But the issues cited in the ads were chosen to demonstrate an ideological distance between the representative and his constituents (seniors in Florida and antiunion, fiscally conservative Indiana voters). Notably, these ads were run fifteen months before the next congressional election, suggesting that congressional campaigns have become ongoing phenomena rather than biannual events restricted to the autumn of even-numbered years. This means that representatives need to be concerned about how their votes will be characterized almost from the moment they are cast.[31]

ACCOUNTABILITY

What then are the consequences of perceived disparities between constituency views and representative behavior? When a representative strays from the views of his constituents—or fails to predict accurately how they will respond to his actions—is he held accountable to the extent that he suffers electoral defeat and, conversely, is fidelity to the constituency sufficient to guarantee victory? Are representatives who fail in their quest for reelection more likely to have strayed from the views of their constituents than those who succeed? Are all deviations equally as likely to have adverse repercussions in the elections?

It is possible that citizens are more likely to call their representatives to account on some types of issues than on others. One study argues that voters care more about "process issues" such as congressional pay raises, term limits, and campaign finance reform than they do about substantive policy issues. Representatives who seem vulnerable to electoral defeat are more likely than their colleagues from safer districts to abandon their own views on these subjects in favor of what they believe to be the views of their constituency. When these issues are broadly publicized, constituency opinion seems a greater constraint on a representative's activity than in instances where there is less publicity. But even in these cases, deviance from constituency views seldom results in electoral defeat; at worst, the incumbent is likely to experience reduced majorities in the next election.[32]

One careful summary of the evidence regarding the effect of deviation from constituency views on reelection success concludes that, "even knowledgeable voters will tolerate a range of ideological positions and will strongly support incumbents so long as they are within that range"; positions adopted by incumbents "are probably decisive in no more than 5 percent of the reelection races."[33] An intensive study of the seventy-three cases in which incumbent representatives were defeated for reelection to the U.S. House of Representatives between 1968 and 1974 found that in only two instances could the defeat be attributed to deviation from the policy wishes of the constituency.[34]

However, these findings are from the era before extensive and expensive television advertising by candidates and the parallel and supposedly independent campaign efforts of national party committees and interest groups. It has been estimated that in more than 40 percent of contested races involving incumbents, at least one outside group mounted a significant effort of this sort.[35] Because modern campaign advertising typically distorts an incumbent's position or focuses on one specific hot button issue, voters may perceive a much greater difference between their views and those of the representative than in fact exists. It also is not clear how wide the acceptable range of deviation from the constituency might be. In 2004, Senator Tom Daschle, a Democratic senator from South Dakota and Democratic minority leader who had served eighteen years in the Senate, lost his reelection bid. Although several factors were at play, one was the increasingly liberal voting record that he had established during his time as the Democratic Party floor leader, a record that no doubt put him at greater variance with the more conservative attitudes of the citizens of South Dakota.

The electoral effect of deviations from constituency preferences also may depend on partisan factors. One scholar argues that Democrats who are to the right of their constituencies and Republicans who are to the left of their constituencies will escape electoral consequences because voters will understand that if they are defeated, their successful opponents will be even further away from district opinion. On the other hand, Democrats who are significantly to the left of their constituencies and Republicans who are significantly to the right of their constituencies may suffer adverse electoral consequences because it is reasonable to believe that their replacements will be closer to the average district opinion.[36] This reasoning, however, does not take into consideration party primary challenges to incumbents. In 2006, for example, Senator Joseph Lieberman, a centrist Democrat, was successfully challenged from the left for his party's nomination by Ned Lamont. And in the 7th Congressional District of Michigan, Representative Joe Schwartz, a centrist Republican, was defeated in the Republican primary by Timothy Walberg, a much more conservative challenger. In other words, moving toward the center may help legislators win an election, but also may make them vulnerable—especially in the current era of hyperpartisan-ship—to a primary challenger who is more in tune with the views of the party's base.

POLICY REPRESENTATION

It may be that when political scientists concentrate on the connection between constituency views and the way in which representatives vote, they are slighting other sorts of policymaking activities that may be just as effective in representing constituency opinions and interests. When representatives are asked about their role in the legislature, one of the most common responses is that they act and speak out on behalf of their constituents.[37] This role orientation is separate from voting as one's constituents wish; rather, it involves introducing legislation, designing amendments that benefit the constituency, making floor speeches, and intervening with bureaucrats, among other activities designed to draw attention to and foster action on behalf of the constituency. Richard Hall shows that "to the extent that members perceive a particular issue as relevant to constituents' interest they invest more of their scarce time and resources," especially the time of their staff, in relevant legislative action, particularly at the committee level. These "constituency driven participation choices" may illustrate the importance of the constituency more vividly than analyses of roll call voting behavior.[38]

In that sense, every member of the United States Congress works to find some issue that will resonate with his constituents. A member from a farm state may seek a place on the Agricultural Committee so that he can address commodity issues. Members from western states often take leadership roles on issues regarding natural resources and the environment. Members from large cities may become advocates for urban mass transit or for housing programs. Or a member may reach out to an area of the constituency where she may be weak. Senator Hillary Clinton, primarily identified with the urban, liberal interests of New York City, made it a point to emphasize agricultural issues as a way to connect with the concerns of the more rural and conservative regions of upstate New York. As a result, she was lauded by farming interests in the state for her help in gaining increased conservation funds, for securing disaster aid for dairy, apple, and grape growers, and for her advocacy of agriculture interests on trade and immigration issues. One farmer told a reporter that "she understands our commodities. She understands eastern dairy. She understands the importance of agricultural trade and the issues that underlie that."[39] In her first campaign for the Senate in 2000, Mrs. Clinton lost the upstate area of New York by 3 percent, but her commitments to agriculture and to other issues of concern to more rural voters (along with a very weak challenger) helped her to win 61 percent of the upstate vote in 2006.

Consider as well the career of Stephanie Herseth, who in 2004 was elected as a Democratic representative from South Dakota with a 2 percent margin of victory. Although Herseth's family had long been involved in South Dakota politics—her father served in the state legislature, her grandfather served as governor, and her grandmother as secretary of state—her victory was still a bit of a surprise given South Dakota's Republican voting habits (she won in the same year that Tom Daschle was losing his Senate race) and the fact that although she is a moderate, she is still less conservative on many issues than her constituents. Upon her arrival in Congress, she identified the development of alternative energy sources, including ethanol, as her highest legislative priority. Ethanol, of course, is an important issue in her farm state because increased ethanol use would likely result in higher commodity prices. According to congressional observers, she immersed herself in this complex issue and mastered it from top to bottom. Her leadership role on ethanol, in the view of local politicians in South Dakota, enhanced her reputation in the state and raised her political stock enormously. In 2006, she won reelection with a stunning 69 percent of the vote.[40]

The alternative energy issue has created constituency oriented legislative options for other members. Another source of alternative energy, for example, is liquid coal, and efforts to provide government incentives for developing that approach, including a guaranteed pricing mechanism, have come from representatives from coal producing regions. One is Representative Nick Rahall of West Virginia, who also chairs the House Resources Committee. He has been supported by, among others, Representative Richard Boucher, whose district in the western part of Virginia includes coal mining, Representative John Shimkus, who represents a downstate Illinois district rich in coal reserves, as well as Senators Barack Obama of Illinois and Jim Bunning of Kentucky.[41] As is the case with Representative Herseth and ethanol, liquid coal may or may not be a good idea for the country, but for these representatives and senators, it is an especially good idea because of the impact that it would have on the economies of their constituencies. These examples suggest as well that we may more readily find evidence of the policy responsiveness of representatives to their constituents in the legislation that they choose to specialize in and sponsor than in their voting records across a wide range of issues about which their constituents may have varying levels of interest and information.

A COMPARATIVE PERSPECTIVE

Although incumbent members of the U.S. Congress typically enjoy the support of some who identify with the opposition party, the most important factor determining a citizen's vote for Congress in the United States continues to be the party with which he or she identifies. In countries with strong political parties, this factor is even more important. When an issue is central to the program of a political party, citizens who identify with the party and legislators who are members of the party are likely to have congruent views. In one study, the views of legislators in four new democracies in Eastern Europe—Bulgaria, Hungary, Poland, and Czechoslovakia—were compared with the views of citizens. Voters and legislators were divided into party groups so that the views of the party's adherents among the public were compared with the views of legislators from that party. On issues that were salient to the party, the most common pattern was for party elites to overstate the divergence of issue preferences among the voters. That is, when voters were divided by party, each group had distinct views, but they were not nearly as divergent from each other as the views of their respective party leaders. Although these legislators could be viewed as being responsive to the views of their voters, another explanation is that the legislators may have been providing issue leadership to their constituents—a case of representatives educating the represented.[42] In the United States, the parallel situation would be the sharply divided views of Republican and Democratic Party representatives on the issue of abortion. Both groups of leaders tend to have virtually uniform and quite distinct positions on the issue. On the other hand, although citizens who identify themselves as Democrats and citizens who identify themselves as Republicans also tend to have distinct views compatible with those of their respective party leaders, the views of the voters overlap to a greater degree than the views of their representatives, and there is among the citizenry more of a willingness than among their leaders to find common ground.[43]

In nations characterized by strong political parties, the representative has a form of dual accountability—to his constituents and to his party—and the influence of the latter is likely to be greater because the party is largely responsible for nominating him for office and organizing and funding his election. In such political systems, citizen views are often represented by the political party for which they cast their vote. That is, voters select a political party in full knowledge (ideally) of its political program and expect (at least implicitly) that the party's representatives will support that political program.

The importance of the political party does not appear to be reduced to any significant degree by single-member district election systems. In Great Britain and Canada—single-member district systems similar to the United States—the political parties are strong enough to command the primary loyalty of their members. Those legislators who look forward to long careers in the parliament and ultimate promotion to ministerial positions are well advised to follow the wishes of their party leaders rather than those of their constituents if the two should conflict.

In the parliaments of France and Italy, legislators view their first obligation as being to their party leadership rather than to the geographic constituency from which they are elected. It is instructive to note that the lower chamber of each of these parliaments is called a "Chamber of Deputies." As noted, the term "deputy" is comparable to the term "delegate" in describing the role of the representative in the sense that it suggests that, unlike the trustee, such a representative is acting under instructions. In Rousseau's formulation, the deputies of the people "are nothing other than its commissaries; they cannot conclude anything definitively."[44] To put it in more popular terms, the sheriff's deputy in the American western film genre has no independent mandate to act. He is simply an extension of his principal—the sheriff—and is to do as he is told. In the case of strong party systems, the deputy is acting under the instructions of his or her political party rather than the instructions of the voter; that is, the deputy is bound to support the party, and the party in turn has a relationship with the voter that is comparable to the trustee's relationship with the voter. In some countries, party control is backed up by the ability of leaders to expel deputies who deviate from party instructions.

Strong political party systems make it difficult to predict what the relationship will be between the opinions of representatives and those of their constituents. In Turkey, a country with highly disciplined political parties operating under a system of proportional representation, one study found that representatives were more likely to have views that were contrary to, rather than congruent with, those of their constituents. For these representatives, the party rather than the voter was the major policy referent.[45] In another study comparing how members of five Nordic parliaments (Denmark, Finland, Iceland, Norway, and Sweden) viewed the importance of various tasks, the most common response (articulated by 52 percent of the respondents across all five countries) was that their job was to represent their parties; respondents also believed that members of parliament should articulate their own views on various public policy issues. Representing their own constituency, or individual voters in the constituency, was thought to be important by only 25 percent of the respondents, and the representation of interest groups seemed to be of relatively little importance.[46] Not surprisingly, therefore, proportional representation systems are characterized by a higher degree of agreement among the views of representatives from the same party than among the voters of each party.[47]

Those members of the parliaments of New Zealand and Germany who are elected from single-member districts seem to have a different and more intimate relationship with their constituency than their colleagues who are elected from the party list. The former are accountable to the constituency; for the latter, accountability is only to the party. However, there is little evidence of significant lapses in party discipline among either country's parliamentarians no matter how they are elected. One study of the mixed system introduced in Ukraine found that other factors, such as the safety of the single-member district and the ability of members to run in a district simultaneously with a place on the list, affected their level of party cohesion.[48]

That is not to say that representatives in nations with strong party systems or proportional representation electoral systems have no incentive to satisfy those who live in their geographic constituency. As noted in chapter 4, representatives in all nations engage in the same constituency activities as their colleagues in single-member district systems with weaker political parties, albeit not to the same extent in terms of time and commitment. The type of proportional representation system in use makes a difference. Incentives for personal campaigning based on one's reputation increase in those systems where the party leadership has little or no control over access to the ballot or the candidate's place on the party list, where candidates can be elected on votes that they receive independently from the votes of their copartisans, or where voters can cast multiple votes for individual candidates rather than a single vote for the party list.[49] In these instances, representatives may show a greater degree of autonomy on policy issues.

As a general rule, in nations where political parties are quite strong, individual legislators have relatively little to say about public policy. In such systems, policies are formulated by "the government"—leaders of the majority party (or majority party coalition) and bureaucrats—and it is the job of the representative to inform his constituents of the policies and explain, defend, or, if he is in the opposition, criticize those policies. However, in some strong party systems, legislators do have a role in shaping the policies and positions of their parties, albeit perhaps not as visibly as their colleagues in weaker party systems. In the Canadian Parliament, voting is characterized by high levels of party discipline, but as one study of that institution suggested, "discipline is voluntary and achieved in consequence of discussion and concession and not imposed upon a passive backbench by an authoritarian group of cabinet ministers."[50] The situation appears to be similar in Great Britain, France, and Germany. In Great Britain, interactions between party leaders and backbenchers can alert leaders to substantive problems with proposed legislation or to the possibility of adverse public reaction; the threat of an internal party revolt, which can be a harbinger of greater than anticipated public opposition, can encourage the government to alter its position and in some instances withdraw a proposal entirely.[51]

COLLECTIVE REPRESENTATION

It is not possible for every citizen to have his opinions reflected by one or even several legislators from his constituency. But it is quite possible for every constituent to have his or her opinions reflected by someone in the legislature, albeit someone who may have no electoral connection to the citizen.[52] If the goal is to have one's views represented, an electoral connection may not be a requirement for such representation to take place. This insight offers an explanation for why individual legislators may be slow to respond to shifts in public opinion in their own constituency but the legislature as a whole may seem to respond to shifts of public opinion at the national level. As John Stuart Mill had hoped, the legislature as a whole may be a representative cross-section of the opinions and interests of the nation, even if individual representatives fail (as they must) to reflect the interests and opinions of all of their constituents.

This suggests that if one truly wishes to represent opinions and interests throughout a large and diverse nation, it may be necessary to rethink the idea of geography as a basis for defining a constituency. As constituencies get larger and more heterogeneous, it becomes difficult indeed to think of them as having a community of interest over a broad range of issues. Given the increasingly tenuous connection between geography and interest, along with the desire to create a legislature that fairly represents the policy priorities of the entire population, political scientist Andrew Rehfield makes the provocative proposal to abandon geography entirely as a basis for constituency. Instead, citizens would be assigned on a random basis to a constituency, and thus the demographic and ideological composition of one representative's constituency would look very much like the composition of every other constituency.[53] The consequences of this radical (and highly unlikely) change in electoral institutions only can be speculated upon, but Rehfield's view that a legislature based on such a representational model would be likely to pursue centrist policies in the national interest and is worth considering.

A more realistic remedy for some of the deficiencies of geographically based constituencies would be replacing or supplementing the single-member district system with a system of proportional representation from multimember constituencies. This system would provide representation for those political parties and their voters that receive less than a plurality of votes. As discussed in chapter 3, proportional representation systems are also more likely than single-member district systems to provide representation that reflects the gender, racial, and ethnic composition of the population. Although single-member district systems can create a legislature that is as a whole reflective of national opinions and interests, it seems clear that in a large, heterogeneous nation, proportional representation would be a more effective means to secure that result.

SUMMARY

How then do we assess the effect of constituencies on the policymaking behavior of legislators? It seems clear that as representatives decide what position to take on a specific issue before the legislature, their first step is to assess the nature of constituency opinion on that issue. As they do that, representatives must ask themselves a series of questions:

1. Is this an issue about which a significant proportion of my constituents are likely to have an opinion?
2. Is this an issue about which a significant proportion of my constituents have a compelling interest?
3. Are the opinions and interests of these constituents on this issue congruent?
4. If the answer to any of the first three questions is yes, how likely is it that these constituents will know how I voted on this issue?
5. Even if the answer to question 4 is "unlikely," how will my constituents react if my vote is publicized to them, either by interest groups who care about the issue, by opinion leaders in the media, or by my opponent and his copartisans in the next election?
6. If the answer to question 5 is that my constituents are unlikely to react even when my vote is publicized, then can I view myself as a trustee on this issue, with the option to do what I think is best or wisest, or I can vote as my party leaders would wish?
7. If the answer to number 5 is that my constituents will react negatively to my vote, will their displeasure outweigh the displeasure of my party leaders if I vote against their wishes?
8. If I believe that a significant segment of my constituency might react adversely to my vote, can I offer a satisfactory explanation for my vote

(or account for my actions) if the issue is raised, particularly if the answer to question 3 is "no"—that is, I cannot explain my vote in terms of their interests?

9. If I cannot offer a convincing explanation, to what extent can the trust that I have built up with my constituents and the support of my party leaders and affected interest groups insulate me from political repercussions?

It is important to note that in the vast majority of situations, the answers to these questions will be self-evident and will not require a great deal of analysis by the representative. In the case of strong political parties, it is extremely rare that constituency pressures will outweigh the views of party leaders when a member casts his vote. Even when constituency views are important, there may not be any conflict between those views and that of the representative or those of party leaders. Remember as well that the representative who has been successful at providing services for his individual constituents and government funding for the district, or who has established strong personal ties with his constituency as well as a reputation as an articulate spokesman for their views, also has established a reservoir of constituency trust. The wider and deeper that reservoir of trust, the more latitude he will have to take risks when he votes in Congress and the more likely it is that his constituents will give him the benefit of the doubt when he casts a vote that may be unpopular with them.

But regardless of the level of trust, representatives always will be uncertain, at least to some degree, about how their constituents will respond to each and every issue. During the Carter administration, Senator Dick Clark of Iowa supported the treaty negotiated by the president to return the Panama Canal to Panama. In his next election campaign, this issue exploded, and Senator Clark was attacked for "giving away" the canal; and that, combined with an unanticipated rise in the importance of the abortion issue in Iowa, cost him an election that he seemed an odds-on favorite to win. These things do not happen on a regular basis, but each instance is a cautionary tale for every representative about the danger of guessing wrong about how one's constituents will react and the importance of staying in touch so that the likelihood as well as the consequences of guessing wrong, or missing a new issue, are minimized.

6

Interest Groups and Representation

Often when representatives appear to be acting contrary to what seems best for the nation or contrary to the wishes of national majorities, or when they seem to be ignoring the views of their constituents, interest groups, or what some call "special interests," are blamed. The percentage of people in the United States who agree with the statement that "the government is pretty much run by the few big interests looking out for themselves" has been above 50 percent ever since the early 1970s and as high as 76 percent in 1994. In another survey, 86 percent of respondents agreed with the statement that "Congress is too heavily influenced by interest groups when making decisions."[1] Although the results of contemporary surveys may vary, concern about the influence of private interests on public policy has been a part of American political culture since the founding period.

In The Federalist No. 10, James Madison warned against the dangers of faction, which he defined as "a number of citizens, whether amounting to a majority or a minority of the whole, who are united and actuated by some common impulse of passion, or of interest, adverse to the rights of other citizens, or to the permanent and aggregate interests of the community." Although these "passions" might have a number of different causes, in Madison's view,

> The most common and durable source of factions has been the various and unequal distribution of property. Those who hold and those who are without property have ever formed distinct interests in society. Those who are creditors, and those who are debtors, fall under a like discrimination. A landed interest, a manufacturing interest, a mercantile interest, a moneyed interest, with many lesser interests, grow up of necessity in civilized nations, and divide them into different classes, actuated by different sentiments and views.[2]

Madison's primary concern was the possibility that a majority faction composed of people with less in the way of economic resources might threaten the position and prerogatives of the wealthier minority; he was less worried about minority factions which, though they might prove disruptive, ultimately would be defeated, he thought, by the republican principle of majority rule.

But today our attention has shifted toward the activities of exactly those factions that constitute less than a majority and sometimes a very small minority and who seem to exercise substantial influence over public policy, the "republican principle of majority rule" notwithstanding. These groups may represent the narrow economic interests to which Madison alluded, such as the Pharmaceutical Research and Manufacturers of America. Others, such as the Sierra Club, may be advocates of a broader public interest. Some, such as the National Abortion Rights Action League or the National Rifle Association, are motivated by public policy concerns that have little to do with economic self-interest. Groups such as the American Association of Retired People (AARP) have a large number of members while others, such as the American Medical Association, have comparatively few. But some groups with few members, such as Exxon Mobil and other energy producers, more than compensate for their small membership with substantial financial resources; other small groups, such as the American Civil Liberties Union, have little in the way of funds. In the United States the activities of all these groups are protected by the First Amendment guarantees of free speech and the right of the people to assemble and petition the government for the redress of their grievances.

THE REPRESENTATIVE ROLE
OF ORGANIZED INTERESTS

As we have observed, on most issues most of the time individual citizens do not have specific policy opinions and may have only the vaguest notion of what would be in their best interest; however, on most issues organized groups do have clearly articulated opinions that speak to the interests of their membership. These groups and their leaders link representatives with their constituents; they inform constituents about the actions of their representatives and they inform representatives about the views and interests of those of their constituents who are members of the group. Many groups employ professional lobbyists based in Washington who monitor the lawmaking process, provide representatives with policy information that supports the interests of the group, and work to persuade them to back the preferences of the group. Groups and their lobbyists also contribute money to the election and reelection campaigns of representatives as a way to facilitate their access to them once they are in office.

From the point of view of their leaders as well as of many political theorists, these organizations, by linking citizens with their political leaders,
serve an indispensable role in a representative system; from the point of
view of critics, many of these organizations distort the policymaking process in favor of those with the financial resources to make their voices
heard. In that way, they undermine the majoritarian principle of representative democracy and weaken the link between constituency opinions and
interests and the policy decisions that representatives make. But whatever
one's view of their merits, even Madison, who wrote of "the mischief of
faction," conceded that such groups were inevitable and could not be eliminated without also eliminating liberty itself; the best that could be hoped
for was to construct political institutions in such a manner that the worst
aspects of factionalism could be controlled.

INTEREST GROUP TECHNIQUES

One of the more important and least appreciated techniques that interest
groups use to gain influence in the policymaking process is to act as a
source of expertise for members of Congress. Because representatives have
a broad range of complex issues to deal with, a limited amount of time,
and multiple interests to hear and to satisfy, they desperately need information. They need to know the details of the policy proposals before them,
their merits and demerits, the problems that each purports to solve, and
the new problems that each may create.

Although representatives can get this information from a variety of
sources—their own staff, committee leaders who specialize in the legislation in question, party leaders, and attentive members of their constituency—interest groups are often more immediate and well-informed
sources. Well-funded interest groups have large research staffs and access to
a great deal of data. The fact sheets, statistics, and talking points that they
provide to members of Congress and to congressional staff members are of
immense assistance to representatives as they plan their approach to a policy area, particularly an area about which they may know very little. Most
important, such information can help them to assess how their constituency will react to a particular piece of legislation, a key element in their
decision-making process, as observed in chapter 5. As one study of the role
of agriculture lobbyists suggests, representatives will listen to some interest
groups simply because they view them as reliable informants; that is, interest groups can tell them which issues concern their constituents, what their
constituents' preferences might be, and which policy alternatives might best
address voters' concerns. At election time, interest groups can make their
members available to representatives and can speak highly of the representative to his constituents who are members of or sympathizers with the

group. These groups exert influence because they can reduce both the informational and electoral uncertainty with which all elected representatives must contend.[3]

Interest groups can assist representatives who are advocates of a particular bill by mobilizing support for the legislation in the constituencies of members of Congress who may be undecided on the issue. As an issue important to a group wends its way through the legislative process, Washington-based offices of interest groups send out notices and alerts to their members throughout the country apprising them of the status of the legislation and, at the appropriate time, urging them to contact their representative or senator. The reasoning is that the most effective way to a representative's heart (and mind) is through his constituency, people to whom he must attend. The American Association of Retired People, for instance, is said to have "4.3 million ready-to-deploy volunteer activists who can descend on politicians' offices anywhere or fire off missives on short notice."[4] In recent years, this strategy has been made much easier by technology. With a few computer key strokes, an organization such as AARP can, in seconds, have a fact sheet and instructions on who to contact, how to contact them, and what to say on all of its members' computer screens. And because for many constituents e-mail is the easiest way to contact representatives, in a matter of moments messages in support of the group's position can come pouring into a representative's office. From beginning to end, the entire process can take only a few minutes. Although representatives are well aware that such campaigns are far from spontaneous, they still represent an indicator of constituency sentiment that they cannot discount.

Groups that do not have large membership lists but wish to apply constituency pressure to representatives can outsource the job to lobbying firms that specialize in running such "grassroots" campaigns. Such firms will identify and mobilize constituents, especially opinion leaders from the business sector or local politicians, and urge them to contact their representative on behalf of the interest group that is employing them. Sometimes this is more of a "grass tops" approach aimed at mobilizing local elites rather than the ordinary voters that the AARP contacts, and it has the potential to be more effective than thousands of stimulated e-mails flooding into a representative's office. This approach is particularly useful for interest groups that have significant amounts of money to hire professionals and a relatively small number of members, or perhaps few members in the constituency of a key representative, so that mobilizing their members alone would do little good. Over an eighteen-month period from 2003 to 2005, the U.S. Chamber of Commerce, working with a Washington lobbying firm to whom they paid more than $1 million in fees, used this technique to sway enough Democratic votes to pass legislation to curb class action lawsuits.[5]

CAMPAIGN FINANCE

The lobbying technique that gets the most attention from scholars and commentators alike is, of course, campaign contributions. The cost of running a successful campaign for a seat in the United States House and Senate increases with each election cycle. A portion of the needed funds comes directly from political action committees (PACs) affiliated with organized interest groups or from individuals and lobbyists connected with interest groups who make private donations to congressional candidates. Although national political party organizations such as the congressional campaign committees of each party in each chamber or the national party committee itself have taken a more active role in raising funds for individual congressional campaigns, a good deal of the money that these committees receive also comes directly or indirectly from interest groups or from employees of or lobbyists for interest groups. During the 2006 midterm election cycle, PACs contributed nearly $372 million to congressional candidates, with $207 million going to Republicans and $161 million to Democrats; the remainder went to Senator Joseph Lieberman of Connecticut who ran as an independent after his defeat in the Democratic primary.[6] More significantly, 81 percent of PAC contributions went to the reelection campaigns of incumbents, Democrats and Republicans alike.[7]

The average House incumbent running for reelection in 2006 spent $1,261,559, and the average challenger spent $510,195; for the 2000 election, the comparable figures were $817,733 for incumbents and $372,931 for challengers.[8] Average figures can, of course, be misleading. In some hotly contested House races, the costs were significantly higher. In the 8th Illinois Congressional District, Melissa Bean, a first-term Democrat, successfully defended her seat against a determined challenge from Republican David McSweeney. Bean raised $5,140,000 for her successful campaign against $4,337,000 by her challenger, for a total of $9,477,000 for the two candidates. Of Bean's contributions, just under $1,500,000 came directly from political action committees; for McSweeney, the figure was $460,000.[9] For Senate races, the dollar numbers are staggering. In 2006, the average incumbent spent $9,426,175 and the average challenger $5,659,763. The comparable figures from 2000 were $4,530,694 for incumbents and $3,153,465 for challengers.[10] In the fiercely contested 2006 Senate race in Virginia, the incumbent, George Allen, raised just under $15,000,000 to $8,590,000 for his challenger, James Webb. Webb received $469,000 from political action committees, while Allen took in just under $2,850,000 from these groups.[11]

Looking only at PAC contributions underestimates the money that comes from or is inspired by interest groups. Without a great deal of careful research through the files of the Federal Election Committee, it is difficult to identify the dollars that come from the personal accounts of individual lobbyists or from business leaders and their families who have interests before Congress or who just wish to stay on good terms with members in the event that their interests come before Congress in the future. It is also not possible to determine how much of the contributions listed as coming from individuals have been provoked or stimulated by an interest group— say an e-mail from a company president to all of her employees extolling the virtues of a particular candidate. Many representatives also benefit through contributions to their campaigns through money raised by senior colleagues who hold influential positions in the Congress and because of that have little difficulty raising campaign funds. Ordinarily, these senior members do not have tough reelection races, and because their leadership positions are based on their membership in the majority party, they support the campaigns of their party colleagues in order to maintain that majority.

Once again, a great deal of those funds comes from PACs or from those with interests before the Congress. In the first half of 2007, for example, Representative Charles Rangel, chair of the House Ways and Means Committee, the jurisdiction of which includes taxation, trade, and social security among other crucial issues, transferred $485,000 from his campaign coffers to the Democratic Congressional Campaign Committee. He had plenty to give. By the end of the third quarter of 2007, only nine months after Rangel became chair, he had raised $2.7 million in campaign contributions, more in such a short time span than any member of the House since records were kept. Prominent among his donors were the tobacco industry, Wall Street entrepreneurs, and a legion of others who had a significant financial stake in tax legislation that might come before Ways and Means. Rangel, who is usually reelected with more than 90 percent of the vote, planned to put most of this money toward supporting the reelection campaigns of fellow Democrats whose success would ensure his continuation as chair of the House's most powerful committee.[12]

None of this takes into account the money that interest groups spend directly on campaigns. Groups can set up independent committees to run radio and television ads for or against a particular candidate as long as these efforts are not coordinated with the candidate's official campaign. Money that groups spend supporting such committees is difficult to track, but it is estimated that groups spent "in excess of $20 million on television alone in the 2002 election. Millions of additional dollars were spent on voter identification, direct mail, mass telephone calls and other communication and voter mobilization activities."[13] Various tax exempt groups can carry out "issue advocacy" campaigns using ads that can praise or criticize a candidate and are legal as long as they do not call explicitly for the candidate's election or defeat. Interest groups can contribute money to these issue advocacy organizations without limit and without formal reporting requirements.

PAYING THE PIPER AND CALLING THE TUNE

As the gross contribution figures show, interest groups spend significantly more of their money on incumbents than on challengers, and this advantage in fundraising is one important reason why incumbents are usually odds-on favorites to win reelection. It is something of a self-fulfilling prophecy: because incumbents are likely to win and groups wish to spend their money on winners, they contribute to incumbents, who because they have the money usually win. The key question is the influence that these campaign contributions have on the actions of the recipients. Instinctively (and perhaps cynically) we assume that if their reelection depends on raising substantial sums of money, politicians will be responsive to those who provide these dollars. The threat that money could be withheld at the next election may encourage the representative to look favorably upon the views of these contributors. We are told, after all, that he who pays the piper generally calls the tune. But, like many other seemingly reasonable assumptions (and clichés) in political science, this is also one that is difficult to nail down empirically.

In some respects, the problem is identical to the empirical issue of documenting constituency control of the representative. If the member's voting behavior agrees with his constituents' views on a particular issue or with their general ideological dispositions, how do we know that constituency views are the motivating force for the representative? As suggested previously, it is possible that the constituency elected the representative because of the compatibility of his views with theirs, and it is also possible that the constituency's views have been influenced by the representative. Similarly, for interest groups, the question is whether or not campaign contributions encourage a member who has no opinion on a proposal to support the interests of the group, or if such contributions can neutralize an opponent of the group or even convert him to a proponent. Alternatively, do groups use campaign donations primarily to reward those who for other reasons are sympathetic to the group and its positions?

A typical finding on this issue comes from a study showing that the sixty-one United States senators who during the 104th Congress (1995–1996) supported a sugar price subsidy that had the effect of increasing the cost of sugar to consumers (and the profits of sugar producers) received over the previous five years an average of $13,473 from sugar industry political action committees, while the thirty-five senators who voted no received an average of $1,461 from these same PACs during the same period.[14] Another study finds a similar disparity in the campaign contributions from the trucking industry to supporters and opponents of trucking deregulation.[15] A recent case involved contributions from executives of major telephone companies to the campaign of Senator John D. Rockefeller IV of West Virginia, chair of the Senate Intelligence Committee. The telephone companies were seeking legislation that would grant them immunity from lawsuits that might arise as a result of their cooperation with President Bush's domestic eavesdropping program, legislation which Senator Rockefeller and his committee ultimately supported. It was reported that executives associated with the two major phone companies involved—ATT and Verizon—had contributed $42,850 to Senator Rockefeller's campaign funds during 2007, compared with a total of $4,050 over the previous four years, and that during deliberations on the bill, Senator Rockefeller had met privately with representatives of the companies.

But the issue in all of these instances is one of causation; did the contribution or the promise of the contribution cause the vote, or was the representative going to vote that way quite apart from the contribution? Would those who supported the sugar subsidy have done so absent a contribution from the sugar growers? Did contributions or the absence of such contributions change anyone's mind on the issue of trucking deregulation? In the case of the telephone companies, Senator Rockefeller's spokesperson was clear: "Any suggestion that Senator Rockefeller would make policy decisions based on campaign contributions," she said, "is patently false. He made his decision . . . based on the Intelligence Committee's careful review of the situation and our national security interests."[16] The fact that Senator Rockefeller is one of the richest people in the Senate, is immensely popular in his home state, and has never faced a tough reelection campaign lends some credence to the position of his spokesperson. On the other hand, those who made campaign contributions did get to make their case to the senator in a private meeting, and it is not clear that others who had not made such contributions would have been afforded the same opportunity. If the empirical issue is difficult to sort out, the ethical issue is equally important and complicated; simply put, can a representative's vote be purchased with a campaign contribution, and even if it cannot, does the intersection of campaign contributions and policy decisions create the impression if not the reality of corruption?

Most major interest groups, in addition to contributing to campaigns, have paid lobbyists in Washington who make contact with representatives, press the views of the group, and, as mentioned, mobilize voters in the representative's district.[17] In the case of organized labor, the volunteers they deploy to assist the campaigns of their favored candidates—people who canvas door to door, who man phone banks, and who get people to the polls—are as important as the money that its PACs contribute to candidates. Although money spent on campaign contributions is a matter of public record, money that lobbyists and interest groups spend on these other activities as well as on the independent committees mentioned earlier is generally unreported.

As the Rockefeller case suggests, a connection also exists between campaign contributions and lobbying. Those seeking access to members of the Congress in order to press their point of view are helped by a record of campaign contributions to the member whom they wish to see. Even if such contributions fail to persuade the representative, it may help a group's lobbyist to get an audience with the member to make her case. As some observers indicate, but only a few less than diplomatic representatives will say, you need to pay to play. There is some evidence that groups use their financial resources to reinforce their contacts with those members who are already disposed to support them,[18] but one study of interest group influence on members of the House Ways and Means Committee concludes that by contributing broadly across partisan and ideological lines, lobbyists gain "flexibility in subsequent choices about whom to lobby."[19] In other words, people who can help (or hurt) are targeted regardless of their past record of support.

COMMITTEES AND INTEREST GROUPS

The Ways and Means example suggests that interest groups act strategically when they make contributions and engage in lobbying activities. One study indicates that members who have demonstrated their ability to guide complex legislation through the Congress receive a disproportionate share of PAC contributions. In other words, groups reward people who can deliver.[20] The members and especially the leaders of committees that have jurisdiction over policy areas that are of concern to a group are also a major focus of interest group activity.[21] For example, PACs associated with the finance industry give significantly more to members of the Senate Banking Committee than they do to other members of the Senate.[22] There is also evidence that PAC contributions tend to rise as election day approaches and as important committee votes come up.[23]

Given the structure of the United States Congress, it makes a great deal of sense for interest groups to focus their efforts on committees. The committees are the workshops of the Congress, the place where the details of legislation are decided and, normally, the arena in which approval must be granted if a legislative proposal is to make its way to the floor of either chamber for a debate and vote. Such an arrangement is necessary if the Congress is to do its work. It is unreasonable to expect every representative to be able to understand and analyze every one of the multiple and increasingly complex policy areas that come before Congress in the form of proposed legislation or as Congress seeks to perform its function of overseeing the executive branch. So Congress divides the labor among standing committees, each with jurisdiction over a particular set of policy areas. These committees, in turn, create subcommittees that have responsibility for an even smaller portion of the full committee's jurisdiction. This division of labor means that when the relevant subcommittee or committee says "no" to a legislative proposal, its chances of final passage are virtually nil. Conversely, although subcommittee agreement does not ensure final approval, it is normally a prerequisite to consideration by the committee and then by the Congress as a whole.

The committee system makes the job of interest groups and lobbyists much easier. The representatives who are most important to a particular policy area are easily identifiable by simply looking at the committee and subcommittee rosters. The names and roles of the staff members who serve the committee are also available. Those interested in agriculture policy, for example, need not seek to influence all of the members of Congress; rather, they concentrate most of their effort on the members and staff of the Agriculture Committee. In addition, the committees, and particularly the subcommittees, operate out of the public eye. The proceedings on the floor of the House and the Senate are highly visible and often receive significant coverage from the media, but what happens in committees usually is a good deal less visible to constituents and to others who are not directly affected by the legislation in question. This environment maximizes the opportunity for interest group influence; there are even stories about lobbyists sitting at the table with subcommittee members and staff as the final details of complex legislation are hashed out. The relative privacy of the subcommittee meeting also can reduce the impact of constituency pressures as well as the pressures from party leaders, who in most instances are inclined to defer to the expertise of the subcommittee. Once a bill makes it to the floor, however, the actions of the representative become more public and more visible to the media and to his constituency, the influence of party leaders increases, and the impact of interest groups may well decline.[24]

One careful study found that the effect of contributions to those members disposed to support a group was most apparent in the members' activity during formal committee sessions finalizing the bill in question and in committee action behind the scenes. The more money a supporter of the group received, the more likely he or she was to allocate time and effort to its interests, including speaking on the group's behalf, attaching favorable amendments to the committee bill, and being present and voting in markup sessions. Money contributed to opponents did not convert them to proponents, but did seem to diminish the intensity of their opposition.[25]

Rather than shielding a representative from constituency pressures, the committee system more often allows him to protect constituency interests. A representative may seek an assignment to a particular committee because the policies that are within the committee's jurisdiction are important to his constituency. In the 110th Congress, Senator Tom Harkin of Iowa and Representative Collin Peterson of Minnesota chaired the Agriculture Committees in their respective chambers. Members who have a large military presence in their districts are often on the Armed Services Committee, and members from oil and gas producing states are attracted to the Energy and Commerce Committee. As indicated in chapter 4, one of the reasons why farm legislation tends to benefit farmers who grow certain crops is because the Agriculture Committee is dominated by representatives from districts and states where those crops are grown.

Often a powerful committee chair may be all that a group needs to protect its interests. For many years, Representative John Dingell of Michigan has either chaired or served as the ranking minority member of the House Energy and Commerce Committee, which among other issues deals with the air emission standards that automobile makers must achieve. Although Representative Dingell, whose district includes the areas south and west of Detroit, has supported some legislation aimed at reducing air pollution and responding to the threat of global warming, he has always worked to make certain that the regulations adopted were less onerous for the automobile industry than the stronger standards and guidelines that have been favored by environmentalists.[26] Not surprisingly, Representative Dingell receives significant campaign contributions from manufacturers involved with the auto industry. In the 2006 election cycle, his top three contributors, accounting for more than $81,000, were the Big Three automakers— General Motors, Ford, and DaimlerChrysler. Contributions from all industries involved in auto manufacturing totaled more than $100,000.[27]

It is also important to remember that Congress is not the only arm of government whose actions can affect a particular interest. The decisions that bureaucrats make can have significant consequences for the manner in which a statute is applied and for how and to whom federal funds are distributed. So interest groups seek friends in Congress not just in the hope that they will design legislation to their liking (or sidetrack legislation that they oppose) but also in the hope that they will use their positions to influence the bureaucracy on their behalf. As demonstrated by the example of Representative Murtha of Pennsylvania and Concurrent Technologies discussed in chapter 4, a company with an interest in receiving a contract from the Defense Department will seek allies on the Armed Services Committee who can press their case with those in the Pentagon who will make the decision. Presumably, the views of those members who serve on the committees that authorize and appropriate the money that the Defense Department spends will count when decisions are made about exactly how and where that money should be spent. This relationship among committee members, bureaucrats, and interest groups, sometimes referred to as an "iron triangle" or a "subgovernment," is one in which all participants work for their self-interest. In the Defense Department example, a company in the representative's district receives a contract, the representative receives electoral support, often in the form of campaign contributions from the grateful company and its employees, and the Defense Department ensures that it maintains its support on the committee responsible for authorizing money for its programs and overseeing its performance.

In this way, the committees represent a nexus between interest group and constituency concerns, or at least the constituency concerns of those in a representative's district who have the greatest economic stake in the legislation that happens to be before the committee. From that perspective, the subgovernment system can be viewed as an example of effective representation, with the efforts of representatives resulting in resources for the constituency, in return for which constituents reward the representative with votes or the money he needs to get votes. The problem with this arrangement, critics say, is that the larger public interest may be less effectively represented by the system. How are the interests of taxpayers who provide the funds to purchase military hardware protected when neither the representative nor the Defense Department has an incentive to reject these projects or to ask that they be brought in at a cheaper price?

CORRUPTION?

Although interest groups certainly play an important and often a constructive role in the policymaking process, it is impossible to ignore the opportunities for corruption, or the appearance of corruption, that inevitably creeps into a system where money is so crucial to success and so much of it is involved. Small changes in tax legislation dealing with the oil industry can produce huge profits for an oil company. The exact manner in which Congress chooses to deal with health care can have tremendous financial consequences for insurance and pharmaceutical companies. For example, when Congress passed the Medicare Part D program providing drug benefits for senior citizens, it declined to include a provision allowing Medicare to negotiate lower prices for its participants—a decision of enormous financial value to the pharmaceutical industry.

In addition to advocating a group's view on general public policy matters, some lobbying firms have developed lucrative specialties in gaining earmarks for clients. Because there are so many applicants for what may well be a limited supply of funds, those seeking earmarks believe that they cannot rely entirely on the efforts of their representatives and senators. It is now more common for municipalities, universities, and companies to engage the services of a Washington lobbyist in the hope that an insider can move their application to the top of the list. When Malone College, a small institution located in Canton, Ohio, sought federal assistance to build a fitness center for its students and a new building for its nursing school, a college spokesperson indicated that it hired a Washington lobbyist "to help us with a 'boots on the ground' program of meeting with various congressional and Senate leaders."[28] Companies that receive a large number of earmarks and government contracts spend a great deal of money paying for professional lobbying services. Raytheon, the giant defense contractor, spent just under $1,000,000 in lobbying fees in 2007 and received approximately $30 million in earmarks. One of its competitors, General Dynamics, was more efficient, spending "only" $580,000 and receiving $26.5 million in earmarks.[29]

Because of the work of lobbying firms, concerns have been raised that earmarks are going to those who have the resources to hire people who are in a position to pull strings on their behalf rather than to those who have the strongest case to make for federal funds. The amount of money involved can be quite large. For example, the lobbying firm of Van Scoyoc Associates reported $26 million in revenue in 2006, with about half of that revenue generated from clients seeking earmarks.[30] Eight companies that received earmarks sponsored by Representative John Murtha used a lobbying firm called the PMA Group, one of whose principals is Paul Magliochetti, a former aide to Mr. Murtha's Defense Appropriations Subcommittee. In 2007, PMA took in $840,000 in fees from those clients. According to contribution records, PMA and its employees gave $58,600 to Mr. Murtha's campaign from 2005 through the 3rd quarter of 2007.[31]

In 2006, a wave of stories hit the press concerning questionable relationships between legislators and lobbyists. Many of these stories highlighted the free flow of personnel between Capitol Hill and lobbying firms. The rosters of the largest and most successful firms in Washington are filled with former members of the House and Senate as well as with people who served as staff to representatives or to congressional committees. Under current law, former members of the House and their senior aides (defined as someone making at least 75 percent of the legislator's salary) must wait one year before engaging in lobbying activities. Legislation passed by Congress in 2007 extended the waiting time for former senators to two years. But for aides whose employer is no longer in Congress (an aide to a member defeated in his reelection bid, for example), there is no waiting period at all. And the waiting period for members does not discourage some from accepting immediate employment with lobbying firms at salaries much higher than what they earned as representatives. To conform with the law, they do not lobby directly during the one-year waiting period, but they are free to offer advice, plan strategies, meet with clients—in other words, to do anything but meet directly with representatives.

Several Republicans who lost their seats in Congress as a result of the 2006 election quickly found positions in lobbying firms. According to *Congressional Quarterly*, "former Rep. Sherwood Boehlert, R-N.Y. (1983–2007), is listed as 'of counsel' with The Accord Group, which also employs his former aide Jeff Moore, a lobbyist since 2000." Former Senator Jim Talent of Missouri became cochairman of government relations for Fleishman-Hillard, a Washington lobbying firm, where his responsibilities were to "develop initiatives and lobbying strategies" while waiting out his one-year moratorium on direct lobbying.[32]

One of the more notorious stories focused on Jeff Shockey, who was an aide to Representative Jerry Lewis of California during the 1990s before joining the Washington lobbying firm of Copeland Lowery. But in 2005, when Representative Lewis became chair of the House Appropriations Committee, Shockey returned to Lewis's employ as deputy director of the committee staff. His lobbying firm gave him a farewell gift of $600,000 in severance pay. In the following year, many of the clients whom Shockey had represented while at the firm as well as some of the firm's other clients did very well in the 2005 appropriations process. This may have been due in part to the decision by Copeland Lowery to share some of its business with a small lobbying firm, Hillscape Associates, operated by Alexandra Shockey, Jeff's wife. Interestingly, some of the clients served by the Shockeys and Copeland Lowery were cities and other interests based in Representative Lewis's California district that were seeking earmarks. Lewis's office apparently had encouraged them to work with (that is, hire) Copeland Lowery. Furthermore, Bill Lowery (the Lowery in Copeland Lowery) was a former member of Congress from California and a close friend of Lewis. It was not clear why these towns and cities in Representative Lewis's district needed to hire a lobbyist when they might well expect their own representative to deliver these earmarks to them as a normal part of his constituency service responsibilities. But clearly this arrangement had great benefits for Shockey, Lowery, and perhaps for Representative Lewis himself.[33]

Another arrangement that raised eyebrows occurred in 2004 when Representative Billy Tauzin of Louisiana left his seat in the House of Representatives to become the top lobbyist for the Pharmaceutical Research and Manufacturers of America at an annual pay package estimated at $2 million. In his last years in the House, Tauzin had served as chair of the House Energy and Commerce Committee, the body that dealt with legislation affecting the drug industry. In fact, Tauzin played a leading role in guiding the Medicare Part D legislation providing drug benefits for senior citizens through the Congress—legislation that has generally been viewed as a boon to the drug industry, especially because it did nothing to control the prices that pharmaceutical companies charge for their products. A bit more disturbing were the rumors that surfaced that Tauzin was in discussions with the lobbying group about his new position while he was still serving in the House.[34] In the year before Tauzin left the House, he had collected $160,000 in campaign contributions from pharmaceutical groups and from others involved in the health industry.[35] Congressional rules allowed him to take that money with him when he left Congress, and he used a portion of the funds to contribute to the campaigns of members of Congress—Democrats and Republicans—serving on the Energy and Commerce Committee and who remain central to legislation dealing with the drug industry.[36]

And if a lobbying firm cannot employ a former member of Congress, a former congressional staff member may do just as well. *National Journal* looked at the careers of senior staff members who worked in the House or the Senate between October 2003 and March 2004 and found that of the 635 people in their study, 107 went from the Congress to lobbying positions. In one not atypical example, Paul Kangas, a senior staffer on the House Financial Services Committee, the jurisdiction of which includes matters relating to the insurance industry, became vice president of government relations for the Property Casualty Insurers Association of America.[37] Although staffers with Hill experience are likely to have an advantage in regard to access, what makes them even more attractive to lobbying firms is their policy expertise. Given the complexity of the legislation that Congress considers and the fact that a small change in the wording of an obscure provision of a statute can have a significant impact on a particular industry, the policy expertise that former staffers bring to their work as lobbyists can be invaluable. Many may even be better informed than current or former members of Congress and their staff.

Although it is difficult to escape the feeling that there is something wrong with all of this, from another perspective it is quite reasonable. If one accepts the premise that organized interests have a legitimate role to play in a representative system, then it makes perfect sense for them to recruit people who know a great deal about the policy areas that are of greatest concern to the group's members. Such people can interpret and convey the interests of those whom they represent to government officials, while at the same time explaining the legislative process to their clients. And what better place to find that expertise than among the ranks of those who have designed these policies while working in the Congress? In this limited way, the interest groups and their lobbyists function in the same way that a representative does: as an intermediary between the government and the citizen, conveying opinions and interests upward and interpreting and explaining policy downward.

With more than 13,000 registered lobbyists in Washington, all cannot gain access to every representative. Lobbyists report that in order to gain or maintain access, they are under tremendous pressure to attend the various fundraising events that representatives and senators host as they engage in the nonstop process of paying off their debts from their previous election campaign and generating funds for their next campaign. After the Republican Party took control of the House of Representatives in 1995, majority whip Tom DeLay launched what he called the "K Street Project," named after the Washington thoroughfare that houses a number of lobbying firms. DeLay made it clear that those groups that wished to gain access to the leadership had to contribute to Republican candidates, and that the lobbying firms that these groups retained had to employ loyal Republicans. When the Democrats regained control of Congress twelve years later, they did not follow DeLay's crass example; nonetheless, lobbying groups that employed highly visible Democrats saw a resurgence in their business, firms that had become top heavy with Republicans so as to conform with the DeLay mandate started hiring Democrats, and PAC contributions to Democrats picked up.

In an arrangement that has raised new ethical questions, some representatives have established personal charities that have a laudable goal of addressing a major social concern of some sort. The problem is that these "charities"—often staffed by relatives, campaign aides, fundraisers, and former staffers of the representative who draw generous salaries for their work—receive a great deal of their contributions from interests that have business before Congress and sometimes business before the committees on which the representative who established the charity serves. The charity will host fundraising dinners, golf tournaments, or junkets that give lobbyists access to the representative involved. It seems that the representative is in effect saying, "I will help you if you will help this organization." In some instances these charities have been direct beneficiaries of earmarks arranged by the representative. Representative Alan Mollohan, Democrat of West Virginia and a member of the House Appropriations Committee, came under scrutiny for his relationship with five such charitable organizations that received millions in earmarks that he had arranged. In addition, Mollohan had a business relationship with the CEO of one of these organizations, and that relationship appeared to net the representative a substantial sum of money.[38]

The most egregious corruption case involved lobbyist Jack Abramoff, who directed funds and other benefits to representatives in return for their support. Representative Bob Ney of Ohio was forced to resign and went to prison for his dealings with Abramoff, as did Mr. Abramoff himself. Ney, the former chairman of the House Administration Committee, admitted sponsoring amendments to legislation and pressuring federal administrators on behalf of Abramoff's lobbying clients between 2001 and 2004. In return, Ney received luxury vacation trips, skybox seats at sporting events, campaign contributions, and expensive meals. One of the connections between Abramoff and Ney was Neil Voltz, Ney's former chief of staff, who had been hired to work for Abramoff's lobbying team along with two former aides to Representative DeLay.[39]

Episodically, Congress attempts to take steps to eliminate these abuses of the interest group system and, seemingly, once a decade vows to do something about the high cost of political campaigning. Almost ritually, a bill is passed with a bevy of new restrictions and limitations, but somehow those with money still find a way to get it to their favored candidates. The latest attempt to deal with campaign finance is the Bipartisan Campaign Reform Act (BCRA) of 2002, sometimes known as the McCain-Feingold bill after the two senators who were its strongest advocates. BCRA was aimed primarily at eliminating contributions to party committees and candidates that had as their ostensible purpose financing voter registration and get-out-the-vote campaigns and other party-sponsored grassroots activity. Funds contributed for these purposes, referred to as "soft money," did not have to be reported to the Federal Election Commission, so interest groups could evade the restrictions on how much they could contribute directly to an individual candidate ("hard money" contributions that needed to be reported) by sending large amounts of unrestricted money to party organizations. The act also attempted to restrict expenditures by independent groups seeking to influence the outcome of elections through "issue ads," and it revised upward the limits on how much hard money individuals and PACs could contribute to candidates and parties, in part to compensate for the loss of soft money.

The Supreme Court has dealt with BCRA in two very close cases. In *McConnell v. FEC*,[40] decided in 2003, the court, in a 5-4 decision, upheld the soft money ban. But four years later, in *FEC v. Wisconsin Right to Life*,[41] in another 5-4 decision, the Court declared the restrictions on issue ads unconstitutional, with the majority viewing these restrictions as an infringement on the First Amendment rights of the regulated groups. In terms of the other provisions, all that really occurred was increased transparency in the system, because dollars and donors now have to be reported. The record cost of the first campaign in which BCRA was in full effect—the 2006 congressional elections—suggests that these provisions have not done much to control the cost of campaigns and have done little to restrict the influence of groups and individuals who have the resources to support political parties and their candidates.

After the scandals that rocked Congress during the 2005–2006 session, other rules and laws were enacted that were designed to limit the perks that lobbyists regularly supplied to legislators. In 2007, Congress passed legislation extending the waiting period on direct lobbying by former senators to two years and by former senior staff members to one year. Senior House aides would be barred from lobbying the personal office, leadership office, or committee where they formerly worked in the House for at least one year after becoming lobbyists. Lobbyists were barred from picking up the tab for a dinner out with a representative, and restrictions were placed on lobbyist funded travel. The latter was aimed at the interest group technique of flying members of Congress, their staff members, and often spouses to exotic locations for "information and study" sessions that sometimes seem longer on fun than on the development of expertise. The new law also required lobbyists to report contributions to organizations controlled by or named for members of Congress (the target here was the "charities"), and lawmakers and their staff were barred from trying to influence hiring decisions by lobbying firms and others in exchange for political access.[42]

Additionally, Congress added more transparency to the earmarking process to discourage members from sponsoring earmarks designed to help friends and campaign donors, particularly those who lived and worked outside of their constituencies. Members were required to take public responsibility for all of the earmarks that they pushed in advance of the final vote on the floor, and the lobbyist who pushed for the earmark also had to be named. On the other hand, little in the new lobbying law affected campaign contributions. Some lobbyists groused that the same legislators who were voting for legislation that prevented a lobbyist from buying a representative a dinner or paying for his travel to a trade association meeting were also sending out invitations to campaign fundraisers—invitations that were difficult to refuse.[43]

INTEREST GROUPS IN
COMPARATIVE PERSPECTIVE

Organized interests exist in all open political systems, but the influence that they are able to exert on representatives varies inversely with the strength of the nation's political party system. The stronger the party, the less likely it is that interest groups will seek to influence a legislator directly. As noted, strong political parties typically control the election process, so once in office representatives are expected to vote with their party leadership, and in some instances representatives who deviate from the party line face significant adverse consequences. In these circumstances, it would seem to make little sense for interest groups to spend their resources and efforts trying to influence individual members of the legislature. Rather, they are more likely to turn their attention to those who are capable of delivering—the political party leadership.

Although efforts to influence party leaders is the general case for strong political party systems, there is some variation among these systems. In Great Britain, for example, interest groups have come to exercise increasing power, even with a political party system substantially stronger than the American system. Michael Rush found that of the 250 organized groups he surveyed, 75 percent reported frequent or regular contacts with MPs, mostly providing information and briefings. Groups also may work with an MP to draft a "private member bill"—a bill not sponsored by the government—for introduction and consideration in the House. Although only a small percentage of such bills are approved—typically about 5 percent of those offered—such legislation can draw public attention to the concerns of a particular group. Groups also can encourage friendly MPs to use the Question Hour to ask questions that will highlight the group's interest.[44] As is the case in the United States, their efforts are directed disproportionately at the members of the standing committees in Parliament that deal with the issues of greatest concern to the group. Although these committees have much less power over legislation than their counterparts in the U.S. Congress, more than 80 percent of the group representatives whom Rush interviewed thought that their efforts had had a significant impact on the committee and its recommendations.

Phillip Norton suggests that these efforts by British interest groups are of relatively recent vintage and attributes them to a weakening of party loyalty among MPs. The government can continue to count on the support of most of its party's MPs, but it cannot, as it did in the past, take this support for granted. Policy adjustments and political accommodations have to be made to ensure that the majority holds, and these arrangements can be arrived at with greater ease in the committee rooms. Thus, as the hold of the party over its members becomes somewhat more problematic, the role of the committee system is enhanced. This in turn makes the MPs more attractive targets of group influence than they have been in the past, when party discipline was unquestioned and when most of the decisions were made by the party leaders.[45]

The connection in the British Parliament between interest group influence and financial considerations is not as clear as it appears to be in the United States. Certainly money counts, and groups with financial resources will have the people and the infrastructure to make their influence felt. Some MPs—about 10 percent in one recent analysis—are paid "consultants" to groups, which is perfectly legal as long as these connections are publicized; however, in the wake of a series of "cash for questions" scandals in the 1990s, Parliament placed some restrictions on such "paid advocacy." The electoral influence of interest groups in British parliamentary elections is also a significant factor. A large number of Labor Party MPs, for example, have their candidacies "sponsored" by union organizations, which means that the union assumes much of the campaign expense for that candidate. There are limits to the amount of money each candidate can spend in his campaign and on how much money parties can spend during the election campaign, but not between elections. At one time, no public reporting was required of campaign contributions to political parties, but that was changed by the Political Parties, Elections, and Referendums Act of 2000, which requires that all donations in excess of 5,000 British pounds be reported and publicized by the Electoral Commission. But Parliament rejected a proposal to include limits on campaign contributions in that bill; in the 2001 general election, there were individual contributions of as much as 5 million pounds to a political party. The act also imposed spending restrictions on political parties of approximately 20 million pounds for parties contesting in all parliamentary districts and 10,000 pounds for each candidate.[46]

As in Great Britain, after the Danish Parliament strengthened its committee system in 1972, policy areas within committee jurisdictions came to be "controlled by groups of legislators characterized by special relationships with the segments of society most directly affected."[47] In Norway, constituency based interests also seem to be a factor in committee assignments, with representatives from coastal areas seeking positions on the Fisheries Committee; teachers sought positions on the Committee for Church and Education; and people connected with industry preferred the Committee on Energy and Industrial Matters.[48] In Finland, committee consultations on pending legislation regularly involve soliciting the views of organized interests.[49] In sum, if interest groups are to play a role in parliamentary systems characterized by strong political parties, it is likely to be through access to committee members. Even then, what individual legislators can accomplish will be limited by the presumption that the views of the party leadership ultimately will determine the outcome.

In countries with list systems of proportional representation, leaders or representatives of interests that are important to the party may be placed on the party's electoral list. This process can provide the interest group with direct representation in the legislature, but the question will be where on the party's list the group's candidates will be placed—high on the list so that they are quite likely to be elected or lower on the list where there is little or no chance of election and where the placement is largely symbolic. In Israel, various factions of the political parties, along with interest groups such as unions and professional associations, "vie for 'safe' places" on the list and "the party leaders must decide which groups' support is most important to them."[50]

When political parties are strong, they rather than individual representatives become the object of interest group attempts to influence public policy. In Venezuela in the period prior to the presidency of Hugo Chavez and in Mexico under the Institutional Revolutionary Party (PRI), political parties penetrated the various interest groups in the nation, including individual labor unions, professional associations, and student groups. Such party control meant electoral benefits for the party at the next election and benefits for the group because alliances with the winning party secured access to the executive leaders, who were the ones making the key policy decisions. If representatives wished to have a long political career, either in Parliament or in other government positions (in Mexico, representatives cannot be reelected), they adhered to the wishes of the party leadership and, as a result, interest groups had little in the way of direct involvement with representatives.[51]

In contrast, in some Latin American nations with weaker political party systems, representatives seem to be virtual captives of large, moneyed interests that often use their influence to block public policies that might move toward a more equitable distribution of land and wealth. In Brazil, election to Congress requires substantial campaign expenditures, with most of the money raised from corporate sources. The "biggest contributors are probably large construction companies" that are dependent on "government projects for their very existence" and "expect their deputies to pressure ministers to liberate previously authorized funds and to sponsor amendments and bills yielding lucrative contracts."[52] In some instances, the control that these groups exercise has little to do with campaign finance and more to do with outright bribery. In nations with fragile representative systems where extraconstitutional attacks on the legislature have occurred and where political parties emerge and disappear in a short period of time, representatives cannot count on making a long-term career in the legislature. Therefore, they may care less about the reputation of the parliament and be more open to the blandishments of those with money who can help them with opportunities outside of the government or who can provide them with the resources that they may need to gain even greater political power.

On the other hand, in some cases interest groups can be more effective representatives of the people than elected legislators. One study of policymaking on issues of violence against women across thirty-six countries finds that a strong women's movement and aggressive policy agencies that deal with issues affecting women may provide more effective avenues of expression and representation on these issues than the presence of women in the legislature.[53] In more authoritarian political systems, the emergence of independent labor organizations as advocates for the rights of workers has served as a vehicle for opening previously closed political systems. In Poland, the rise of the labor movement Solidarity sparked the long transition from a one-party state to a more open republic. The point is that interest groups can influence policy, politics, and political systems in ways quite independent of their capacity to influence individual representatives and, especially in less open political systems and in those systems dominated by moneyed elites, some groups may be more effective representatives of particular constituencies than those who have been formally elected to discharge such responsibilities.

THE INTEREST GROUP SYSTEM

Certainly in the United States, there are many examples of interest groups that articulate broad public interests that are not likely to be represented on the floor of the legislature. Early in the twentieth century, suffrage groups were instrumental in gaining women the right to vote. In mid-century, civil rights organizations like the National Association for the Advancement of Colored People did more to represent the interests of African-Americans than most elected politicians. Today, groups such as the Sierra Club have forced environmental issues onto the national agenda, and the American Association of Retired People has acted as a key player on issues affecting the elderly. Interest groups then are not necessarily a force separate from and counter to either constituency interests or the national interest. Although individual citizens may not spend very much time monitoring the behavior of their representatives, interest groups do, and they share this information with their members as well as with the public at large. From this perspective, groups can amplify constituency interests, enhance constituency control by providing information to voters, and strengthen accountability. Groups inform the political debate by providing expert policy information to their members and to policymakers. They also provide a means for minority interests within different constituencies to join together. Gun owners, for example, probably constitute a minority in every state of the union, but through the activities of the National Rifle Association, they have, for better or worse, become a national force with which representatives from across the nation must contend.

Those who believe that interest groups and their activities are an integral part of the representative process frequently suggest that for every group on one side of an issue, there is a group on the other side that exerts a countervailing pressure.[54] But the interest group system does not provide equitable representation to every minority interest, and there is no disputing the fact that money is the price of admission to the interest group system—money to contribute to campaigns, money to hire lobbyists, money to organize grassroots activities on behalf of a particular interest, or, in the United States as well as other nations, money to bribe representatives. Because economically disadvantaged groups are by definition those with less or no money, they are further disadvantaged by their virtual exclusion from the interest group system. In many cases, it is not that an organized but underfunded group is working on the other side. Rather, there is no organized group on the other side. When welfare reform is considered, where is the group that has organized those who are on welfare? When bankruptcy laws are tightened, who speaks for those on the economic margins who may be adversely affected by attempts to make these laws more punitive? When those representing financial interests such as banks and credit card companies gain access to those who design the regulations governing their business practices, which if any groups represent the interests of those who use credit cards or borrow money from banks? And not simply the poor are underrepresented. Rather, it may be that the underrepresented have the resources but are underorganized. When Congress considers windfall profit taxes on oil companies, who represents the interests of the disorganized gasoline purchasing public opposite the well-financed oil company lobbyists?

Finally, even if all groups could be equitably represented in the interest group system, it is not clear that the result would be public policies that serve the public interest. The assumption of interest group politics is that by aggregating and seeking compromises among the various private interests represented by organized groups, the public interest will emerge. If one associates the public interest with such terms as justice, fairness, wisdom, or policy effectiveness, there is no reason to assume that, for example, an energy policy that satisfies the interests of all actual or potential producers of energy—oil and gas companies, coal producers, ethanol entrepreneurs, solar and wind energy enthusiasts—will be either just, fair, wise, or effective. It may turn out to be any or all of these things, but the self-interest that motivates these various points of view seldom elevates these larger concerns to actual decision-making criteria. It is just as likely that the chosen policies will be designed to serve the interests of those at the table, and doing so does not necessarily add up to the public interest.

But the advocates of interest group representation have little or no problem with this. In her critical analysis, Melissa Williams makes the point that the interest group system is "self-legitimating"—all policy outcomes are deemed fair as long as every interest has the right to participate.[55] If some interests have not participated and their views are not reflected in the policies adopted, it is because they have not worked hard enough, organized sufficiently, raised enough money, or made powerful enough arguments to be included.

This thought returns us to the role of the representative. It should be his job, more than anyone else's, to be an advocate for the more inchoate and typically disorganized public interest in the policymaking process. But to the extent that representatives view themselves as advocates for more narrow private interests—for constituency based reasons, reelection campaign finance concerns, or more selfish or nefarious reasons—their role as representatives of the broad public interest is drawn into question. Madison and many of his colleagues at the Constitutional Convention hoped that representatives would exhibit what they liked to call civic virtue—an ability to rise above their own or their constituents' narrow concerns to discover and protect the public interest.[56] Whether that does in fact occur with any regularity is open to question. As noted at the outset of this chapter, large segments of the United States population believe that "big interests" dominate public policymaking in general and the Congress in particular and, as explored in the next chapter, these views seem to contribute to the poor opinion that American citizens have of the Congress.

7

Representative Government and Its Critics

Representative institutions have multiple critics and relatively few defenders. The criticisms come from a variety of distinct ideological perspectives. Committed democrats argue that representative institutions undermine the principle of popular sovereignty. Those who advocate major changes in public policy believe that representative institutions are too slow to act and too protective of the powerful interests that benefit from the status quo. Proponents of strong centralized executive power agree, and add that representative institutions lack expertise, are too parochial in their focus on local constituency interests, too disposed toward compromise, and therefore unable to make good public policy that speaks to the national interest. And there are some in each of these groups who take a dim view of the representatives themselves, suggesting that they are more disposed toward political posturing, personal ambition, and corruption than toward the civic-minded pursuit of the public interest.

THE DEMOCRATIC CRITIQUE

Taking seriously the notion of democracy as government by the people, the democratic critique begins with the obvious assertion that when citizens select someone to govern them, clearly they are not governing themselves. Ardent democrats claim that what representatives do diverges too frequently and too far from the attitudes and interests of the people whom they represent. Furthermore, representative institutions marginalize the political role of the average citizen by telling her that her chance to participate in the politics of her nation is in essence restricted to those occasional days when she casts her vote for a representative or for other officeholders. Otherwise, representative government tells the citizen that she knows too little, her opinions are uninformed or fatally infected by narrow self-interest, and that public policy is too complicated for her to understand. Therefore it is beyond citizens' competence to take part in designing and deciding on the policies under which they will live. With citizens' views of little importance, democrats argue, representatives become more responsive to narrow, highly organized, well-funded interests than to the interests of their constituents or the public at large

The democratic critique of representation carries a more optimistic view of the citizen than the available data suggests. It is beyond dispute that most citizens know very little about their representative institutions, about how they operate, and in most instances about who their representatives are and what they are doing. Attempts to draw connections between what representatives do and the wishes of their constituents find that on some issues some citizens are quite attentive and their views have some degree of influence on the behavior of their representatives. But on most issues, there is little indication that most citizens know very much about public policy beyond their support for broad general themes (e.g., good schools, clean air, a strong national defense). In most surveys, citizens cannot even agree on which problems facing the nation are most important, let alone what might be done to solve them.

Ironically, despite their lack of information and interest, many citizens seem to have concluded that their legislative institutions are not doing a very good job. One analysis of public opinion in fourteen representative democracies over the last two decades of the twentieth century found that in eleven of these nations confidence in legislative institutions had declined. By the early 1990s, in only five of nineteen advanced industrial democracies (Iceland, Norway, the Netherlands, West Germany, and Ireland) was 50 percent or more of the public prepared to say that they had a great deal or quite a lot of confidence in parliament.[1] These attitudes were accompanied by increases in the number of citizens who thought that representatives tend to lose touch with their constituents, that they are only interested in votes, and that they do not really care about those they represent. These attitudes about the legislatures and its members are to some extent part of a larger picture of growing distrust of politics and political institutions more generally. In twelve of the thirteen nations for which data were available, confidence in all "politicians" had declined.[2]

In the United States, most surveys of public confidence in political institutions find that Congress ranks near the bottom, and often in last place. In one 1992 poll, 75 percent of a national sample thought that Congress was doing a "poor" job handling the nation's most important problems; only 2 percent thought Congress was doing a good job.[3] In May 2007,

President Bush, facing some of the lowest presidential approval ratings in recent American history, must have taken some comfort in a Gallup Poll that showed that although his job approval rating was at 33 percent (about where it had been for the previous six months or so), the job approval rating of the new Democratic Congress was even lower—at 29 percent. And by late June 2007, although President Bush's job approval rating had dropped 1 percent since the May reading, Congress had dropped to an all-time low, with only 14 percent of the public indicating they had a great deal or quite a lot of confidence in Congress.

The average citizen has more positive views of his own representative, but this seems to have as much to do with the personality and reputation of the representative and the particularized services that he is able to deliver to his constituents as it has to do with the policy positions he takes or the votes he casts. This favorable view of their representative, the artful manner in which congressional districts are drawn, and the ability of incumbents to attract substantial campaign contributions virtually ensure the reelection of incumbent members of Congress. Members of the House of Representatives who seek reelection generally succeed at rates in excess of 95 percent. Although senators are a bit more vulnerable to electoral defeat, their reelection success rate seldom falls below 80 percent.

Every election year, in other words, Americans reelect the individual members of a body whose collective performance they seem to hold in contempt. Although they may make an exception for their own member of Congress, they view representatives in general as self-seeking politicians out to take care of themselves who will do or say anything to get reelected, rather than as public servants out to protect and advance the public interest. In one survey, 60 percent of respondents pronounced themselves "angry" or "disgusted" with Congress; a similar evaluation of the president and Supreme Court justices was offered by only 33 percent and 7 percent respectively of the respondents.[1] Citizens view Congress as an arena for partisan bickering and conflict, where people spend a lot of time talking and very little time actually doing something. They are convinced that big, well-financed interests have much more influence on what their representatives do than they themselves have. This alienation is reflected in the general lack of faith that voters have that the election results will make much difference in their lives or that the vote will alter the course of the nation's politics to any significant degree, a sentiment that in the view of some contributes to the low voter turnout and general political apathy that characterizes elections and attitudes in the United States.

If people know very little about the Congress, what are the sources of these negative, even hostile impressions of the institution and its members? Media coverage of the Congress is certainly one factor. The institution is typically depicted in ways "that highlight conflict and controversy, on the one hand, and personal ambition and ethical lapses, on the other."[5] The issue is the old one of what constitutes news. It is not news when the public's business is being handled efficiently and honorably by hardworking public servants, but heated debates, the sometimes angry clash of ideas and personalities, and the inability to reach a decision is news. And when the business imperative to increase newspaper circulation and television ratings is combined with the public's seemingly unquenchable thirst for scandal, individual and usually isolated cases of corruption and personal misbehavior are overemphasized, and these stories can last through several news cycles. Nearly all of my students, for example, could identify Senator Larry Craig of Idaho in autumn 2007 because of his well-publicized behavior in an airport rest room in Minneapolis that summer, but few knew who the majority leader of the Senate was. This sort of selective reporting leaves voters with the impression of Congress as a body riddled by corruption and bad behavior—"as a bunch of politicians squabbling over the distribution of benefits to special interests and jockeying for personal power while the needs of the country are ignored."[6]

The tendency of representatives to run for reelection by running against the Congress also plays a role. Members often curry favor with their constituents by depicting themselves as lonely crusaders against the ills that plague the Congress, thus lending credence to citizen perceptions that something is fundamentally wrong with the institution. Further reinforcing that view is the campaign rhetoric of those candidates running to unseat incumbents who typically tell voters that their goal if elected is to "clean up the mess in Washington," a sentiment which if expressed often enough leads voters who have no idea what is going on in Washington to conclude that indeed it must be a mess. Negative advertising that depicts incumbents as out of touch with the constituency, the captives of special interests, and sometimes corrupt contributes further to citizen distaste for the Congress.

Finally, congressional procedure seems complicated to the point of incomprehensibility, and it may be simple human nature to be critical of that which one cannot understand.[7] In the view of one scholar, the somewhat lower levels of confidence that Americans display in their political institutions when compared with the attitudes of citizens in other representative systems is attributable in large measure to the extreme complexity of the United States Congress and the U.S. political system in general.[8] Another analysis concludes that "Congress embodies practically everything Americans dislike about politics. It is large and therefore ponderous; . . . it is open and therefore disputes are played out for all to see."[9]

All of these factors were at play in the spring 2007 bottoming out of confidence in the Congress. In November 2006 the Democrats gained majority control of both houses of Congress in the midst of great public discontent with the Iraq war and an impression of a Republican majority wracked by an endless series of well-publicized scandals. The voters and the media expected massive changes from the first Congress in twelve years that had Democratic majorities in both chambers. Although much of the Democratic Party's legislative agenda moved rather quickly through the House of Representatives—including a plan to wind down the war in Iraq—little got through the Senate, where the Republican minority was able to prevent action by threatening to filibuster anything with which they disagreed. Under Senate rules, the only way to force a vote is to get sixty senators to support shutting off debate, a feat that would require nine Republican votes, assuming that all Democratic senators were on board. The Democrats seldom succeeded, especially on the major issue of the day, Iraq. And even on those occasions when they were able to get to sixty votes, or when the Republicans allowed a majority vote to take place, President Bush was set to wield his veto pen, as he did with the one Iraq withdrawal plan that got through Congress, and the two-thirds vote in both chambers necessary to override these vetoes simply did not exist. Citizens, of course, have little or no understanding of the rules of the Senate and, despite their high school civics classes, the necessity for both chambers to agree, or even the nature of the president's veto power. All they understood is that they changed party control of Congress, that they were promised policy changes as a result of their electoral decision, and that Congress was not able to deliver. This served to reinforce the view of many that election outcomes do not matter and that Congress is an ineffectual body that talks and bickers and ultimately fails to deal with the issues of the day.

From the point of view of representation theory, the paradox of high reelection rates of members of Congress in the context of this widespread public dissatisfaction with the performance of the institution suggests problems of accountability. From the point of view of democratic theory, the negative opinion of representative institutions that citizens hold is a reflection of the distance and distinction between representative government and self-government. If citizens rather than representatives were making the major decisions, or if somehow the voice of citizens in public policy decisions could be amplified, the democratic argument goes, citizens would conclude that their views make a difference, they would not be as politically alienated as they seem to be, and their participation rates would increase. And citizen participation would make a difference because they themselves would be making the decisions, and the decisions therefore would be closer to their opinions and interests than the decisions made in their representative institutions. With upwards of two-thirds of the American people wanting an end to American involvement in Iraq, democrats argue that policy should reflect this fact and, to the extent that it does not, our representative institutions have failed.

THE CONSERVATIVE LEGISLATURE

Another school of thought, associated with democrats as well as some scholars of a more authoritarian bent, views legislatures as too slow to act and, when they do act, inclined toward minimal, incremental policies. They argue that the policies that legislatures enact are notable only for their capacity to gain majority support rather than their capacity to deal with the problem at hand. This critique goes to the very nature of a representative institution as well as to the definition of what constitutes "good public policy."[10]

Legislatures are collective bodies representing the diverse interests and opinions of the nation. They provide an arena in which these multiple, often diverging views can be aired. Because such institutions are relatively large, many will wish to have their say about the policy options before them, and such discussions take time. If the different views are to be respected, the final policy outcome often will be a compromise version speaking to the needs of different interests and publics. As such, legislative institutions implicitly define good public policy as policy that can get the most votes rather than policy that will deal most effectively with the problem at hand. But the compromises that emerge from this process can leave everyone unhappy. Those among the affected groups who have gotten much of what they want will still complain because they believe that the necessary compromises have gutted the legislation; of course, those who have come out on the short end of the bargains that have been struck will be even more upset.[11] And those who believe that the process has produced an ineffective policy become even more convinced that good public policy cannot emerge from the legislative process.

Part of the problem, as noted in chapter 4, is that because of the representative nature of legislative institutions, the narrow demands of the constituencies to which representatives must account often will be emphasized over what may appear to be the interests of the nation as a whole. Because major departures from established public policy may upset the universalistic distributive arrangements—the "something for everyone" approach—to which representative institutions are disposed, representatives will resist major changes. Proposals, for example, to distribute federal highway funds on the basis of need rather than on the basis of geography will be nonstarters. Wasteful subsidies for agricultural products that serve narrow regional interests will be preserved even though there may be insufficient government funds available to address more pressing national needs, such as health care. By responding in this manner to these localized concerns, legislative institutions present themselves as inherently conservative bodies that instinctively resist change and protect the status quo.

Legislatures also may be accused of being conservative in the more contemporary sense of the word. By the time people become representatives, they already are among the more privileged classes of society even if they did not start out that way. At a minimum, their ascent to office has been facilitated by campaign contributions and support from the wealthier segments of society. Proposals to redistribute wealth through, for example, more steeply progressive taxation or, in some countries, measures that look to a more equitable distribution of land are certain to be opposed by those who benefit from the current distribution of resources. Such interests, because of who the legislators are and the sources of their campaign funds, have much greater influence on representatives than those who might benefit from such measures; therefore, legislatures are likely to resist such proposals. As Samuel Huntington observed in the late 1960s, the most ambitious programs to redistribute resources in less developed nations characterized by great inequalities in wealth have come through executive action; "a basic incompatibility exists between parliament and land reform," in large measure because parliaments in these countries tend to be dominated by rural landholding elites.[12]

In Latin America, populist presidents elected to office promising major socioeconomic change often find their initiatives frustrated by legislative assemblies beholden to those who are advantaged by the status quo. At this writing, popularly elected reformist presidents in Bolivia and Ecuador have found themselves at loggerheads with their legislative assemblies as they have pushed land reform programs and initiatives designed to secure greater government control of the private and often foreign-operated industries involved with natural resource extraction. In Brazil, a popularly elected president from the left, Lula da Silva, has seen his most radical ideas frustrated by an inability to marshal support from the legislature, many of whose members have been co-opted by the more privileged members of society. This is not a new phenomenon. One case study of land reform in Spain in the years prior to the Spanish Civil War attributes the Parliament's inability to deal with this crucial issue to the essential nature of the legislature itself. By doing what a representative institution is supposed to do—representing the various political forces interested in the issue, engaging in prolonged deliberations, and searching, sometimes unsuccessfully, for compromise on what was essentially a zero-sum issue—the legislature ultimately ended up doing nothing. That stalemate, in turn, contributed to extraparliamentary, often violent actions that set the stage for civil war.[13]

Legislatures do not just resist change instigated from the left. Proposals for major changes from the right also run into trouble. More conservative leaders who have attempted to impose changes that would move their nations to a more market-oriented system and reduce the government's commitment to a welfare state role have met strong legislative resistance. Between 1985 and 1994, congressional opposition prevented Brazilian presidents from implementing a number of measures that aimed to stabilize the economy in the face of triple-digit inflationary pressures. Most economists had agreed that earlier legislation that resulted in the indexing of wages and pensions to the cost of living had contributed to a dangerous level of inflation. However, proposals to end the practice were resisted in parliament by representatives beholden to trade unions and even by more conservative politicians who, though rhetorical supporters of such steps, were loath to act for fear of electoral repercussions. Congress also resisted executive attempts to reduce public sector employment, to increase taxes, to collect debts owed to the government by private businesses, and to reform the social security system.[14]

Representatives then and now have been reluctant to support such measures because of the popular outrage that would likely ensue. In other words, it is not very difficult for them to predict how their constituents would react to such measures and what the electoral repercussions might be. In such instances, executive leaders have called for constitutional changes that would restrict the budgetary and financial roles of Congress and enhance the role of the presidency in such matters. The 1973 military coup in Chile had as one of its goals "a new constitutional order characterized by a far more powerful president [and] a weakened parliament" that would create a new society where "market forces and an open, export-oriented economy would unleash entrepreneurial skills, and boost production and economic growth."[15] When representative democracy returned in the late 1990s, the new constitution restored some of the prerogatives of the congress, but the budgetary powers that had been exercised by the congress in the period prior to the coup were moved to the president. The reasoning behind such an approach is clear. Representative systems, as noted earlier, often create incentives for incumbents to push local projects that will gain them favor among their constituents so they will be reelected. Budget deficits are more likely as the institution seeks to accommodate as many of these requests as possible. This tendency can be combated either by enhancing the executive's power in budget making or by introducing electoral reforms that reduce the incentive to pursue funding for local projects—for example, moving from an open to a closed list proportional representation system.[16]

Of course, the military does not always have or need an economic justification for attacking representative institutions. In countries throughout Asia, Africa, and Latin America, coups d'etat have resulted in the disbanding of the legislature and the installation of military juntas. Such events happen for a variety of reasons, but the military leaders typically cite the corruption of members of parliament, threats to public order, and other dangers to the nation that they claim are the result of the petty politics of representative institutions and their inability to deal with major public problems. Such criticisms are often not far from the mark, and although they may not justify unilateral military action against democratically elected institutions, it is often difficult to muster a great deal of sympathy for the deposed legislators and their institutions. For example, in 1972, President Ferdinand Marcos of the Philippines suspended the legislature. One scholar, no fan of President Marcos, summarized the situation this way:

> Over the years, Congress has fallen into disrepute. . . . [It] had become an object of scorn, hated and despised. To many Filipinos, Congress stands as a massive symbol of all that is dirty and evil in Philippine politics. To think of the legislature as an assemblage of learned men, many believe is to be out of one's mind. . . . Absenteeism is prevalent, discipline is sadly lacking, and intellectual bankruptcy characterized congressional discussions. To some, Congress is virtually a theater of the absurd.[17]

Such attitudes are not restricted to less developed political systems. Given our earlier discussion, it is not clear that many Americans would disagree if that same assessment were applied to the United States Congress. In France in 1958, one survey conducted at the nadir of the Fourth Republic found that 75 percent of the French population agreed with the statement that "parliamentary morality is inadequate," and nearly half thought that Parliament had too much power. With the advent of the Fifth Republic under President Charles de Gaulle, the power of Parliament was reduced and, interestingly, popular support for the institution rose.[18]

THE DECLINE OF THE LEGISLATURE AND THE RISE OF THE ADMINISTRATIVE STATE

There has long been a view that representative institutions, no matter whether one thinks well or ill of them, inevitably will lose power and authority to the executive. In the late nineteenth century, the political sociologist Max Weber predicted that a trend toward a bureaucratic state was inexorable and posed a significant threat to representative and democratic institutions.[19] Today, the imperatives of governing the modern nation-state require all governments to rely more heavily on presumably more rational and certainly more expert technocrats based in the executive branch who fully understand the details of public policy. In the case of foreign and defense policy issues, speed and secrecy are imperative, and a greater degree of executive control is necessary. All that the best politicians can ever be, say advocates of the administrative state, are generalists who have some familiarity with a wide range of policy areas. Therefore, the actions of legislators are more likely to be guided by considerations of political expediency rather than by what is best from a policy perspective. As governments strive for the best policy solutions, legislatures and their members will become increasingly marginalized and their power and influence must decline.[20]

As countries attempt to move to neoliberal market driven economies, such efforts are often led by Western trained economists in bureaucratic or private sector posts. As Weber would have predicted, in some instances, such as Chile, this transition was accompanied by a more authoritarian political system. In a whole range of other areas, from climate change to international trade to energy policy, good public policy requires expertise of the sort that legislative institutions cannot muster and a commitment to do what is needed rather than what is politically expedient. One leading European scholar notes a cross-national phenomenon of "creeping authoritarianism," in which ways are found to bypass parliament on important policy issues. Indicators of this are the increasingly powerful roles for nonrepresentative institutions such as central banks and independent judiciaries, along with the usual delegation of decision-making to bureaucracies through the enactment of "skeleton" laws that establish broad goals and leave the details to be worked out by those who administer the law.[21]

Ironically, the argument for such institutions and practices is similar to the argument that justified the replacement of direct democratic practices with representative institutions—that public policy was too complicated for the ordinary citizen to understand and would need to be left to representatives who would be better equipped to handle these complexities. In its current form, the critique is extended to the representatives themselves. In this sense, the argument for the administrative state constitutes an even stronger rejection of the principles of popular sovereignty than the argument for representative government. Now it is the elected representatives who do not know enough about public policy; that is why their policymaking role has been eclipsed by technocrats who have the capacity to develop the best solutions to complex problems.

On the other hand, some have argued that at least in the United States the bureaucracy may be more representative than many give it credit for. Its employees are more demographically representative of the population than the membership of the Congress. The military better reflects population demographics than elected representatives, especially so in less developed nations. Elements of the bureaucracy also have demonstrated a greater willingness than elected politicians to stand up for and defend those at the bottom of the socioeconomic scale. Government agencies that deal with social services, education, and health benefits for the poor may be more passionately committed to these programs and may be less under the sway of moneyed interest groups than the politicians who ostensibly are their masters. They also may have stronger connections with public advocacy groups and nongovernmental organizations that speak for these populations than legislators do, given the fact that such groups usually do not have sufficient funds or control sufficient votes to attract the attention and concern of politicians.[22]

The response to these presumed policy deficiencies of representative institutions takes a number of forms. In nations such as the United States, characterized by stable constitutional systems, some argue for a shift in power from the legislature to the executive. With some barely concealed admiration for the British political system, they suggest that Congress should emphasize its role as the overseer of the executive, but when it comes to policymaking, defer for the most part to the expertise resident in the political and bureaucratic components of the executive branch. The means to accomplishing such a goal without resorting to the bulky process of constitutional amendment is typically found in a strengthened party system that would link the president more firmly with his copartisans in Congress. In instances when Congress and the president are controlled by the same political party, the executive, assured in general of congressional support, could move ahead expeditiously on policy priorities.[23] However, if Congress and the president happen to be controlled by different political parties, this remedy would fail because these more disciplined parties would increase the likelihood of policy stalemate.[24]

Situations of unified party control along with relatively high levels of party discipline have existed for short periods in recent United States history. After his landslide election victory in 1964, President Lyndon Johnson had overwhelming Democratic majorities in both the House and Senate and saw most of his legislative priorities, including significant changes in public welfare and civil rights policies, approved by Congress. Similarly, during the 2002–2006 period, when George W. Bush had disciplined Republican majorities in both houses of the United States Congress (albeit much narrower majorities than Johnson enjoyed), he was able to gain approval for a number of items on his agenda, most notably a huge reduction in the tax rates for the most well-off Americans and the establishment of a testing regime in the public schools through the No Child Left Behind Act.

But these periods of presidential domination through strong parties have been episodic in the United States, and presidents typically have been unable to depend on the consistent and loyal support of their copartisans in Congress. Increasingly, they have been attracted to strategies and measures that avoided Congress in order to accomplish their goals. This has been especially the case in foreign and defense policy, areas in which presidents have asserted the right to act unilaterally without legislative support. But it also has appeared domestically, most recently in the assertion by President George W. Bush of the theory of a unitary executive, which, taken to an extreme, suggests significant limitations on the power of the Congress (and even the Supreme Court) to control the actions of the president and the bureaucracy. Along with signing statements that may include presidential interpretations of legislation that are at odds with the intention of Congress, the unitary executive notion suggests a much stronger executive and a much diminished legislative branch of government.[25]

In less stable political systems, attempts to reduce the role of the legislature often have been more forceful. At various times military leaders have sent tanks rolling toward the parliament buildings, either to intimidate legislators into following a particular course or to force the suspension or closing of the legislature so that juntas and strongmen could rule. As indicated earlier, such steps are often accompanied by at least short-term popular approbation, given the reputation for corruption that legislators sometimes have. Alternatively, such steps are taken at a time of domestic crisis or foreign danger, and the military in that context is seen as a force to restore order and protect the nation. In the end, representative institutions have no defense against such steps, no power to command or raise alternative military forces to protect their own prerogatives. This has been the case in Myanmar (formerly Burma), in Thailand, and at various times throughout the twentieth century in Greece and several Latin American and African nations.

The threat to representative institutions may not come directly from the military. There are instances when charismatic, popularly elected presidents can diminish the power of other institutions and centralize power in their own hands. Hugo Chavez was elected president of Venezuela and enjoyed enormous support, especially among the poorer citizens of his country. Once in office, he moved to consolidate his power and diminish the role of the congress. President Robert Mugabe of Zimbabwe, a hero in the fight against British colonialism, has been in essence president for life in that country and rules with an iron fist that has eliminated the power of the parliament as well as opposition political parties.

Even in the United States, there have been proponents of the view that in times of crisis, power should move toward a president capable of acting with dispatch and away from a Congress that is characterized by slow, often too deliberate action. Such a perspective has a long theoretical pedigree. Machiavelli made the point that assemblies are not up to the task of "remedying a situation which will not brook delay." Members of representative institutions "have to consult with one another, and to reconcile their diverse views takes time," but the single executive can act with dispatch.[26] Alexander Hamilton, writing in The Federalist No. 70, advocated energy in the executive which was conducive to "decision, activity, secrecy, and dispatch," which in turn is "essential to the protection of the community against foreign attacks." Hamilton went on to argue that another benefit of an energetic executive was the ability of the public to fix responsibility for government actions. Plural executives and assemblies would be likely to shift the blame from one person to another when public policies had bad results.[27]

Although the circumstances and events in each nation will vary, attacks on the prerogatives and in some cases the existence of the legislature share in common the notion that power must reside in the person of a single leader who will be in charge. These attacks are a rejection of the idea that differing political views need to be aired and discussed, that policy needs to be deliberated, that the views of different parts of the society need to be considered and incorporated in government action, and if that cannot be done, then inaction is not an unreasonable alternative. In brief, proponents of power in a strong single leader reject the core principles of representative democracy, and in the United States, the principle of institutional checks and balances embedded in the constitutional system of separate institutions sharing power. Although some of the executive leaders who have sought to enhance their own power at the expense of the legislature continue to call themselves democrats because they have been elected by the people, the steps that they take to aggrandize the power of their office appear to move their nations further from, rather than closer to, the democratic end of the continuum.

Then there are authoritarian systems with marginal legislative institutions that are not necessarily the product of either popular election or military coup. The Saud family of Saudi Arabia rules that country with little interference from a thoroughly co-opted legislature, and Moammar Gadhafi has ruled Libya in much the same way for nearly forty years. In Iran, a legislative body of marginal importance under the shah was replaced with another weak legislative body under the theocratic rule of the ayatollahs who overthrew the shah. And in China, the legislature has never been very strong, with all power residing in the hands of the Central Committee of the Communist Party.

In brief, although representative institutions in established constitutional systems vary significantly in their ability to influence public policy, many representative institutions have little or no ability to participate in the policymaking process. Contrary to the democratic critique of representative institutions, the most common alternative to representation is not democracy but authoritarianism with a single person, a military junta, or a hegemonic political party in control, no significant role for the legislature, and even less of a role for citizens than a representative system contemplates. To be sure, there may be other representative institutions that exist in these nations—some would argue that the Communist Party in China provides a form of representation, and others will argue that the connections of military and bureaucratic personnel with mass publics has been underestimated—but certainly representation as we have come to understand the term does not exist.

MORE DEMOCRACY

If one response to the weaknesses of representative institutions is to move in the direction of a more authoritarian model, the other alternative is to move toward a more robustly democratic model. From this perspective, the primary commitment of a political system should be to popular sovereignty, and the primary failing of representative institutions is that they undermine that commitment. As one of the leading advocates of this point of view puts it, representative government "steals from individuals the ultimate responsibility for their values, beliefs, and actions. . . . Representation is incompatible with freedom because it delegates and thus alienates political will at the cost of genuine self-government and autonomy." As a result, "citizens become subject to laws they did not truly participate in making; they become passive constituents of representatives who, far from reconstituting the citizens' aims and interests, usurp their civic functions and deflect their civic energies."[28]

Traditionally, these critics have been advocates for institutions and practices that bypass representative bodies or provide enhanced opportunities for citizens to hold their representatives accountable. In the United States in the early twentieth century, the progressive movement sought to return power to the people by proposing a triumvirate of reform measures. The first of these, the referendum, would require that the legislature place certain issues directly before the people for a vote; if approved, the proposal would become law without the need for further legislative action. A second reform, the initiative, would allow individual citizens or groups of citizens to bypass the legislature entirely by placing public policy questions, or propositions, directly on the ballot. Currently, just over half of the states in the union have provisions for referenda or initiatives or both. A third reform was the recall, which would allow citizens to force an officeholder to submit to reelection in the middle of his term in office. This process, which exists in only a few states, was used most recently in California in 2003 to remove incumbent governor Grey Davis from office and replace him with Arnold Schwarzenegger.

In most states where it is permitted, the initiative is rarely used, with an average of two initiatives per state a year on the ballot in recent decades. In a few states, however, they are much more frequent occurrences. Oregon voters dealt with seventy-five initiatives between 1990 and 2001, twenty-six in 2000 alone, and California had sixty-six during that same period. In Colorado, which averages about four initiatives a year, the mechanism was used to prevent the state legislature from raising taxes unless it gained approval through a public referendum. In the 2006 midterm elections, there were more than 200 initiatives and referenda on the ballots of the various states, dealing with issues as diverse as stem cell research, the minimum wage, smoking, abortion, gay marriage, and affirmative action.[29]

Although there is undoubtedly a democratic quality to initiatives, referenda, and recall, there are serious problems with these techniques as well. The first two reduce politics to a yes/no affair—that is, the deliberative element that is so essential to good public policy is minimized or eliminated entirely. Although democrats worry that expertise is overly valued, initiatives and referenda allow little if any room for informed policy discussion. Like elections, initiative and referendum battles are fought with expensive ad campaigns that reduce the issue at hand to a slogan and seldom expose what is truly at stake and what the real implications of the proposal are. And, of course, money is important in determining the outcome. Groups favoring stem cell research spent more than $12 million in support of the 2006 Missouri referendum on this issue, and the R. J. Reynolds Tobacco Company vowed to spend $40 million fighting antismoking referenda that appeared on various state ballots.[30] As for the recall, if widely used it would make it less likely that representatives would take political risks or do anything that might offend the voters, no matter how necessary such a step might be, lest they be subject to recall petitions. The device might even make representatives more vulnerable to those with financial resources, given the money that an incumbent would need to spend in order to defend himself against a recall campaign.

TERM LIMITS

Among the most wrongheaded approaches to the perceived problems of representation has been the movement toward limiting the number of terms that a representative can serve. In the United States, this became a particularly popular reform in the 1990s and, as indicated earlier, a few other countries also have legislative term limits. One rationale for term limits is that politicians who stay in office too long inevitably lose touch with their constituents. Another, in some ways at odds with the first, is that legislators are too focused on reelection and therefore do what is popular rather than what is necessary. Moreover, because of the cost of election campaigns, they are too vulnerable to the corrupting impact of money in politics. The way to prevent these problems, the argument runs, is to limit the amount of time a person can serve in the legislature. Ostensibly, this would put an end to government by professional politicians who view public service as a vocation and return the country to the romantic notion of the citizen representative who enters public service on a temporary basis to do what is best for his community and his country and then returns to his home to resume his nonpolitical life.

The connection between term limit proposals and the democratic critique of representative institutions focuses on the high reelection rates of incumbents and, therefore, their virtual permanence in office. The term oligarchy is used to refer to those who hold political power on a nearly permanent basis, and oligarchs, by definition, tend to be less responsive and accountable. From another perspective, some proponents of term limits argue that such measures would reduce the disposition of representatives to focus only on those policies that would help their local constituencies. Without the possibility of building a long political career, representatives would be more likely to concentrate on policies that addressed the national interest rather than those that served local interests or the moneyed interests that are essential to reelection success. As opposed to the anti-oligarchic justification for term limits, this argument suggests that the desire for reelection makes the representative too responsive to his constituents.

The most common method for instituting term limits has been through citizen initiatives. In those states that require a constitutional amendment to enact term limits, these proposals have been put before the voters as well. The term limit idea has been voluntary as it has applied to members of the United States Congress, because the general understanding is that there are constitutional barriers to a state passing legislation imposing term limits on federal officeholders. But term limits for members of the state legislature exist in fifteen states, have been passed but ruled contrary to the state constitution in four states, and have been repealed by the legislatures of two states.[31] The limits range from three to six two-year terms in the lower chamber of state legislatures and two to three four-year terms for the upper chamber. Although a majority of the states with term limits specify that the limit applies to consecutive terms, six states impose lifetime bans on legislative service once the limit is reached.

The problems with term limits are almost too many to list. First, they restrict membership in the legislature to those who have alternative nonpolitical positions to which they can return. Those with more modest resources who need to think of politics as a vocation rather than an avocation would find it difficult to serve. Second, if one is worried that representatives tend to drift away from the opinions and interests of their constituents, what sense does it make to eliminate reelection, the primary institution that democracies have for holding politicians accountable to their constituents? No empirical evidence indicates that term limits increase the responsiveness of legislators to their constituents.[32] Third, if one of the goals of term limit advocates is to improve the performance of the legislature, what sense does it make to require members to leave just at the point when they have acquired the experience and knowledge of the legislature and its procedures to be effective representatives and when they may well have acquired at least some degree of public policy expertise? In many legislatures with term limits, leadership positions of necessity have been assumed by members who have barely had enough time to learn how the institution functions and how to get things done. Fourth, rather than weakening the ties between representatives and those with significant financial interests, term limits may strengthen that tie. Representatives who will need to leave office at a specified time may be tempted to work more cooperatively with those interest groups that will have the capacity to provide them with lucrative employment at the time they need to step down. Even if they do not strengthen their ties with these groups, it stands to reason that as members begin to approach the end of their legislative service, they may spend less time concentrating on their legislative responsibilities and more time thinking about what they will do afterward. Contrary to the views of term limit advocates, if one wishes to have high quality people in Congress, it stands to reason that members should see their service as a profession, with good salaries and with the prospect of continuation in their jobs as long as their performance satisfies their employers—in this case, the citizens who vote for them. Finally, term limits are fundamentally antidemocratic in that they deprive citizens of the opportunity to select the person whom they wish to represent them; although they would be barred from returning an incompetent representative to office, they also are prevented from returning to office someone who has a demonstrated record of honest, informed public service.[33]

DEMOCRACY AND TECHNOLOGY

If the referendum, initiative, and recall were early twentieth century devices for facilitating more direct democracy, the early twenty-first century proposals are characterized by their reliance on electronic technology. One of the arguments for representative rather than direct democracy was that it was impossible to gather together the citizenry of a large nation for discussion and deliberation; but now, the Internet can provide a means for a "virtual" gathering of large numbers of citizens. The Internet also has placed a vast amount of information at the fingertips of the average voter. Although newspaper readership has declined, most major newspapers can be easily accessed online, as can high quality public policy sources such as *Congressional Quarterly* and *National Journal*. The "blog" has emerged as a way for individual citizens with no media connections to reach large numbers of people, and because those who read blogs tend to be politically attentive and active, politicians have begun to pay almost as much attention to these writers as to mainstream journalists. E-mail has provided a convenient, nearly instantaneous means for an interest group to reach all of its members with information, talking points, and action alerts. Although no hard evidence indicates that citizen information has increased dramatically because of these technological advances, some inferences can be drawn from the fact that every political campaign now relies heavily on Internet based fundraising appeals, and that organizations like MoveOn.org, which operates entirely through the Internet, have become significant political players. Finally, the proliferation of television channels that has accompanied the move to cable TV has spawned an array of 24-hour news stations and networks that provide information, opinion, and partisan commentary. At a minimum, these changes, taken as a whole, challenge the assumption that it is too difficult for citizens to gain the information they need to make informed public policy decisions. In some respects, citizens may have too much information available, maybe so much that it is difficult or impossible to sort through it all and to evaluate its reliability, but that is a problem for another book.

The next step, some democrats argue, is to move toward electronic decision-making. Assuming that the near future will produce widespread, low cost access to the web in much the same way that almost everyone now has access to a telephone, television, and radio, it becomes possible to imagine a voting process not unlike a national referendum on key issues, except much easier and less expensive to conduct than the traditional voting process. Such an innovation could place decision-making power directly into the hands of the people, or at least provide citizens with the opportunity to give specific, timely instructions to their representatives on important issues as they come up.[34] Already, organizations like MoveOn.org have empowered their members to decide through electronic balloting which candidates the organization should back. And although it is more frivolous, more people vote for contestants on "American Idol" than participate in many elections. Some states are seriously discussing electronic voting options that would enable citizens to cast their votes from their home computers, and it is only a short step from computerized election systems to computerized systems that would allow citizens to choose among policy options.

Endowing citizens with the right to assemble in a virtual town meeting to choose among policy options returns us once again to the issue of deliberation. Referenda and initiatives already provide citizens with an opportunity to say *yea* or *nay*, but do not provide them with the opportunity to deliberate. If we are to consider computer assisted direct democracy, ways need to be found to bring citizens into the discussion of policy options by creating "a public space between individuals and the state" where ordinary citizens "could develop, express, and share their views." Ways also would need to be found to make experts available as providers and translators of technical information.[35] This approach suggests that the remedy for the bureaucratic state as well as supposedly nonresponsive representatives lies not in the strengthening of representative institutions but rather in the strengthening of democracy itself.

Perhaps the most detailed argument for such a participatory approach is offered by Benjamin Barber, who advocates "strong democracy" that "rests on the idea of a self-governing community of citizens who are united less by homogeneous interests than by civic education and who are made capable of common purpose and mutual action by virtue of their civic attitudes and participatory institutions." In Barber's opinion, the machinery of representative government constitutes "thin democracy" characterized by a passive, ill-informed, and inarticulate citizenry. Strong democracy, in contrast, "is the politics of amateurs, where every man is compelled to encounter every other man without the intermediary of expertise" and where public participation "is a way of defining the self, just as citizenship is a way of living."[36]

Barber makes a number of concrete suggestions that in his view would strengthen democracy. These include such steps as the creation of neighborhood assemblies so that the spirit and form of the New England town meeting could be replicated across the nation; the use of technology to create a national town meeting; steps to make it easier for all citizens to get information; and nationwide initiatives and referenda. To the argument that various experiments of this sort show that citizens will not participate, Barber responds that in the past, decisions made through these processes have not had any actual impact on public policy. But if consequential decisions resulted from these processes, citizens would participate. In this reasoning, the citizen apathy and lack of information noted earlier as a justification for representative institutions is in fact caused by representative institutions that take away any meaningful role citizens might have in deciding the issues that are important to them.

"Deliberative polling" is a technique to enhance the role of citizen opinion and to address the concern that direct democracy does not allow enough room for debate and discussion. One approach, devised by James Fishkin of the University of Texas, is called face-to-face deliberative polling. With deliberative polling, one begins by surveying a random sample of the public to discover their attitudes on a major policy question. Then the people in the sample engage in a dialogue on the issue, assisted by a balanced set of briefing materials and the opportunities to interact with experts and with each other. A second survey is then conducted, producing a snapshot of more informed opinion on the issue. Dr. Fishkin has conducted various experiments with this process, and the final polls are almost always at marked variance with the initial predialogue polls taken on the issue.[37] At a minimum, these experiences suggest that uninformed voters are educable, and, under the right circumstances, they can learn about an issue and adjust their opinions based on new information.

In April 2007, an experiment in deliberative polling was conducted in Bulgaria. A sample of 1,344 people was polled on what the nation's policies toward the country's Roma population (Gypsies) should be. Of the initial sample, 255 people were selected for the deliberative stage, where they received "briefing materials, including proposals from political parties, the government, and nongovernmental organizations." Over a two-day period, "they debated with competing experts and politicians, posing questions they formed in small groups." A second poll, conducted when the debates and discussions concluded, found that the percentage of respondents who thought the Roma should live in separate neighborhoods declined from 43 percent to 21 percent, and the percentage who thought there should be more Roma police officers increased to 52 percent from 32 percent. The higher postdeliberation levels of tolerance were surprising given the more hostile tone of the debate on these issues among the nation's elites.[38]

If the outcome of the second poll is meant to be only advisory to politicians who may or may not be guided by its results, then participants will have less incentive to take the process seriously. But if such a process assumed referendum-like status, with the results binding at some level on government officials, then it is more likely that citizens will take it seriously. In the case of Bulgaria, the prime minister said that he would use the results of the poll to shape policy, but to this point there are few indicators that these experiments have been used to actually settle controversial issues or that they are being formally adopted as a regular part of the political decision-making process. Presumably, if there is merit in this model, it also may be possible to involve larger groups of people through the Internet; although the face-to-face aspect of deliberation would be lost, information can be exchanged and some dialogue presumably can take place.

It is difficult and uncomfortable for supporters of representative institutions, most of whom view themselves as democrats at heart, to criticize the notion of direct democracy or to find fault with something as reasonable as deliberative polling, but it is important to note the problems before one takes the plunge. One concern is that systems that utilize forms of direct democracy are, as the Founders noted, vulnerable to being taken over by demagogues who appeal to the passions and emotions of the population rather than to their reason. After all, it was the citizens of Athens who voted to put Socrates to death. A second concern is the inability of deliberative democracy to come to grips with systemic issues. The political theorist Iris Marion Young makes the point that deliberative democracy explicitly accepts the structural realities and inequalities of the nation along with its prevailing ideology, and these factors shape the terms and terminology of its deliberative processes. Attempts to achieve social or economic justice through deliberative democracy are frustrated because participants in these arenas are confronted with what she refers to as "constrained alternatives that cannot question existing institutional priorities and social structures." Therefore, "deliberation is as likely to reinforce injustice as to undermine it." She concludes by making a case for political activism that goes beyond a willingness to engage in discussion with one's opponents to embrace street demonstrations and forms of civil disobedience that are designed to "expose the sources and consequences of structural inequalities in law."[39]

It is not at all obvious that the outcome of citizen-based deliberative processes would be public policies that are wiser and more reasoned than what emerges from the legislature. As examined in chapter 1, its deliberative capacity is one of the defining characteristics of, and compelling arguments for, representative rather than direct democracy. Although deliberative democracy advocates argue that they have solved the practical problems of assembling citizens (by using random samples and perhaps technology) as well as the expertise problem (by providing participants with access to expert opinion) it is not clear that average citizens will, over a broad array of policy issues, be able to make effective use of this expertise. It is more likely that professional politicians who engage in policymaking as a full-time occupation will be better able to utilize expert information and even may possess some of that expertise themselves.

RENEWING CIVIC LIFE

Another category of democratic reforms focuses on proposals for strengthening civic engagement. One train of thought argues for the renewal of local community life by encouraging citizens to become active in organizations such as parent-teacher associations, bowling leagues, garden clubs, and the like. Exponents of this point of view argue that the reason why people are alienated from and distrustful of politics and politicians is because they are alienated from each other. The decline in the membership in these community organizations has meant a decline in personal interaction with others, and it is through such personal interaction with others at the local level that people acquire a broader sense of trust in others. Civic engagement of this sort would lead to a fuller engagement with issues and problems and a more active and informed citizenry.[40] The representation problem that this set of reforms would address presumably is the large number of apathetic, alienated, and uninformed citizens. At the local level, the renewal of civic life would create greater public involvement in local issues. More active and involved citizens would be more attentive to public policy at the national level and to what their representatives are doing, and the tie between constituents and representatives would be strengthened.

This reasoning, however, assumes that citizens have a strong desire to participate at much higher levels than they currently do. Based on extensive focus group discussions and analysis of public opinion data, political scientists John Hibbing and Elizabeth Theiss-Morse come to a different conclusion. They find that mass publics have little or no interest in policy representation; rather, they are more concerned with issues such as corruption, the ability (or the inability) of leaders to solve problems and reach solutions, and what they perceive to be the unfair way in which the policymaking process works. Citizens, in their view, do not wish to be directly involved in the policymaking process as democrats argue; rather, they are comfortable with the trustee model of representation and are willing to defer to their representatives as long as these representatives are honest and produce results.[41]

Further support for this view comes from Jane Mansbridge's study of New England town meetings. She discovered that the number of people who actively participated in these meetings was actually quite small and that most people were not interested in getting involved in the conflict, debate, criticism, and hard feelings that are, of course, the very stuff of political deliberation and decision-making.[42] Similarly, Morris Fiorina marshals evidence that questions the democratic assumption that people really do wish to participate in politics and political decision-making; he concludes that most people are not, in fact, political animals.[43] If the trustee model is in fact the system that citizens implicitly prefer, it obviates the concern about the absence of policy or even general political knowledge among mass publics, and reduces the democratic complaint about the extent to which representatives succeed or fail to reflect public opinion in their policymaking activities.

In this same vein, when I was discussing representation in one of my courses, a student suggested that she thought of her representative in the same way that she thought of her automobile mechanic. She had no interest in learning what makes her car run, or what to do to make it run better; nor did she wish to give the mechanic instructions on how to take care of her car. She just wanted the mechanic to fix the car so that it would run. In the same way, she had little interest in learning the mechanics of public policymaking (odd, of course, for a student in a political science class, but I digress) or the details of particular public policy proposals; she just wanted the political system to run well and that was what she expected her representative to ensure. It is from this perspective that we might best understand the frustration that Americans have with their Congress. Apart from committed activists, most may not care about the details of how the issue of immigration, for example, should be dealt with; they simply want it dealt with, and Congress's inability to muster the supermajority in the Senate in 2007 to pass legislation to deal with this or several other important issues leads them to the conclusion that their representative institutions just are not working.

CONTROLLING THE MONEY?

Another approach begins from the premise that the real problem with representation is the disproportionate influence that powerful interest groups have on the actions of elected representatives. Proposed reforms typically focus on steps designed to restrict the flow of money from these groups to the campaign coffers of candidates. Public funding of legislative campaigns and significant restrictions or a total ban on private donations has been a perennial proposal of reformers, although it has not gotten very far in the United States. The experience with the laws that have been enacted to tighten regulations on campaign contributions has been less than edifying. Interest groups and those with significant financial resources always seem to find imaginative ways to circumvent the legislation and get money to their favored politicians. And, as noted, the Supreme Court has raised questions about the compatibility of such legislation with the Constitution's free speech guarantees.

It may be more realistic to accept the fact that in a capitalist society such as the United States a connection between money and political power is inevitable. Rather than seeking to sever this tie, the goal should be to find ways to broaden the spectrum of interest groups who have financial resources so that politicians will not be beholden to only one side of a policy issue. Theda Skocpol has emphasized the importance of mass membership organizations that collect dues and use these funds in much the same way that smaller, moneyed groups use their dollars to influence politicians. She notes how effective trade unions and organizations such as the AARP have been in raising and spending money on behalf of candidates and funding professional lobbying efforts, thereby providing a counterweight to the funds from large business concerns. The success of MoveOn.org as a virtual interest group composed for the most part of small donors connected only by the Internet is another newer example of this approach.[44]

THE CRITIQUE IN SUMMARY

What are we to make, then, of representation and its critics? It is easy and probably accurate to accept many of the charges leveled against representative institutions. They certainly are slow to act, often inefficient and uninformed in what they do, and their members are vulnerable to the corrupting influence of campaign contributions, their own ambition, and occasionally outright bribery. The linkage between what they do and the opinions and interests of their constituents (not to mention the national interest) is often difficult to discern. On the other hand, when they do respond to their constituents, they seem motivated more by the desire for reelection than by the desire to produce good public policy. The citizens who are supposed to be represented by members of these institutions usually are unaware of what their representatives are doing and even who they are. In several Western democracies, the level of public approval of the legislature is consistently low, and in many other nations the legislature is under threat of suspension by political forces backed by military power.

Even the most committed exponents of representative institutions find it difficult at times to rise to the defense of an institution that so frequently seems alienated from those whom they are supposed to "make present" in government. The various proposals and practices designed to bypass the legislature and return power to the people do hold a certain attraction. And for those whose primary goal is achieving good public policy—public policy that yields long-term and effective solutions to the plethora of problems and challenges that every nation confronts—more centralized, executive-centered power and the expertise that it commands from professional bureaucrats can sound attractive.

Although there is a danger that centralized executive power can deteriorate into authoritarianism, it is also the case that decisions taken by such leaders might well be more responsive to the interests of the people than decisions taken by a conservative, oligarchic legislative body. In nations with conservative legislatures dominated by the forces in society most resistant to change, radical departures from established policies—either from the right or the left—are more likely to come from the executive. And for better or worse, executives, as Hamilton suggested, can supply energy to government that legislatures cannot; in brief, they can act, and at least in the United States, it is the Congress's failure to act that seems to arouse the sharpest public criticism.

REPRESENTATION AND THE PROBLEMS OF REPRESENTATIVE INSTITUTIONS

Certainly, people want their government to solve problems, and they are usually less concerned with which institution does the solving or with the specifics of the solution that is adopted. But citizens put representatives and the institutions in which they serve in a no-win situation. When they act as their constituents wish them to act, we criticize them for any number of reasons: for being overly responsive to public opinion; for focusing solely on getting reelected; for decisions that result in incoherent or lowest-common-denominator policies designed to satisfy as many constituencies as possible rather than to solve problems; and for their tendency to avoid long-term solutions in favor of short-term fixes, because the former carry greater electoral risks than the latter. But if they do not act or do not act with dispatch, we accuse them of being wedded to the status quo, enslaved by special interests, consumed by partisan bickering, overly fearful of adverse electoral repercussions, and tied down by Byzantine rules designed to frustrate rather than facilitate action. And if they act contrary to our wishes or they do not act when we wish them to act, we indict them on the most heinous charge of all—that they have frustrated the will of the people and are therefore antidemocratic.

Ironically, what citizens find most repellent about their representative institutions is the deliberation, argumentation, and compromise that lies at the very heart of policymaking in a representative body. But when these same citizens are asked what they expect of their representatives, they are very likely to say that they expect representatives to speak up for them and their interests and to advocate in the strongest terms the policy positions that they support—in other words, to argue! Meeting this expectation is likely to produce exactly the highly visible and seemingly nonproductive conflict that contributes to the low approval ratings for the United States Congress and other legislatures and that can provide a justification for executive attacks on legislative prerogatives—constitutional attacks in relatively stable systems such as the United States, or extraconstitutional attacks led by the military in less stable systems.

The point is that the most obvious failings of the United States Congress as a policymaking institution are directly tied to the connection between its members and their constituents. Although making good public policy often involves taking risks, reelection—the essential process for holding representatives accountable for their actions—makes representatives risk averse. It would be good if members of Congress supported highway legislation that would direct funds only to those areas where the roads were in greatest need of repair, but reelection incentives ensure that Congress spreads the money equally across the nation regardless of need. It would be good if Congress took action to ensure the long-term viability of social security and Medicare—two immensely popular programs that currently face uncertain actuarial futures. But solving this problem requires policy actions that members will find electorally risky—some combination of steps that would raise the payroll tax that supports these programs, raise the retirement age, or reduce the benefits that all or some retirees receive. So Congress avoids this issue as it looks for the elusive, painless solution and draws comfort from stray studies that say we really do not have to worry about these problems for decades. It would be good if Congress dealt with our dependence on foreign oil, but all the solutions on the table would involve some combination of higher prices for gasoline, conservation, the reconsideration of nuclear power, or more aggressive exploration in wilderness areas. So rather than act, Congress looks for the painless solutions of alternative and clean energy sources, obviously a good idea but one that is unlikely to yield any concrete results for many years to come.

Legislative inaction stemming from its members' aversion to risk is made more likely by the manner in which congressional campaigns are now conducted. Members of Congress seem to live in fear of the thirty-second ad, financed by their opponents or by interest groups, highlighting and often distorting a particular vote that they cast. Congressional inaction on immigration during 2006 and 2007 may be explained in large measure by the reduction of this complex debate to a single word: "amnesty." Advocates for comprehensive immigration reform were accused by opponents of offering amnesty to undocumented immigrants and their families who had entered the country illegally. It seems that few members of either party were prepared to run for reelection as proponents of amnesty, fearing that should they support a bill that provided a path to citizenship for undocumented workers, no matter how difficult the path and no matter how many penalties the law imposed, that one word would become the centerpiece of every advertisement opposing their reelection. All of this takes place in the increasingly bitter partisan atmosphere that has characterized the United States Congress from 1994 to the present, a win at all costs philosophy that relies on demonizing one's opponents with an eye toward gaining an advantage in the next election, rather than finding common ground that will allow the legislative process to move forward.

When representatives are not responding to electoral concerns by avoiding risk, they may opt for "individual responsiveness at the expense of collective responsibility." Members have every electoral reason to promote narrowly targeted programs, projects, and tax breaks for their constituents but little incentive to consider the impact that such measures have on the federal budget as a whole. Recipients notice and appreciate such benefits and presumably show their gratitude to the legislator at election time. "But when members in large numbers follow this individually productive strategy, spending rises, revenue falls, deficits accumulate, and inefficient government programs and projects proliferate."[45] Citizens hold the Congress as a whole responsible for these adverse budgetary results and seldom trace the fault back to their own representatives and the individual actions they have taken that, although supporting the immediate interests of their constituencies, contribute to these long-term problems of the nation as a whole.

As an example of how individual responsiveness can lead to collective irresponsibility, consider the actions of the House Appropriations Subcommittee on Financial Services during the 110th Congress. Representative Jose Serrano of New York, who chaired the subcommittee, reported that one hundred of his colleagues in the House had requested earmarks from the portion of the budget for which his subcommittee was responsible. After reviewing the requests and eliminating the more frivolous ones, Representative Serrano was hard pressed to figure out how to proceed given the funds available to his committee and his and his staff's inability to judge the relative merits of each request. So he simply took the total amount of dollars that he had and divided them equally among all of the requesters, with each member receiving $231,000. Representative Serrano was not convinced that this was the wisest or the best thing for him to do, but he concluded that it was "the fairest approach" available to him.[46] Thus, individual responsiveness trumps collective responsibility.

Members of Congress seem to be engaged in what amounts to a permanent reelection campaign, to the point where they spend so much of their time and so much of their personal and staff resources on the reelection process, or on activities closely associated with reelection such as constituency service and securing project funds, that public policy concerns get short shrift. As observed earlier, members of Congress go home to their constituencies, often once a week, to visit and to listen. They deploy a significant percentage of their office staffs to service the concerns of individual constituents and to handle, record, tally, and respond to the mountains of communications that they receive from them. Meanwhile, they are constantly engaged in the process of raising money to support their next election campaign. With the cost of the average House reelection campaign far in excess of $1,000,000, that means that each year every incumbent member needs to raise more than $11,000 a week in campaign contributions. For the Senate, the average reelection campaign costs in excess of $9,000,000, which translates into almost $30,000 a week in campaign contributions throughout the six-year term; and in large, competitive states, the figure could easily be double that. Leaving aside the implicit (and in some cases explicit) policy commitments that a representative may be tempted to make in return for these funds, the sheer time committed to this activity must put a significant dent in the time that members have to devote to legislative matters.

WHAT CAN BE DONE?

In a 1947 speech in the British House of Commons, Winston Churchill famously said that, "democracy is the worst form of government, except for all those other forms that have been tried from time to time." Churchill of course was referring to representative rather than direct democracy, and the discussion in this book supports his basic point. The problems with and shortcomings of representative systems are numerous and varied, but the solutions that have been proposed, such as more direct democracy or enhanced power to the executive branch, each carry risks of their own. In other words, these supposed cures for the problems of representative democracy may be worse than the disease. What then can be done to improve representative systems in general, and particularly the system in the United States, without relegating representative institutions to the periphery of our political system?

One option is to accept the fact that an increased policymaking role for the executive is inevitable for all of the most frequently cited reasons: expertise; the ability to act with dispatch, particularly in the international arena; and the expectation of citizens that they will be led. If that is the case, then representative institutions need to reorient their emphasis toward overseeing and controlling the executive so that abuses of executive authority can be avoided or ameliorated. To watch and control the government and to hold executive leaders and professional civil servants to a public accounting for their actions was in John Stuart Mill's view the most appropriate function for representative institutions, more appropriate than having a direct role in the shaping of public policy. As the legislators exercise their representative function of being the public voice of the people and articulating the views that are abroad in the nation, they can develop the capacity to constrain executive action.

Students of the United States Congress have argued that representatives have relatively little interest in oversight because it is tedious, time-consuming work that almost never pays electoral dividends. The only exceptions are when highly publicized scandals arise and the representative's efforts can be popularly viewed as standing up for government integrity and effectiveness. The general disinterest in oversight means that Congress is derelict in one of a legislature's most important functions, especially in the United States where our constitutional system is built on the principle of institutions checking the abuses of one another so that ambition will counteract ambition, to use Madison's phrase from The Federalist No. 51. Reinvigorated oversight will require not just a change in the attitude of representatives but in the attitudes of executives as well. In the United States, that means less presidential reliance on executive privilege and governmental secrecy and a greater willingness to share information with Congress. The price to the president for greater legislative deference to him on major policy questions must be greater accountability of the president to the Congress.

If Congress is to turn greater attention to oversight as well as to other key policymaking functions, steps need to be taken to diminish the permanent campaign atmosphere within which the Congress operates. Members who are always concerned with raising money for the next election and with how their positions will be depicted in their opponent's television ads during the next campaign cannot give their full attention to the challenges of governing. Too often, the goal of good, long-term public policy solutions seems subverted by short-term political expediency. And the constant money chase will always raise questions about the ethics and integrity of representatives and, fairly or not, undermine the confidence that citizens have in their representative institutions. When those with financial resources have unfettered access to political leaders, it is natural for those without such resources to ask whether or not their views and interests are receiving equal consideration and protection. The connection between at least some earmarks and campaign contributions discussed in chapter 4 suggests a quid pro quo arrangement that, no matter how it might be justified, emits an odor of corruption to all who read about it. Even though it is difficult to tie campaign contributions to specific actions by members, the appearance of corruption is probably as important as actual corruption, at least from the point of view of the average citizen. As Supreme Court Justice David Souter said in a majority decision upholding state limits on campaign contributions, "Leave the perception of impropriety unanswered, and the cynical assumption that large donors call the tune could jeopardize the willingness of voters to take part in democratic governance."[47]

Public funding of congressional campaigns, although never a politically popular alternative, holds out the hope of weakening (although certainly not eliminating) the tie between representatives and moneyed interests. The cost of instituting public funding would be large, but certainly not much larger than the total amount of funds that representatives and their challengers raise privately during each election cycle. Such reforms also might be accompanied by greater restrictions on political advertising, although such steps have encountered constitutional objections from the judiciary. Canada has adopted a system of public funding for its national campaigns, banned corporate and union contributions, and placed a $5,000 limit on individual contributions while providing partial tax deductibility for such contributions. However, those with financial resources still have the option of running independent "third party" campaigns that could support or oppose particular candidates.[48] Australia restricts the amount of money individual candidates for Parliament can spend but places no restrictions on political parties. The parties are supported by a system of public funding based on the number of votes they receive and by private donations, the amount and source of which are unregulated. As in Canada, smaller donations from individuals are encouraged by limited tax deductibility.[49]

Perhaps more important is for Congress to establish an independent office to monitor the behavior of its members and to deal with ethical issues that arise. Congressional attempts to police their own ethics have failed abysmally. Members, no matter how well intentioned they might be, are under tremendous pressure to look the other way and to ignore or minimize the peccadilloes of their colleagues. Slaps on the wrist for obvious conflicts of interest are rare, and significant disciplinary action virtually nonexistent. Responding to these concerns, the House in March 2008 agreed to establish a panel of six nonmembers, three recommended by the speaker and three by the minority leader, who would have the power to receive and initiate ethics complaints, examine the allegations, and decide whether or not to forward them to the House Committee on Standards of Official Conduct for a formal investigation. Whether or not this panel actually will be established—there was substantial opposition to the proposal on both political and constitutional grounds—is an open question at this writing.[50] But what is not an open question is that the appearance of corruption contributes to citizen alienation from the Congress.

Finally, the complex procedures that characterize the House and the Senate need to be overhauled. In the Senate, the filibuster seems to have assumed sacred, quasiconstitutional status even though it is found nowhere in law and certainly nowhere in the Constitution. There is no indication at all that the Founders wished the Senate to operate on a supermajority basis. By giving small states the same representation as large states, they had gone far enough in ensuring that a minority of the nation's population (the fifty senators from the twenty-five smallest states in terms of population) could thwart the wishes of the majority. Allowing forty-one senators to stop the majority from acting seems a step too far and undermines the confidence that people have in the ability of their government to act. Although the House works more efficiently than the Senate, its rules and procedures could use some airing and renovation as well.[51] This is not the place to get into the specifics, but it is good to remember that if one is concerned with what members of the public think about their representative institutions, it would be good to have institutions whose operations are readily understandable. Better reporting by the mass media also would be helpful in this respect. Rather than running the simple, predictable story about legislators deliberating (the usual term is the more demeaning "bickering") and nothing getting done, or concentrating excessively on political scandals, clear, comprehensible reporting on what Congress is discussing, what is at stake, and what the different opinions are that need to be reconciled might explain to citizens why democratic decision-making often can be such a slow, time-consuming affair.

In some respects, however, the most important remedy lies with we the people and with our attitudes toward and expectations of our representatives. As mentioned earlier, we tend to place our representatives in a no-win situation. On the one hand, we expect them to fight vigorously for the interests of our communities; we elect them, and we reward them for responding to our views and for securing federal support for projects that will benefit us locally. On the other hand, we condemn them for being responsive to local interests and for not doing what is good for the nation as a whole. We get upset at federal spending but never, it seems, about the spending that takes place in our constituency or the spending on programs that benefit us. Everyone wants to have roads, buildings, bridges, and airports paid for by the federal government, a strong national defense, better schools, a cleaner environment, low-interest student loans, protection for veterans and for the elderly, and better medical care, but not everyone is happy to pay the taxes that allow the government to provide these benefits. The only way then to meet these conflicting expectations is through the budget deficits and accounting shenanigans that so many take as emblematic of a dysfunctional representative body.

And in the current age, the great mass of citizens who want government to act on the major problems that we confront as a nation and who are willing to support and even pay for the compromises that address these problems have allowed their political system to be hijacked by strong partisans who view compromise, conciliation, and the search for common ground as a betrayal of principle. During the summer of 2007, Senator John McCain's candidacy for the Republican presidential nomination temporarily foundered in large measure because the right wing of his party disavowed him for his willingness to work with Democrats on issues such as immigration and campaign finance reform. In an environment of nasty television commercials, sound bite politics that summarize complex policy issues in three-word slogans, and the easy demonizing of candidates, it is understandable that representatives become risk averse, avoid opportunities to find common ground, and operate on the assumption that doing nothing may be better than doing something that might offend someone. Such a strategy leads to the paradox of highly popular representatives who get reelected to a representative institution that is held in contempt by those who are being represented.

This is exactly the situation that those who wrote the United States Constitution hoped to avoid by establishing a representative rather than a democratic system and by restricting both the number of officeholders who would be elected directly by the people and the number of people who would have the right to vote. They feared the debilitating impact of popular passions on the quality of public policy and hoped that these arrangements would produce representatives characterized by a level of civic virtue that would enable them to rise above narrow personal and regional interests to do what the national interest required. Of course, no one today is seriously considering rolling back the franchise or appointing rather than electing representatives. But the Founders' concerns are still relevant, perhaps more so today than they were 220 years ago. In The Federalist No. 10, Madison took comfort in the large size of the republic, where "the influence of factious leaders may kindle a flame within their particular states, but will be unable to spread a general conflagration through the other states."[52] But in our modern age of instantaneous mass communication, the size of the nation is no longer a barrier to the influence of "factious leaders" who rely on slogans, thirty-second television ads, and simplistic solutions rather than on thoughtful deliberation and hard choices. On the contrary, the ability to communicate widely and instantaneously amplifies their influence and their messages and contributes mightily to an environment in which representatives choose to be cautious and safe rather than courageous and sorry.

It is important to note that although Congress' failings as a policymaking body are well known, the institution also succeeds in a number of less visible ways. Representatives work productively in a number of policy areas, and in many instances their work is influenced neither by narrow pressures from their constituents, nor by pressures from interest groups, nor by worries about their next election campaign. Representatives by and large are people who have committed themselves to public service, who care about achieving good public policy, and who aspire to do what is right. At some level, they are good people caught in a bad system. At the beginning of the 110th Congress, *National Journal*, one of the most influential Washington publications, published brief profiles of the representatives who would be people of influence in the new Democratic-controlled House. What is striking about these profiles is how little of what makes these representatives stand out to their colleagues and to journalists has to do with constituency pressures. Representative Donna DeGette of Colorado is mentioned as a person who has worked across party lines to coauthor legislation on stem cell research. Representative Edward Markey of Massachusetts "embraces technology and explores its impact on average people." Representative David Price of North Carolina is cited as an influential force on issues of congressional reform, including tightening ethics rules, and Representative Carolyn McCarthy of New York has been an activist on gun control legislation.[53] Obviously these efforts and positions may be political pluses when these representatives run for reelection, and although representatives do not necessarily pick these areas for the electoral advantage that they may offer, they are unlikely to select an area that will cause them problems in their constituency. If Carolyn McCarthy were the representative from Wyoming, she likely would find an area of policy emphasis other than gun control. The point is that in each of these instances, legislative priorities and concerns are not provoked by constituency or interest group pressures but rather by the interest that these members have in making good public policy, in accomplishing something, and in making his or her mark.

Former Senator Clairborne Pell of Rhode Island never had to worry about reelection, so his work to establish a program of federal grants to low-income students that would help them to attend college had little to do with constituency pressures and a great deal to do with what he thought was good public policy. The Pell grants that have benefited many readers of this book are his legacy. The late Senator William Fulbright of Arkansas had little to gain in his state for fostering better relations among the people of different countries, but he worked to do that by championing legislation that provides funds for foreign students and scholars to study in the United States and for American students and scholars to study abroad. The Fulbright program is his legacy. Keeping these examples in mind is a healthy counterbalance to the simplistic view of the representative who constantly is checking with his constituency—voters, interest groups, and electoral financiers—as he decides how he wishes to allocate his time in Washington. It also helps us to understand that being a good representative carries with it an injunction to work in the public interest broadly conceived.

Appendix

30 Questions for Discussion

1. If democracy means government by the people and representation means government by someone else, is the concept of "representative democracy" a contradiction in terms?
2. Is popular sovereignty, the very core of democratic theory, either possible or desirable? Can average people make good public policy decisions? Is it not better for us to be governed by "the best and the brightest"?
3. What criteria would a representative system have to meet in order for you to feel comfortable classifying it as a reasonable approximation of democracy? There are both practical and philosophical arguments for representative rather than democratic systems. Which, if either, do you find more persuasive?
4. What problems does one encounter in attempting to apply the principal-agent model of constituency control to elected representatives?
5. From a democratic perspective, what are the advantages and the dangers of concentrating political power in the hands of a popularly elected president?
6. What challenges do members of representative institutions face as they seek to control and check who holds power in executive institutions such as the presidency and the bureaucracy?
7. Under what circumstances should representatives be more attuned to minority voices and interests in their constituency rather than to the majority view of their constituents?

8. From the point of view of democracy, should representatives be more concerned with advocating the opinions or the interests of their constituents?

9. Under what conditions might the interests of a representative's constituency conflict with the interests of the nation as a whole? Under those circumstances, which should take precedence for the representative?

10. If the actions of representatives are congruent with the opinions of their constituents, does that mean that the representative is following the instructions of his constituents? What alternative explanations might there be for policy agreement between representatives and their constituents?

11. How effective are elections as mechanisms for holding representatives accountable for their actions? What role should promises made during the course of a campaign play in the decisions of representatives once they are in office?

12. Are demographic groups such as women, African-Americans, and Latinos always better represented by someone who is "like" them? What are the strongest arguments in favor of this point of view? Can a man be just as effective a representative of women? Can a white person provide effective representation for an African-American or Latino constituency?

13. It has been argued that the composition of a legislature should reflect the divisions among the population of the nation. What are the best arguments in support of this position? What are the practical and philosophical objections to this position?

14. Should state legislatures be encouraged to draw district boundaries with an eye toward facilitating the election of African-American or Latino representatives? What is wrong with such measures? What is right with them?

15. Should the United States replace its system of single-member district elections with a proportional representation system? What would be gained by such a change?

16. What are the justifications for maintaining geographically based constituencies? Can one argue that these justifications are outmoded and that geography is no longer an appropriate way to define a constituency?

17. What are the factors that contribute to a high level of trust between representatives and their constituents? Is trust a good thing or a bad thing? For the representative? For the constituent?

18. What are the best arguments to make in support of the practice of representatives earmarking money for specific projects in their constituencies? Does the earmark process have adverse consequences for the

relationship between representatives and their constituents? What are the public policy consequences of this practice?

19. Do you know the names of your representative and your two United States senators? Do you know their positions and their votes on the major issues of the day, or the issues that are important to you? What are the implications of your answers for the ability of constituents to control or influence the behavior of their representatives?

20. If citizens have little information about their representatives and their activities and one assumes that representatives are aware of that, what accounts for the concern that members have about the views of their constituents?

21. What factors explain the generally weak connection that researchers have found between constituency opinion and the voting behavior of representatives in the legislature? Does the absence of such a connection mean that representatives are not responsive to their constituents? Are there other ways to be responsive aside from conforming to constituents' opinions when they vote on policy proposals?

22. What influence does the political party have on the behavior of representatives? Is this influence greater or lesser than the influence of constituents? How does the answer to that question vary from nation to nation?

23. Large numbers of American citizens believe that their representatives are overly influenced by so-called special interests. To what extent is this perception accurate? From the point of view of representation, is the influence of interest groups good or bad?

24. What difficulties does one encounter in trying to demonstrate that well-funded interest groups purchase the support of representatives through campaign contributions?

25. Do interest groups have more influence on the behavior of representatives in the United States than they do in other representative democracies? If so, what factors explain the difference?

26. To what extent can legislatures be viewed as "conservative" bodies? Is this a strength or a weakness of representative institutions?

27. What are the arguments for characterizing representative systems as a "soft" form of democracy that marginalizes the influence of citizens over political decision-making? What are the problems with the major proposals that aim to strengthen the involvement of citizens in their political system?

28. What are the arguments for and against limiting the number of terms a representative can serve in office? Would doing so make representative systems more or less democratic?

29. To what extent can it be said that the low level of popular support for the legislature as an institution is directly connected with the roles that

its members play as representatives of the people and to the attitudes and expectations that citizens hold concerning their representatives?

30. Would those who wrote the United States Constitution be pleased or displeased with the current state of representative government in America? Why?

Notes

NOTES TO CHAPTER 1

1. See Nadia Urbanati, *Representative Democracy: Principles and Genealogy* (Chicago: University of Chicago Press, 2006), 60.

2. Benjamin R. Barber, *Strong Democracy: Participatory Politics for a New Age* (Berkeley: University of California Press, 1984), 145.

3. Bernard Manin, *The Principles of Representative Government* (Cambridge: Cambridge University Press, 1997), 236.

4. Ibid., 13–16.

5. See Andrew Rehfield, "Toward A General Theory of Political Representation," *Journal of Politics* 68, no. 1 (February 2006): 1–21.

6. John Stuart Mill, *Considerations on Representative Government* (New York: The Liberal Arts Press, 1958), 55.

7. See Urbanati, *Representative Democracy*, 62.

8. See Manin, *Principles of Representative Government*, 3. For a fuller treatment of Sieyes, see Urbanati, *Representative Democracy*, chap. 4.

9. Joseph Schumpeter, *Capitalism, Socialism, and Democracy* (New York: Harper, 1947).

10. Clinton Rossiter, ed. *The Federalist Papers*, (New York: New American Library, 1961), No. 1, 35.

11. Rossiter, *The Federalist Papers*, No. 10, 82.

12. See Charles A. Beard, *An Economic Interpretation of the Constitution of the United States* (New York: The Macmillan Company, 1913); and Richard Hofstadter, *The American Political Tradition* (New York: Vintage Books, 1948), chap. 1. For a rebuttal of the Beard and Hofstadter viewpoint, see John P. Roche, "The Founding Fathers: A Reform Caucus in Action," *American Political Science Review* 55, no. 4 (December 1961): 799–816.

13. Max Farrand, ed., *The Records of the Federal Convention of 1787* (New Haven: Yale University Press, 1966), 1:48.

14. Rossiter, *The Federalist Papers*, No. 10, 81.

15. According to Yates' notes on Hamilton's June 18, 1787 speech at the Constitutional Convention. See Thomas P. Govan, "Notes and Documents: The Rich, the

Well-Born, and Alexander Hamilton." *The Mississippi Valley History Review* 36:4 (March 1950), 675.

16. Farrand, *Records of the Federal Convention of 1787*, 1:48.

17. Quoted in Hofstadter, *American Political Tradition*, 4.

18. Rossiter, *The Federalist Papers*, No. 10, 82.

19. See Michael L. Mezey, *Congress, the President, and Public Policy* (Boulder, CO: Westview Press, 1989), 39–40; Daniel Wirls and Stephen Wirls, *The Invention of the United States Senate* (Baltimore: The Johns Hopkins University Press, 2004).

20. For a brief but good summary of the history, see Michael Rush, *Parliament Today* (Manchester: Manchester University Press, 2005), chap. 2.

21. John Locke, *Of Civil Government, Second Treatise*, Gateway Edition (Chicago: Henry Regnery and Company, 1955), 125.

22. Mill, *Considerations*, chap. 3.

23. Quoted in Charles C. Thach, Jr., *The Creation of the Presidency, 1775–1789* (Baltimore: The Johns Hopkins University Press, 1923), 27.

24. J. R. Pole, *Political Representation in England and the Origins of the American Republic* (Berkeley: University of California Press, 1971), 70, 74.

25. Rossiter, *The Federalist Papers*, No. 51, 322.

26. James Madison, *Letters of Helvidius*, (1793), http://press-pubs.uchicago.edu/founders/documents/a2_2_2-3s15.html (accessed July 14, 2008).

27. J. Capo-Giol, R. Cotarelo, D. Lopez-Garrido, and J. Subirats, "By Consociationalism to a Majoritarian Parliamentary System: The Rise and Decline of the Spanish Cortes," in *Parliament and Democratic Consolidation in Southern Europe*, ed. Ulurike Liebert and Maurizio Cotta (London: Pinter Publishers, 1990), 96–98.

28. Attila Agh, "Bumpy Road to Europeanization: Policy Effectiveness and Agenda Concentration in the Hungarian Legislation (1990–93)," in Attila Agh, ed., *The Emergence of East Central European Parliaments: The First Steps* (Budapest: Hungarian Center of Democracy Studies Foundation, 1994), 72.

29. James Sundquist, *The Decline and Resurgence of Congress* (Washington, DC: The Brookings Institution, 1981); Andrew Rudalevige, *The New Imperial Presidency: Renewing Presidential Power After Watergate* (Ann Arbor: University of Michigan Press, 2005).

30. Farrand, *Records of the Federal Convention of 1787*, 2:31.

31. See Melissa Williams, *Voice, Trust, and Memory: Marginalized Groups and the Failings of Liberal Representation* (Princeton: Princeton University Press, 1998), 33–38, for a discussion of Burke.

32. In Farrand, *Records of the Federal Convention of 1787*, 1:51.

33. Arthur M. Schlesinger, Jr., *The Imperial Presidency* (Boston: Houghton Mifflin, 1973).

34. Urbanati, *Representative Democracy*, 5. See also Geoffrey Brennan and Alan Hamlin, "On Political Representation," *British Journal of Political Science* 29 (1999): 109–27.

NOTES TO CHAPTER 2

1. The seminal work on the topic is Hanna Fenichel Pitkin, *The Concept of Representation* (Berkeley: University of California Press, 1967). See also Andrew Rehfield,

The Concept of Constituency: Political Representation, Democratic Legitimacy, and Institutional Design (New York: Cambridge University Press, 2005); Nadia Urbanati, *Representative Democracy: Principles and Genealogy* (Chicago: University of Chicago Press, 2006); Bernard Manin, *The Principles of Representative Government* (Cambridge: Cambridge University Press, 1997); and Jane Mansbridge, "Rethinking Representation," *American Political Science Review* 97, no. 4 (November, 2003): 515–28.

2. Mansbridge uses the term "promissory representation." See her "Rethinking Representation," 516. For a discussion of "principal-agent" theory, see Robert Barro, "The Control of Politicians: An Economic Model," *Public Choice* 14 (1973): 19–42; and Barry Weingast, "The Congressional-Bureaucratic System: A Principal-Agent Perspective," *Public Choice* 44 (1984): 147–92.

3. Of course, the typical sports agent also has multiple clients, but she works for each of them separately; she does not negotiate one contract for all of her clients. The political representative, in contrast, has one vote to cast on behalf of all of his clients.

4. Richard F. Fenno, Jr., *Home Style: House Members in Their Districts* (Boston: Little Brown, 1976), chap. 1.

5. Fenno does not include the attentive public as a separate circle. He moves from the reelection constituency to a "primary" constituency (a representative's strongest supporters) and then to a "personal" constituency composed of his intimates.

6. For a brief discussion of the differences between single-member district and proportional representation systems, see Arend Lijphart, *Patterns of Democracy* (New Haven: Yale University Press, 1999), chap. 8.

7. See Scott Morgenstern, *Patterns of Legislative Politics: Roll-Call Voting in Latin America and the United States* (Cambridge: Cambridge University Press, 2004), chap. 2.

8. Andrew Rehfield makes the point that an actor can claim to represent even in the absence of authorization, as when a delegate to the United Nations claims to represent the people of his nation. See Andrew Rehfield, "Toward A General Theory of Political Representation," *Journal of Politics* 68, no. 1 (February 2006): 1–21.

9. William T. Bianco, *Trust: Representatives and Constituents* (Ann Arbor: University of Michigan Press, 1994), 18.

10. See the Introduction to Adam Przeworski, Susan Stokes, and Bernard Manin, eds., *Democracy, Accountability and Representation* (Cambridge: Cambridge University Press, 1999), 7.

11. Michael X. Delli Carpini and Scott Keeter, *What Americans Know about Politics and Why It Matters* (New Haven: Yale University Press, 1996), 269.

12. See Bernard Manin, Adam Prezeworski, and Susan Stokes, "Elections and Representation," in *Democracy, Accountability, and Representation*, ed. Przeworski, Stokes, and Manin, 30–40.

13. Susan Stokes, "What Do Policy Switches Tell Us About Democracy?" in *Democracy, Accountability, and Representation*, ed. Przeworski, Stokes, and Manin, chap. 3.

14. See Pitkin, *Concept of Representation*, chap. 7; John Wahlke, Heinz Eulau, William Buchanan, LeRoy Ferguson, *The Legislative System: Explorations in Legislative*

Behavior (New York: John Wiley and Sons, 1962); and Warren Miller and Donald Stokes, "Constituency Influence in Congress," *American Political Science Review* 57 (March 1963): 45–57.

15. Clinton Rossiter, ed., *The Federalist Papers* (New York: New American Library, 1961), No. 57, 350.

16. *The Federalist Papers*, No. 10, 82.

17. See http://press-pubs.uchicago.edu/founders/documents/v1ch13s7.html for the text of Burke's speech to the electors of Bristol.

18. See Mansbridge, "Rethinking Representation," 520. These previous two paragraphs draw on the insights of Andrew Rehfield, "Trustees, Delegates, and Gyroscopes: Democratic Justice and the Ethics of Political Representation," paper prepared for the annual meeting of the American Political Science Association, Philadelphia, August 30–September 3, 2006.

19. Jose Maria Maravall, "Accountability and Manipulation," in Przeworski, Stokes, and Manin, eds., *Democracy, Accountability, and Representation*, 159.

20. Robert A. Bernstein, *Elections, Representation, and Congressional Voting Behavior: The Myth of Constituency Control* (Englewood Cliffs, N.J.: Prentice-Hall, 1989), 18.

21. Pitkin, *Concept of Representation*, 209–10.

22. Douglas Arnold, *The Logic of Congressional Action* (New Haven: Yale University Press, 1990).

23. Richard Hall, *Participation in Congress* (New Haven: Yale University Press, 1997).

24. See Heinz Eulau and Paul Karps, "The Puzzle of Representation: Specifying Components of Responsiveness," *Legislative Studies Quarterly* 2 (1977): 233–54, for a discussion of the service and allocational dimensions of representation.

25. See David Mayhew, *Congress: The Electoral Connection*, 2nd ed. (New Haven: Yale University Press, 2004); and Morris Fiorina, *Congress: Keystone of the Washington Establishment*, 2nd ed. (New Haven: Yale University Press, 1989).

26. Fenno, *Home Style*, chap. 5.

27. See Mansbridge, "Rethinking Representation," for a discussion of anticipatory representation.

28. Lawrence R. Jacobs and Robert Y. Shapiro, *Politicians Don't Pander: Political Manipulation and the Loss of Democratic Responsiveness* (Chicago: University of Chicago Press, 2000), xiii.

29. Arnold, *Logic of Congressional Action*, 10–11.

30. Geoffrey Brennan and Alan Hamlin, "On Political Representation," *British Journal of Political Science* 29 (1999): 109–27.

31. William T. Bianco, *Trust: Representatives and Constituents* (Ann Arbor: University of Michigan Press, 1994), 23.

32. See Mansbridge, "Rethinking Representation," 520–22.

33. Melissa S. Williams, *Voice, Trust, and Memory: Marginalized Groups and the Failings of Liberal Representation* (Princeton: Princeton University Press, 1998), 14.

34. Jane Mansbridge, "Should Blacks Represent Blacks and Women Represent Women? A Contingent 'Yes,'" *Journal of Politics* 61, no. 3 (August 1999): 643–48.

35. Williams, *Voice, Trust, and Memory*, 13.

36. Richard Fenno, *Going Home: Black Representatives and Their Constituents* (Chicago: University of Chicago Press, 2003), 260.

37. Anne Phillips, *The Politics of Presence* (Oxford: Clarendon Press, 1995), cited in Williams, *Voice, Trust, and Memory*, 229.

38. Mansbridge, "Should Blacks Represent Blacks," 636.

39. See Will Kymlicka, *Multicultural Citizenship: A Liberal Theory of Minority Rights* (Oxford: Oxford University Press, 1995).

40. Mansbridge, "Rethinking Representation."

41. In Pitkin, *Concept of Representation,* 173.

42. See Mansbridge, "Rethinking Representation," 518; and Brennan and Hamlin, "On Political Representation," 115.

43. John Stuart Mill, *Considerations on Representative Government* (New York: The Liberal Arts Press, 1958), 82.

44. Robert Weissberg, "Collective vs. Dyadic Representation in Congress," *American Political Science Review* 72, no. 2 (June 1978): 535–47.

45. See Lijphart, *Patterns of Democracy,* 147–50.

46. See G. Bingham Powell, "Political Representation in Comparative Politics," *Annual Review of Political Science* 7 (2004): 273–96.

47. Brian Crisp and Scott Desposato, "Constituency Building in Multimember Districts: Collusion or Conflict," *Journal of Politics* 66, no. 1 (2004): 136–56.

NOTES TO CHAPTER 3

1. Andrew Rehfeld, *The Concept of Constituency: Political Representation, Democratic Legitimacy, and Institutional Design* (New York: Cambridge University Press, 2005), 75.

2. Jack P. Greene, "Legislative Turnover in British America, 1696–1776," *The William and Mary Quarterly* 38, no. 3 (1981): 461.

3. Stanley B. Parsons, William W. Beach, and Dan Hermann, *United States Congressional Districts, 1788–1841* (Westport, CT: Greenwood Press, 1978).

4. Ibid., 73.

5. Alan Rosenthal, Burdett A. Loomis, John R. Hibbing, and Karl T. Kurtz, *Republic on Trial: The Case for Representative Democracy* (Washington, DC: Congressional Quarterly Press, 2003): 98–99.

6. www.britannica.com/eb/article-9064202/rotten-borough (accessed July 14, 2008).

7. Michael Rush, *Parliament Today* (Manchester: Manchester University Press, 2005), chap. 2.

8. *Colegrove v. Green,* 328 U.S. 549 (1946).

9. *Baker v. Carr,* 369 U.S. 186 (1962).

10. *Wesberry v. Sanders,* 376 U.S. 1 (1964).

11. *Reynolds v. Sims,* 377 U.S. 533 (1964).

12. John C. Courtney, *Commissioned Ridings: Designing Canada's Electoral Districts* (Montreal: McGill-Queen's University Press, 2001), 165–71, and chap. 9.

13. R. J. Johnston, "Constituency Redistribution in Britain: Recent Issues," in

Electoral Laws and Their Political Consequences, ed. Bernard Grofman and Arend Lijphart, (New York: Agathon Press, 1986).

14. www.official-documents.gov.uk/document/cm70/7032/7032.pdf (accessed July 14, 2008).

15. Richard Snyder and David Samuels, "Devaluing the Vote in Latin America," *Journal of Democracy* 12, no. 1 (January 2001): 150–51.

16. www.delimitation-india.com/index.asp (accessed July 14, 2008).

17. David Samuels and Richard Snyder, "The Value of a Vote: Malapportionment in Comparative Perspective," *British Journal of Political Science* 31 (2001): 651–71.

18. These figures are calculated from U.S. Census Data reported at www.demo graphia.com/db-2000stater.htm (accessed July 14, 2008). Also see Frances E. Lee and Bruce I. Oppenheimer, *Sizing Up the Senate: The Unequal Consequences of Equal Representation* (Chicago: University of Chicago Press, 1999).

19. Gerhard Loewenberg and Chong Lim Kim, "Comparing the Representativeness of Parliament," *Legislative Studies Quarterly* 3 (February 1978): 38.

20. See Peter Esaiasson, "How MPs Define Their Task," in *Beyond Westminster and Congress: The Nordic Experience,* Peter Esaiasson and Knut Heidar, ed. (Columbus: The Ohio State University Press, 2000), 53.

21. J. Djordjevic, "Interest Groups and the Political System of Yugoslavia," in *Interest Groups on Four Continents,* ed. H. W. Ehrmann (Pittsburgh: University of Pittsburgh Press, 1960), 214.

22. Arend Lijphart, "Proportionality by non-PR Methods: Ethnic Representation in Belgium, Cyprus, New Zealand, West Germany, and Lebanon," *Electoral Laws and Their Political Consequences,* Grofman and Lijphart, ed.

23. www.ipu.org/wmn-e/world.htm (accessed July 14, 2008).

24. See www.state.gov/r/pa/ei/bgn/2874.htm (accessed July 14, 2008).

25. *Shaw v. Reno,* 509 U.S. 630 (1993); the quotation from *Shaw* is found in David T. Canon, *Race, Redistricting and Representation: The Unintended Consequences of Black Majority Districts* (Chicago: University of Chicago Press, 1999), 77.

26. *Davis v. Bandemer,* 478 U.S. 109 (1986).

27. See Canon, *Race, Redistricting, and Representation;* David Lublin, *The Paradox of Representation: Racial Gerrymandering and Minority Interests in Congress* (Princeton: Princeton University Press, 1997); and Charles Cameron, David Epstein, and Sharyn O'Halloran, "Do Majority-Minority Districts Maximize Substantive Black Representation in Congress?" *American Political Science Review* 90, no. 4 (1996): 794–812.

28. *Easley v. Cromartie,* 532 US 234 (2001). Also see Roger Davidson, Walter Oleszek, and Frances Lee, *Congress and Its Members,* 11th ed. (Washington, DC: Congressional Quarterly Press, 2008), 55–58.

29. Courtney, *Commissioned Ridings,* 223–32.

30. John Stuart Mill, *Considerations on Representative Government* (New York: The Liberal Arts Press, 1958), p. 111.

31. See Pippa Norris, "Women's Legislative Participation in Western Europe," *Western European Politics* 8 (1985): 90–101; Wilma Rule, "Parliaments Of, By, and For the People: Except for Women?" in *Electoral Systems in Comparative Perspective: Their Impact on Women and Minorities,* Wilma Rule and Joseph Zimmerman, ed. (Westport, CT: Greenwood Press, 1994); and Richard Matland, "Women's Repre-

sentation in National Legislatures: Developed and Developing Countries," *Legislative Studies Quarterly* 23, no. 1 (1998): 109–25.

32. Melissa S. Williams, 217.

33. Mi Yung Yoon, "Explaining Women's Legislative Representation in Sub-Saharan Africa," *Legislative Studies Quarterly* 29:3 (August 2004), 447–468.

34. Melissa S. Williams, 210. Also see Lisa Baldez, "Elected Bodies: The Gender Quota Law for Legislative Candidates in Mexico," *Legislative Studies Quarterly* 29, no. 2 (May 2004): 231–258.

35. Lani Guinier, *The Tyranny of the Majority: Fundamental Fairness in Representative Democracy* (New York: The Free Press, 1994).

36. David Brockington, Todd Donovan, Shaun Bowler, and Robert Brischetto, "Minority Representation under Cumulative and Limited Voting," *Journal of Politics* 60, no. 4 (1998): 1108–25.

37. Jane Mansbridge, "Should Blacks Represent Blacks and Women Represent Women? A Contingent 'Yes,'" *Journal of Politics* 61, no. 3 (August 1999): 653.

38. Carol Swain, *Black Faces, Black Interests: The Representation of African-Americans in Congress* (Cambridge, MA: Harvard University Press, 1993).

39. Canon, *Race, Redistricting and Representation*, 200.

40. Bernard Grofman, Lisa Handley, and Richard Niemi, *Minority Representation and the Quest for Voting Equality* (New York: Cambridge University Press, 1992).

41. Katherine Tate, "The Political Representation of Blacks in Congress: Does Race Matter?" *Legislative Studies Quarterly* 26, no. 4 (November 2001), 623–38.

42. Richard Fenno, *Going Home: Black Representatives and Their Constituents* (Chicago: University of Chicago Press, 2003), 259.

43. Claudine Gay, "The Effect of Black Congressional Representation on Political Participation," *American Political Science Review* 95, no. 3 (2001): 589–602; and "Spirals of Trust? The Effect of Descriptive Representation on the Relationship Between Citizens and Their Government," *American Journal of Political Science* 46, no. 4 (2002): 717–33.

44. Susan A. Banducci, Todd Donovan, and Jeffrey Karp, "Minority Representation, Empowerment, and Participation," *Journal of Politics* 66, no. 2 (2004): 534–56.

45. Gay, "Effect of Black Congressional Representation"; and "Spirals of Trust."

46. See Lublin, *Paradox of Representation*.

47. Michele Swers, "Are Women More Likely to Vote for Women's Issue Bills Than Their Male Colleagues?" *Legislative Studies Quarterly* 23, no. 3 (August 1998): 435–48.

48. John D. Griffin, Brian Newman, and Christina Wolbrecht, "Sex, Party, and the Representation of Women," paper delivered at the annual meeting of the American Political Science Association, Philadelphia, August 30–September 3, 2006.

49. Karen Beckwith and Kimberly Cowell-Meyers, "Sheer Numbers: Critical Representation Thresholds and Women's Political Representation," *Perspectives on Politics* 5, no. 3 (September 2007): 553–66.

50. Karen Ross, "Women's Place in 'Male' Space: Gender and Effect in Parliamentary Contexts," *Parliamentary Affairs* 55, no. 1 (2002): 189–99.

51. Sue Thomas, *How Women Legislate* (New York: Oxford University Press, 1994); Susan Gluck Mezey, "Increasing the Number of Women in Office: Does It

Matter?" in *The Year of the Woman: Myths and Realities,* ed. Elizabeth Adell Cook, Sue Thomas, and Clyde Wilcox (Boulder, CO: Westview Press, 1994).

52. Manon Tremblay, "Do Females MPs Substantively Represent Women? A Study of Legislative Behavior in Canada's 35th Parliament," *Canadian Journal of Political Science* 31, no. 3 (1998): 435–65.

53. Kathleen Bratton and Leonard Ray, "Descriptive Representation, Policy Outcomes, and Municipal Daycare Coverage in Norway," *American Journal of Political Science* 46, no. 2 (2002): 428–37.

54. Sarah Childs, "Hitting the Target: Are Labour MPs 'Acting For' Women?" *Parliamentary Affairs* 55, no. 1 (2002): 143–53.

55. Jennifer Lawless, "Politics of Presence? Congresswomen and Symbolic Representation," *Political Research Quarterly* 57, no. 1 (2004): 81–99.

56. Narud and Valen, p. 102.

57. Arend Lijphart, *Electoral Systems and Party Systems* (New York: Oxford University Press, 1994).

58. See Michael L. Mezey, *Comparative Legislatures* (Durham: Duke University Press, 1979), 240–41.

59. Michael Rush, *The Role of the Member of Parliament Since 1868: From Gentlemen to Players* (Oxford: Oxford University Press, 2001), 98ff.

60. Iris Marion Young, *Justice and Politics of Difference* (Princeton: Princeton University Press, 1990), 185. Also see Young, *Inclusion and Democracy,* 141–48.

NOTES TO CHAPTER 4

1. See Michael L. Mezey, *Comparative Legislatures* (Durham: Duke University Press, 1979), chap. 9.

2. John Frears, "The French Parliament: Loyal Workhorse, Poor Watchdog," in *Parliaments in Western Europe,* Philip Norton, ed. (London: Frank Cass, 1990), 46.

3. Mezey, *Comparative Legislatures,* 168.

4. S. R. Maheshewari, "Constituency Linkages of National Legislators in India," *Legislative Studies Quarterly* 1 (August 1976): 338.

5. C. L. Baker, "Costa Rican Legislative Behavior in Perspective," PhD diss., University of Florida, Gainesville, 1973, 235–36.

6. Maheshewari, "Constituency Linkages," 338; Michael L. Mezey, "The Functions of a Minimal Legislature: Role Perceptions of Thai Legislators," *Western Political Quarterly* 25 (December 1972): 697.

7. R. D. Morey, "Representational Role Perceptions in the Japanese Diet: The Wahlke-Eulau Framework Reexamined," paper delivered at the annual meeting of the American Political Science Association, Chicago, September 1971.

8. Frears, "French Parliament," 47.

9. S. E. Franzich, "A Comparative Study of Legislative Roles and Behavior," PhD diss., University of Minnesota, Minneapolis, 1971, 153, 155.

10. Frances Lee, "Interests, Constituencies, and Policy Making," in *The Legislative Branch,* ed. Paul J. Quirk and Sarah H. Binder (New York: Oxford University Press, 2005), 284.

11. Peter Esaiasson, "How MPs Define Their Task," in *Beyond Westminster and*

Congress: The Nordic Experience, ed. Peter Esaiasson and Knut Heidar (Columbus: The Ohio State University Press, 2000), 60.

12. Ilter Turan, "The Turkish Legislature: From Symbolic to Substantive Representation," in *Parliaments in the Modern World: Changing Institutions,* ed. Gary Copeland and Samuel Patterson (Ann Arbor: University of Michigan Press, 1994), 124.

13. See R. J. Cayrol, J. L. Parodi, and C. Ysmal, "French Deputies and the Political System," *Legislative Studies Quarterly* 1 (February 1976): 74–76; and Frears, "French Parliament," 47.

14. Roger Davidson, Walter Oleszek, and Frances Lee, *Congress and Its Members,* 11th ed. (Washington, DC: Congressional Quarterly Press, 2008), 127–35.

15. Chong Lim Kim, Joel D. Barkan, Ilter Turan, and Malcolm Jewell, *The Legislative Connection: The Representative and the Represented in Kenya, Korea, and Turkey* (Durham: Duke University Press, 1983), chaps. 5 and 6.

16. R. O. De La Garza, "The Mexican Chamber of Deputies and the Mexican Political System," PhD diss., University of Arizona, Tucson, 1972, 89.

17. Morris Fiorina, *Congress: Keystone of the Washington Establishment,* 2nd ed. (New Haven: Yale University Press, 1989).

18. Alan Rosenthal, Burdett A. Loomis, John R. Hibbing, and Karl T. Kurtz, *Republic on Trial: The Case for Representative Democracy* (Washington, DC: Congressional Quarterly Press, 2003), 100.

19. Bruce Cain, John Ferejohn, and Morris Fiorina, *The Personal Vote: Constituency Service and Electoral Independence* (Cambridge, MA: Harvard University Press, 1987), 54–55.

20. Malcolm Jewell and Chong Lim Kim, "Sources of Support for Legislative Institutions: Kenya, Korea, and Turkey," paper delivered at the annual meeting of the Southern Political Science Association, Atlanta, Georgia, November 1976. Data reported in Mezey, *Comparative Legislatures,* 165.

21. See David Mayhew, *Congress: The Electoral Connection,* 2nd ed. (New Haven: Yale University Press, 2004); and Glenn Parker and Roger Davidson, "Why Do Americans Love Their Congressman So Much More Than Their Congress?" *Legislative Studies Quarterly* 4 (1979): 53–61.

22. Cited in Rosenthal et al., *Republic on Trial,* 96.

23. Bruce Oppenheimer, "The Representational Experience: The Effect of State Population on Senator-Constituency Linkages," *American Journal of Political Science* 40, no. 4 (1996): 1280–99.

24. Frances E. Lee and Bruce I. Oppenheimer, *Sizing Up the Senate: The Unequal Consequences of Equal Representation* (Chicago: University of Chicago Press, 1999), 190–92.

25. Jeff Stein, Jeremy Toobin, David Clarke, Chris Logan, and Jim McGee, "Is Homeland Security Keeping America Safe?" *Congressional Quarterly Weekly Report,* June 14, 2003.

26. Tim Starks, "House Votes to Change Formulas for First-Responder," *Congressional Quarterly Weekly Report,* May 16, 2005.

27. Diana B. Henriques and Andrew W. Lehren, "Religious Groups Reaping Share Of Federal Aid for Pet Projects," *New York Times,* May 13, 2007.

28. Brian Friel, "A Sink or Swim Issue," *National Journal,* September 9, 2006, 71–72.

29. Ron Nixon, "Pork Barrel Remains Hidden in U.S. Budget," *New York Times,* April 7, 2008.

30. John Solomon and Jeffrey H. Birnbaum, "Pet Projects' Veil Is Only Partly Lifted: Lawmakers Find Other Paths To Special-Interest Funding," *Washington Post,* September 9, 2007.

31. David Baumann, "Attention, Earmark Shoppers," *National Journal,* March 3, 2007.

32. Alex Wayne, "Bill Benefits Hospitals in Democrats' Districts," CQ.com, August 1, 2007.

33. Robert Pear, "Selected Hospitals Reap a Windfall Under Child Bill," *New York Times,* August 12, 2007.

34. Frances Lee, "Geographic Politics in the U.S. House of Representatives: Coalition Building and Distribution of Benefits," *American Journal of Political Science* 47, no. 4 (2003): 714–28; Frances Lee, "Bicameralism and Geographic Politics: Allocating Funds in the House and Senate," *Legislative Studies Quarterly* 29, no. 2 (May 2004): 185–213.

35. See Mayhew, *Congress: The Electoral Connection,* 52–61.

36. John Solomon, Alec MacGillis, and Sarah Cohen, "How Rove Directed Federal Assets for GOP Gains," *Washington Post,* August 19, 2007.

37. Lee and Oppenheimer, *Sizing Up the Senate,* 193.

38. All of Representative Boyda's requests can be found at http://boyda.house .gov/?sectionid = 21&sectiontree = 3,21&itemid = 112 (accessed July 14, 2008).

39. http://boyda.house.gov/?sectionid = 21&sectiontree = 3,21&itemid = 112 (accessed July 14, 2008).

40. The complete list is at http://boyda.house.gov/?sectionid = 21&section tree = 3,21&itemid = 166 (accessed July 14, 2008).

41. Edmund L. Andrews and Robert Pear, "With New Rules, Congress Boasts of Pet Projects," *New York Times,* August 5, 2007.

42. Rahm Emanuel, "Don't Get Rid of Earmarks," *New York Times,* August 24, 2007.

43. Scott Lilly, "Despite Earmarks, Many Districts Are Worse Off," *Roll Call,* October 6, 2005.

44. Thomas Mann and Norman Ornstein, *The Broken Branch: How Congress Is Failing America and How to Get It Back on Track* (New York: Oxford University Press, 2006), 176–78; Norman Ornstein, "Don't Take Civility Out of the House," *Roll Call* November 5, 2003.

45. Jonathan Allen, "The Earmark Game: Manifest Disparity," *Congressional Quarterly Weekly Report,* October 1, 2007, 2843.

46. Bart Jansen and Jonathan Allen, "Critics See Ruse in Senate Earmark Rules," CQ.com, September 25, 2007.

47. Despite this, Representative Walsh decided not to seek reelection in 2008.

48. Jonathan Allen, "Earmark Dollars Follow Politics, Power," CQ.com, July 27, 2007.

49. Jonathan Allen, "Earmark Game," 2836.

50. Paul Martin, "Voting's Rewards: Voter Turnout, Attentive Publics, and Congressional Allocation of Federal Money," *American Journal of Political Science* 47, no. 1 (2003): 110–27.

51. R. Michael Alvarez and Jason L. Saving, "Deficits, Democrats, and Distributive Benefits: Congressional Elections and the Pork Barrel in the 1980s," *Political Research Quarterly* 50, no. 4 (1997): 809–31.

52. Patrick J. Sellers, "Fiscal Consistency and Federal District Spending in Congressional Elections," *American Journal of Political Science* 41, no. 3 (1997): 1024–41.

53. Jonathan Allen, "Earmark Game," 2843.

54. See Robert M. Stein and Kenneth N. Bickers, "Congressional Elections and the Pork Barrel," *Journal of Politics* 56, no. 2 (May 1994): 377–99.

55. Ibid.; Lee, "Geographic Politics."

56. Avery Palmer, "House Passes Connecticut River Conservation Bill," *Congressional Quarterly Weekly Report*, August 6, 2007, 2385.

57. John Johannes and John McAdams, "The Congressional Incumbency Effect: Is it Casework, Policy Compatibility, or Something Else? An Examination of the 1978 Election," *American Journal of Political Science* 25, no. 3 (1981): 512–42.

58. Bruce Oppenheimer, "Deep Red and Blue Congressional Districts: The Causes and Consequences of Declining Party Competition," in *Congress Reconsidered*, ed. Lawrence C. Dodd and Bruce I. Oppenheimer, 8th ed. (Washington: Congressional Quarterly Press, 2005).

59. Cain, Ferejohn, and Fiorina, *Personal Vote*, 154–62.

60. Diane Yiannakis, "The Grateful Electorate: Casework and Congressional Elections," *American Journal of Political Science* 25 (1981): 568–80; Stein and Bickers, "Congressional Elections and the Pork Barrel."

61. Jonathan Rauch, "The Democrats' Best Shot at Reform," *National Journal*, January 6, 2007, 12–13.

62. David M. Herszenhorn, "Farm Subsidies Seem Immune to an Overhaul," *New York Times*, July 26, 2007.

63. David M. Herszenhorn, "A Bid to Overhaul a Farm Bill Yields Subtle Changes," *New York Times*, October 24, 2007.

64. Mann and Ornstein, *Broken Branch*, 178.

65. Calculations of the number and value of earmarks in the FY 2008 appropriations vary depending on who is doing the counting and what is being counted. The figure of 11,043 earmarks worth $14.1 billion comes from a December 18, 2007, press release from the watchdog group Citizens Against Government Waste and is available on their web site at www.cagw.org/site/News2?page = NewsArticle&id = 11166 (accessed July 14, 2008).

66. Jonathan Cohn, "Roll Out the Barrel: The Case Against the Case Against Pork," in *Fault Lines: Debating The Issues in American Politics*, ed. David T. Canon, John J. Coleman, and Kenneth R. Mayer, 2nd ed. (New York: W.W. Norton, 2007), 219. Also see Diana Evans, *Greasing the Wheels: Using Pork Barrel Projects to Build Majority Coalitions in Congress* (Cambridge: Cambridge University Press, 2004).

67. Elizabeth Williamson, "Spending Bills Still Stuffed With Earmarks," *Washington Post*, December, 21, 2007.

68. Jeff Flake, "Transportation Earmarks Tying Hands of States," *Arizona Republic*, August 28, 2007.

69. John Chase and Mickey Ciokajlo, "Pork Helps Sweeten the Deal," *Chicago Tribune*, August 12, 2007.

70. Robert O'Harrow, Jr., "A Contractor, Charity and Magnet for Federal Earmarks," *Washington Post*, November 2, 2007; and "Millions in Earmarks Produce Little of Use," *Washington Post*, December 29, 2007.

71. Marilyn Thompson and Ron Nixon, "Even Cut 50 Percent, Earmarks Clog Military Bill," *New York Times*, November 4, 2007. According to Citizens Against Government Waste, the final number of earmarks in the Defense Appropriations Bill was 2,076 at a cost of $6.6 billion, or just over 1 percent of the total Defense Appropriations Bill. See www.cagw.org/site/News2?page = NewsArticle&id = 11166 (accessed July 14, 2008).

72. William Yardley, "Stevens and Alaska: A Longtime Partnership," *New York Times*, August 18, 2007.

73. Karl Vick, "'I'll Sell My Soul to the Devil': Corruption Scandals Involve Alaska's Biggest Political Names," *Washington Post*, November 12, 2007.

74. Kathryn Wolfe, "Stevens' Earmark Funds Airport Project That Benefits One Company," CQ.com, August 1, 2007.

75. David Kirkpatrick, "A Congressman's $10 Million Gift for Road Is Rebuffed," *New York Times*, August 18, 2007.

76. Sarah Binder, Thomas Mann, and Molly Reynolds, "One Year Later: Is Congress Still the Broken Branch? A Report on the 110th Congress," in *Mending the Broken Branch*, vol. 2, January 2008, The Brookings Institution, Washington, DC. www.brookings.edu/papers/2008/01_uscongress_mann.aspx (accessed July 14, 2008).

77. Edmund Andrews and Robert Pear, "Pet Projects are Flourishing," *New York Times*, August 5, 2007; David Clarke and Liriel Higa, "House Takes Sharper Knife to Earmarks than Senate," CQ.com, July 17, 2007; Jonathan Allen, "Earmark Game."

78. Andrews and Pear, "Pet Projects are Flourishing."

79. Elizabeth Williamson, "Spending Bills Still Stuffed With Earmarks."

80. Andrews and Pear, "Pet Projects are Flourishing." As the 2008 election season moved into high gear, the rhetoric on earmarks became more strident. President Bush attacked earmarks in his State of the Union address; many Republicans in the Congress demanded a one-year moratorium on earmarks, a demand that was endorsed by the two leading Democratic candidates for the presidency, Senators Obama and Clinton, as well as the Republican nominee, Senator McCain.

81. Mark P. Jones, "Evaluating Argentina's Presidential Democracy: 1983–1995," in *Presidentialism and Democracy in Latin America*, ed. Scott Mainwaring and Matthew Soberg Shugart (Cambridge: Cambridge University Press, 1997), 277–78.

82. Michael Rush, *The Role of the Member of Parliament Since 1868: From Gentlemen to Players* (Oxford: Oxford University Press, 2001), 207–11.

83. Cain, Ferejohn, and Fiorina, *Personal Vote*, 66–67.

84. Frears, "French Parliament," 46–47.

85. See Mezey, *Comparative Legislatures*, 168.

86. David Denemark, "Partisan Pork Barrel in Parliamentary Systems: Australian Constituency-Level Grants," *Journal of Politics*, 62, no. 3 (August 2000): 909.

87. See Rush, *Role of the Member of Parliament Since 1868*, 206; Philip Norton and David Wood, *Back from Westminster: British Members of Parliament and Their Constituencies* (Lexington: University Press of Kentucky, 1993); and Donald Searing, *Westminster's World: Understanding Political Roles* (Cambridge, MA: Harvard University Press, 1994).

88. Michael Jogerst, *Reform in the House of Commons: The Select Committee System* (Lexington: University of Kentucky Press, 1993), 160–61.

89. Valerie Heitshusen, Garry Young, and David Wood, "Electoral Context and MP Constituency Focus in Australia, Canada, Ireland, New Zealand, and the United Kingdom," *American Journal of Political Science*, 49, no. 1 (January 2005): 32–45.

90. Mattei Dogan, "Parliamentarians as Errand Boys in France, Britain, and the United States," *Comparative Sociology* 6 (2007): 438, 447.

91. John M. Carey, *Term Limits and Legislative Representation* (New York: Cambridge University Press, 1996).

92. Barry Ames, "Electoral Rules, Constituency Pressures, and Pork Barrel: Bases of Voting in the Brazilian Congress," *Journal of Politics* 57, no. 2 (1995): 331.

93. John M. Carey, Richard Niemi, and Lynda W. Powell, "The Effects of Term Limits on State Legislatures," *Legislative Studies Quarterly* 23, no. 2 (May 1998): 271–300.

94. A. Valenzuela and A. Wilde, "The Congress and Chilean Democracy," paper presented at the Conference on Legislatures and Development, Carmel, California, August 1975. A revised version of this paper by the same authors is entitled "Presidential Politics and the Decline of the Chilean Congress," in *Legislatures in Development: Dynamics of Change in New and Old States*, ed. Joel Smith and Lloyd D. Musolf (Durham: Duke University Press, 1979).

95. Peter M. Siavelis, "Executive-Legislative Relations in Post-Pinochet Chile: A Preliminary Assessment," in *Presidentialism and Democracy in Latin America*, ed. Mainwaring and Shugart, 329–30.

96. Heitshusen, Young, and Wood, "Electoral Context and MP Constituency Focus."

97. Dogan, "Parliamentarians as Errand Boys," 432.

98. David M. Wood and Garry Young, "Comparing Constituency Activity by Junior Legislators in Great Britain and Ireland," *Legislative Studies Quarterly* 22, no. 2 (May 1997): 217–32.

99. Scott Mainwaring and Matthew Shugart, "Conclusion: Presidentialism and the Party System," in *Presidentialism and Democracy in Latin America*, ed. Mainwaring and Shugart, 426–27.

100. Brian F. Crisp et al., "Vote-Seeking Incentives and Legislative Representation in Six Presidential Democracies," *Journal of Politics* 66, no. 3 (August 2004): 823–46.

101. Brian Crisp, "Presidential Behavior in a System with Strong Parties: Venezuela, 1958–1995," in *Presidentialism and Democracy in Latin America*, ed. Mainwaring and Shugart.

102. Mark Hallerberg and Patrik Marier, "Executive Authority, the Personal Vote, and Budget Discipline in Latin American and Caribbean Countries," *American Journal of Political Science* 48, no. 3 (2004): 571–87.

103. Thomas D. Lancaster and W. David Patterson, "Comparative Pork Barrel Politics: Perceptions from the West German Bundestag," *Comparative Political Studies* 22 (1990): 458–77.

104. Heitshusen, Young, and Wood, "Electoral Context and MP Constituency Focus," 38.

105. Joel Barkan, "Bringing Home the Pork: Legislator Behavior, Rural Develop-

ment, and Political Change in East Africa," in *Legislatures in Development: Dynamics of Change in New and Old States*, ed. Smith and Musolf.

106. Ronald P. Archer and Matthew Soberg Shugart, "The Unrealized Potential of Presidential Dominance in Colombia," in *Presidentialism and Democracy in Latin America*, ed. Mainwaring and Shugart, 117, 138.

107. Brian Crisp and Felipe Botero, "Multicountry Studies of Latin American Legislatures: A Review Article," *Legislative Studies Quarterly*, 29, no. 3 (August 2004): 338.

108. Scott Mainwaring, "Multipartism, Robust Federalism, and Presidentialism in Brazil," in *Presidentialism and Democracy in Latin America*, ed. Mainwaring and Shugart, 85.

109. Barry Ames, "Electoral Rules, Constituency Pressures, and Pork Barrel," 342.

NOTES TO CHAPTER 5

1. See John Wahlke, Heinz Eulau, William Buchanan, and LeRoy Ferguson, *The Legislative System: Explorations in Legislative Behavior* (New York: John Wiley and Sons, 1962). For comparative findings, see Michael L. Mezey, *Comparative Legislatures* (Durham: Duke University Press, 1979), 170–75.

2. See John Kingdon, *Congressmen's Voting Decisions*, 3rd ed. (Ann Arbor: University of Michigan Press,1989).

3. In the case of delegates versus trustees, or nationally oriented versus locally oriented role orientations, it is advisable to think in terms of distinctions and degrees rather than in terms of dichotomies and absolutes. See Andrew Rehfield, "Trustees, Delegates, and Gyroscopes: Democratic Justice and the Ethics of Political Representation," paper presented at the annual meeting of the American Political Science Association, Philadelphia, August 30–September 3, 2006.

4. Jose Maria Maravall, "Accountability and Manipulation," in *Democracy, Accountability and Representation*, ed. Adam Przeworski, Susan Stokes, and Bernard Manin (Cambridge: Cambridge University Press, 1999), 156.

5. Christopher Jan Carman, "Public Preferences for Parliamentary Representation in the UK: An Overlooked Link?" *Political Studies* 54 (2006): 111.

6. John Hibbing and Elizabeth Theiss-Morse, *Congress as Public Enemy: Public Attitudes Toward American Political Institutions* (Cambridge: Cambridge University Press, 1995), 64.

7. Mattei Dogan, "Parliamentarians as Errand Boys in France, Britain, and the United States," *Comparative Sociology* 6 (2007): 435.

8. Warren Miller and Donald Stokes, "Constituency Influence in Congress," *American Political Science Review* 57 (March 1963): 45–57.

9. Walter Stone, "The Dynamics of Constituency Electoral Control in the House," *American Politics Quarterly* 8 (1980): 399–424.

10. Robert Erikson, "Constituency Opinion and Congressional Behavior: A Reexamination of the Miller-Stokes Representation Data," *American Journal of Political Science* 22 (1978): 511–35.

11. Kim Quaile Hill and Patricia Hurley, "Dyadic Representation Reappraised," *American Journal of Political Science* 43, no. 1 (1999): 109–37; Patricia Hurley and

Kim Quaile Hill, "Beyond the Demand-Input Model: A Theory of Representational Linkages," *Journal of Politics* 65, no. 2 (2003): 304–26.

12. Robert A. Bernstein, *Elections, Representation, and Congressional Voting Behavior: The Myth of Constituency Control* (Englewood Cliffs, NJ: Prentice-Hall, 1989), 76–77, 93.

13. Vincent L. Hutchings, *Public Opinion and Democratic Accountability: How Citizens Learn About Politics* (Princeton: Princeton University Press, 2003), 132.

14. Philip E. Converse, "The Nature of Belief Systems in Mass Publics," in *Ideology and Discontent*, ed. David Apter (New York: The Free Press, 1964).

15. Vincent L. Hutchings, "Issue Salience and Support for Civil Rights Legislation among Southern Democrats," *Legislative Studies Quarterly* 23, no. 4 (November 1998): 521–44.

16. B. Dan Wood and Angela Hinton Anderson, "The Dynamics of Senatorial Representation, 1952–1991," *Journal of Politics* 60, no. 3 (1998): 705–36.

17. Sarah Binder, Forrest Maltzman, and Lee Sigelman, "Senators' Home State Reputations: Why Do Constituents Love a Bill Cohen So Much More Than an Al D'Amato?" *Legislative Studies Quarterly* 23, no. 4 (November 1998): 545–60.

18. Greg Giroux, "Republicans Seek Entrant in Must Win Bayou State," *Congressional Quarterly Weekly Report*, August 13, 2007, 2453; Jessica Benton Cooney, "A Rare Yankee Moderate's Future Defined by the War," *Congressional Quarterly Weekly Report*, August 13, 2007, 2454.

19. Brian F. Schaffner, "Local News Coverage and the Incumbency Advantage in the U.S. House," *Legislative Studies Quarterly* 31, no. 4 (November 2006): 491–511.

20. Richard F. Fenno, Jr., *Home Style: House Members in Their Districts* (Boston: Little Brown, 1978); Richard F. Fenno, Jr., *Going Home: Black Representatives and Their Constituents* (Chicago: University of Chicago Press, 2003); Richard F. Fenno, Jr., *Congressional Travels: Places, Connections, and Authenticity* (New York: Pearson, Longman, 2007).

21. Hibbing and Theiss-Morse, *Congress as Public Enemy*, 64.

22. Fenno, *Congressional Travels*, 26.

23. Jesse McKinley, "Iraq War and Other Issues Follow Lawmakers Home," *New York Times*, April 15, 2007.

24. David T. Canon, "Electoral Systems and the Representation of Minority Interests in Legislatures," *Legislative Studies Quarterly*, 24, no. 3 (August 1999): 333–36.

25. Bruce Oppenheimer, "Deep Red and Blue Congressional Districts: The Causes and Consequences of Declining Party Competition," in *Congress Reconsidered*, ed. Lawrence C. Dodd and Bruce I. Oppenheimer, 8th ed. (Washington, DC: Congressional Quarterly Press, 2005).

26. Binder et. al., "Senators' Home State Reputations."

27. Benjamin Bishin, "Subconstituencies and Competition: A subconstituency based explanation for the conflicting results of the competition and representation literature," paper presented at the annual meeting of the American Political Science Association, Philadelphia, August 30–September 3, 2006.

28. Girish Gulati, "Revisiting the Link Between Electoral Competition and Policy Extremism in the United States Congress," *American Politics Research* 32 (2004): 495–520.

29. Tracy Sulkin, *Issue Politics in Congress* (Cambridge: Cambridge University Press, 2005).

30. Kathleen Hunter, "Republican Motions Try to Force Freshman Democrats into Difficult Votes," CQ.com, October 1, 2007.

31. Jonathan Weisman, "A Rush To Frame Views on Congress," *Washington Post,* August 20, 2007.

32. Sean Theriault, *The Power of the People* (Columbus: Ohio State University Press, 2005).

33. Bernstein, *Elections, Representation, and Congressional Voting Behavior*, 30.

34. Robert Weissberg, "Have House Elections Become a Meaningless Ritual?" in *Public Opinion and Public Policy: Models of Political Linkage*, ed. Norman Luttbeg, 3rd ed. (Itasca, IL: F. E. Peacock, 1981).

35. Paul S. Herrnson, *Congressional Elections: Campaigning at Home and in Washington* (Washington: Congressional Quarterly Press, 2004), 245.

36. Bernstein, *Elections, Representation, and Congressional Voting Behavior*, 49–57.

37. Mezey, *Comparative Legislatures*, 174.

38. Richard Hall, *Participation in Congress* (New Haven: Yale University Press, 1997), 237.

39. Jerry Hagstrom, "The Apple of Their Eyes," *National Journal*, October 14, 2006.

40. Erin McPike, "Fueling a Young Career," *National Journal*, July 8, 2006, 42–43.

41. Margaret Kitz, "Liquid Coal," *National Journal*, January 6, 2007, 30–35.

42. Herbert Kitschelt, Zdenka Mansfeldova, Radoslaw Markowski, and Gabor Toka, *Post-Communist Party Systems: Competition, Representation, and Inter-Party Cooperation* (Cambridge: Cambridge University Press, 1999), 340.

43. Morris P. Fiorina and Matthew S. Levendusky, "Disconnect: The Political Class Versus the People," in *Red and Blue Nation? Characteristics and Causes of America's Polarized Politics*, vol. 1, ed. Peter S. Nivola and David W. Brady (Washington, DC: The Brookings Institution, 2006), 64–66.

44. Nadia Urbanati, *Representative Democracy: Principles and Genealogy* (Chicago: University of Chicago Press, 2006), 63.

45. Ilter Turan, "The Turkish Legislature: From Symbolic to Substantive Representation," in *Parliaments in the Modern World: Changing Institutions*, ed. Gary Copeland and Samuel Patterson (Ann Arbor: University of Michigan Press, 1994).

46. Peter Esaiasson, "How MPs Define Their Task," in *Beyond Westminster and Congress: The Nordic Experience*, ed. Peter Esaiasson and Knut Heidar (Columbia: Ohio State University Press, 2000), 59.

47. G. Bingham Powell, "Political Representation in Comparative Politics," *Annual Review of Political Science* 7 (2004): 285–90.

48. Erik S. Herron, "Electoral Influences on Legislative Behavior in Mixed-Member Systems: Evidence from Ukraine's Verkhovna Rada," *Legislative Studies Quarterly* 27, no. 3 (August 2002): 361–82.

49. John Carey and Matthew S. Shugart, "Incentives to Cultivate a Personal Vote: A Rank Ordering of Electoral Formulas," *Electoral Studies* 14 (1995): 417–39.

50. Allan Kornberg and William Mishler, *Influence in Parliament: Canada* (Durham: Duke University Press, 1976), 174–81.

51. See Mezey, *Comparative Legislatures*, 94.

52. Robert Weissberg, "Collective vs. Dyadic Representation in Congress," *American Political Science Review* 72, no. 2 (June 1978): 535–47.

53. Andrew Rehfield, *The Concept of Constituency: Political Representation, Democratic Legitimacy, and Institutional Design* (New York: Cambridge University Press, 2005).

NOTES TO CHAPTER 6

1. John Hibbing and Elizabeth Theiss-Morse, *Congress as Public Enemy: Public Attitudes Toward American Political Institutions* (Cambridge: Cambridge University Press, 1995), 64.

2. Clinton Rossiter, ed., *The Federalist Papers* (New York: New American Library, 1961), No. 10, 78–79.

3. John Mark Hansen, *Gaining Access: Congress and the Farm Lobby, 1919–1981* (Chicago: University of Chicago Press, 1991).

4. Julie Kosterlitz, "The World According to AARP," *National Journal*, March 10, 2007.

5. Peter H. Stone, "Under the Radar," *National Journal*, March 31, 2007.

6. Lisa Caruso, "Leaders of the PAC," *National Journal*, March 17, 2007. Slightly different figures can be found at the web site of the Campaign Finance Institute, www.cfinst.org/data/pdf/VitalStats_t11.pdf (accessed July 14, 2008).

7. Campaign Finance Institute, www.cfinst.org/data/pdf/VitalStats_t11.pdf (accessed July 14, 2008).

8. Figures calculated from data supplied by the Campaign Finance Institute, www.cfinst.org/data/pdf/VitalStats_t3.pdf (accessed July 14, 2008).

9. www.politicalmoneyline.com.

10. Figures calculated from data supplied by the Campaign Finance Institute, www.cfinst.org/data/pdf/VitalStats_t6.pdf (accessed July 14, 2008).

11. www.politicalmoneyline.com/cgiwin/x_racepg.exe?DoFn=VA002006S (accessed July 14, 2008).

12. Jonathan Allen, "Rangel's Fund Raising Soars—Thanks to Corporate America," CQpolitics.com, November 2, 2007.

13. Paul S. Herrnson, *Congressional Elections: Campaigning at Home and in Washington* (Washington: Congressional Quarterly Press, 2004), 13.

14. Leslie Wayne, "Lobbyists' Gifts to Representatives Reap Benefits, Study Shows," *New York Times*, January 27, 1997.

15. John Frendreis and Richard Waterman, "PAC Contributions and Legislative Behavior: Senate Voting on Trucking Regulation," *Social Science Quarterly* 66 (1983), 401–12.

16. Eric Lichtblau and Scott Shane, "Phone Companies Seeking Immunity Gave to Senator," *New York Times*, October 22, 2007.

17. Janet Grenzke, "Shopping in the Congressional Supermarket: The Currency is Complex," *American Journal of Political Science* 33 (1989): 1–24.

18. Raymond A. Bauer, Ithiel de Sola Pool, and Lewis Anthony Dexter, *American Business and Public Policy* (New York: Atherton, 1963).

19. John R. Wright, "Contributions, Lobbying and Committee Voting in the U.S. House of Representatives," *American Journal of Political Science* 84, no. 2 (June 1990): 434.

20. Janet Box-Steffensmeier and J. Tobin Grant, "All in a Day's Work: The Financial Rewards of Legislative Effectiveness," *Legislative Studies Quarterly* 24, no. 4 (November 1999): 511–23.

21. Marie Hojnacki and David Kimball, "Organized Interests and the Decision of Whom to Lobby in Congress," *American Political Science Review* 92, no. 4 (1998): 775–90.

22. Christine Loucks, "Finance Industry PAC Contributions to U.S. Senators: 1983–88," *Public Choice* 89 (1996): 219–29.

23. Thomas Stratmann, "The Market for Congressional Votes: Is Timing of Contributions Everything?" *Journal of Law and Economics* 41, no. 1 (1998): 85–113.

24. Glenn R. Parker and Suzanne L. Parker, "The Economic Organization of Legislatures and How it Affects Congressional Voting," *Public Choice* 95 (1998): 117–29.

25. Richard L. Hall and Frank W. Wayman, "Buying Time: Money Interests and the Mobilization of Bias in Congressional Committees," *American Political Science Review* 84, no. 3 (September 1990): 797–820.

26. In December 2007, Dingell, under pressure from Democratic leaders, reluctantly agreed to a deal calling for significant increases in fuel-efficiency standards. See Jonathan Broder and Micheline Maynard, "Lawmakers Set Deal on Raising Fuel Efficiency," *New York Times*, December 1, 2007.

27. Data from Opensecrets.org.

28. Diana B. Henriques and Andrew W. Lehren, "Religious Groups Reaping Share of Federal Aid for Pet Projects," *New York Times*, May 13, 2007.

29. Marilyn Thompson and Ron Nixon, "Even Cut 50 Percent, Earmarks Clog Military Bill," *New York Times*, November 4, 2007.

30. Courtney O. Walker, "Leaders of the Pack," *National Journal*, March 31, 2007.

31. Thompson and Nixon, "Even Cut 50 Percent, Earmarks Clog Military Bill."

32. CQ.com, June 25, 2007.

33. David Baumann, "Lobbying Lewis," *National Journal*, June 10, 2006; David Baumann, "The Shockeys' Family Business," *National Journal*, July 29, 2006; David Baumann, "The Lewis-Lowery Lobbying Loop," *National Journal*, September 16, 2006.

34. Robert Pear, "House's Author Of Drug Benefit Joins Lobbyists," *New York Times*, December 16, 2004; William Welch, "Tauzin Switches Sides From Drug Industry Overseer to Lobbyist," *USA Today*, December 18, 2004.

35. Data from OpenSecrets.org.

36. CQ.com, July 17, 2007.

37. Gregg Sangillo, "K Street Moves," *National Journal*, December 2, 2006.

38. Eliza Newlin Carney, "Charitable Chicanery," *National Journal*, June 24, 2006.

39. Peter H. Stone, "The Fallen," *National Journal*, September 30, 2006.

40. *McConnell v. FEC*, 540 U.S. 93 (2003).

41. *FEC v. Wisconsin Right to Life*, 546 U.S. 410 (2007).

42. Jeff Zeleny and David Kirkpatrick, "House, 411–8, Passes a Vast Ethics Overhaul," *New York Times*, August 1, 2007.

43. David Kirkpatrick, "Tougher Rules Change Game for Lobbyists," *New York Times*, August 7, 2007.

44. Michael Rush, *Parliament Today* (Manchester: Manchester University Press, 2005), 189, 257.

45. Phillip Norton, "Representation of Interests: The Case of the British House of Commons," in *Parliaments in the Modern World: Changing Institutions*, ed. Gary Copeland and Samuel Patterson (Ann Arbor: University of Michigan Press, 1994).

46. A. W. Bradley and K. D. Ewing, *Constitutional and Administrative Law*, 14th ed. (Harlow, England: Pearson Longman, 2007), 161–72; and K. D. Ewing, *The Cost of Democracy* (Portland, OR: Hart Publishing Company, 2007), chap. 3.

47. Erik Damgaard, "Denmark: Experiments in Parliamentary Government," in *Parliamentary Change in the Nordic Countries*, ed. Erik Damgaard (Oslo: Scandinavian University Press, 1992), 40.

48. Hilmar Rommetvedt, "Norway: From Consensual Majority Parliamentarism to Dissensual Minority Parliamentarism," in *Parliamentary Change in the Nordic Countries*, ed. Damgaard, 93.

49. Dag Anckar, "Finland: Dualism and Consensual Rule," in *Parliamentary Change in the Nordic Countries*, ed. Damgaard, 185.

50. Gregory S. Mahler, *The Knesset: Parliament in the Israeli Political System* (Madison, NJ: Fairleigh Dickenson University Press, 1981), 47.

51. Brian Crisp, "Presidential Behavior in a System with Strong Parties: Venezuela, 1958–1995," in *Presidentialism and Democracy in Latin America*, ed. Scott Mainwaring and Matthew Soberg Shugart (Cambridge: Cambridge University Press, 1997), 164ff.

52. Barry Ames, "Electoral Rules, Constituency Pressures, and Pork Barrel: Bases of Voting in the Brazilian Congress," *Journal of Politics* 57, no. 2 (1995): 331.

53. S. Laurel Weldon, "Beyond Bodies: Institutional Sources of Representation for Women in Democratic Policymaking," *Journal of Politics* 64, no. 4 (2002): 1153–74.

54. The classic statement of this position is David Truman, *The Governmental Process: Political Interests and Public Opinion* (New York: Alfred A. Knopf, 1953). Among the many critiques is Theodore Lowi, *The End of Liberalism: The Second Republic of the United States*, 2nd ed. (New York: W. W. Norton, 1979).

55. Melissa S. Williams, *Voice, Trust, and Memory: Marginalized Groups and the Failings of Liberal Representation* (Princeton: Princeton University Press, 1998), 88.

56. See Gordon Wood, *The Creation of the American Republic, 1776–1778* (Chapel Hill, NC: University of North Carolina Press, 1969), 65–70 for a discussion of "republican virtue."

NOTES TO CHAPTER 7

1. Kenneth Newton and Pippa Norris, "Confidence in Public Institutions: Faith, Culture, or Performance?" in *Disaffected Democracies: What's Troubling the Trilateral*

Countries? ed. Susan J. Pharr and Robert Putnam (Princeton: Princeton University Press, 2000), 56.

2. Robert Putnam, Susan Pharr, and Russell Dalton, "What's Troubling the Trilateral Democracies?" introduction to *Disaffected Democracies*, ed. Pharr and Putnam, 14–20.

3. John Hibbing and Elizabeth Theiss-Morse, *Congress as Public Enemy: Public Attitudes Toward American Political Institutions* (Cambridge: Cambridge University Press, 1995), 54.

4. Ibid., 58.

5. Joseph Cooper, "Performance and Expectations in American Politics: The Problem of Distrust in Congress," in *Congress and the Decline of Public Trust*, ed. Joseph Cooper (Boulder, CO: Westview Press, 1999), 150.

6. Ibid.

7. Alan Rosenthal, Burdette A. Loomis, John Hibbing, and Karl Kurtz, *Republic on Trial: The Case for Representative Democracy* (Washington, DC: Congressional Quarterly Press, 2003), 17–29.

8. Anthony King, "Distrust of Government: Explaining American Exceptionalism," in *Disaffected Democracies*, ed. Pharr and Putnam.

9. Hibbing and Theiss-Morse, *Congress as Public Enemy*, 60.

10. This point is explored more fully in Michael L. Mezey, *Congress, the President, and Public Policy* (Boulder, CO: Westview Press, 1989), chap. 1.

11. David M. Shribman, "Insiders With a Crisis from Outside: Congress and the Public Trust," in *Congress and the Decline of Public Trust*, ed. Cooper.

12. Samuel Huntington, *Political Order in Changing Societies* (New Haven: Yale University Press, 1968), 374.

13. Gerard Alexander, "Parliament and Land Reform in Spain," in *Working Papers on Comparative Legislative Studies*, ed. Lawrence D. Longley, Research Committee on Legislative Specialists, International Political Science Association (Lawrence, WI: Lawrence University, 1994).

14. Scott Mainwaring, "Multipartism, Robust Federalism, and Presidentialism in Brazil," in *Presidentialism and Democracy in Latin America*, ed. Scott Mainwaring and Matthew Soberg Shugart (Cambridge: Cambridge University Press, 1997).

15. Arturo Valenzuela, "Party Politics and the Crisis of Presidentialism in Chile: A Proposal for a Parliamentary Form of Government," in *The Failure of Presidential Democracy*, ed. Juan Linz and Arturo Valenzuela (Baltimore: John Hopkins University Press, 1994), 166.

16. Mark Hallerberg and Patrik Marier, "Executive Authority, the Personal Vote, and Budget Discipline in Latin American and Caribbean Countries," *American Journal of Political Science* 48, no. 3 (2004): 571–87.

17. Robert Stauffer, *The Philippine Congress: Causes of Structural Change*, Sage Research Papers in the Social Sciences, Comparative Legislative Studies Series, No. 90–024 (Beverly Hills, CA: Sage Publications, 1975), 36–37.

18. Samuel Patterson, John Wahlke, and G. R. Boynton, "Dimensions of Support for Legislative Systems," in *Legislatures in Comparative Perspective*, ed. Allan Kornberg (New York: David McKay, 1973), 309.

19. See Reinhard Bendix, *Max Weber: An Intellectual Portrait* (Garden City, NY: Doubleday-Anchor Books Edition, 1962), particularly 423–30.

20. See K. C. Wheare, *Legislatures* (London: Oxford University Press, 1963) for the classic statement of the decline of legislatures theme. For a rebuttal, see Gerhard Loewenberg, "The Role of Parliaments in Modern Political Systems," in *Modern Parliaments: Change or Decline?* ed. Gerhard Loewenberg (Chicago: Aldine-Atherton, 1971).

21. Ralf Dahrendorf, afterword to *Disaffected Democracies*, ed. Pharr and Putnam, 312.

22. Francis E. Rourke, "Bureaucracy in the American Constitutional Order," *Political Science Quarterly* 102, no. 2 (Summer 1987): 217–32.

23. See, for example, Mezey, *Congress, the President, and Public Policy*.

24. Sarah A. Binder, *Stalemate: Causes and Consequences of Legislative Gridlock* (Washington, D.C.: The Brookings Institution, 2003).

25. Christopher Kelly and Ryan Barilleaux, "The Past, Present, and Future of the Unitary Executive," paper presented at the annual meeting of the American Political Science Association, Philadelphia, PA, September 2006; Louis Fisher, "The Unitary Executive: Ideology Versus the Constitution," paper presented at the annual meeting of the American Political Science Association, Philadelphia, PA, September 2006.

26. Machiavelli, *Discourses*, trans. L. J. Walker (London: Penguin, 1970), 194–95. See also Harvey Mansfield, Jr., *Taming the Prince: The Ambivalence of Modern Executive Power* (New York: The Free Press, 1989), chap. 6.

27. Clinton Rossiter, ed., *The Federalist Papers* (New York: New American Library, 1961), No. 70, 423.

28. Benjamin R. Barber, *Strong Democracy: Participatory Politics for a New Age* (Berkeley: University of California Press, 1984), 145, 147.

29. Brian Friel, "Direct Democracy: Version '06," *National Journal*, October 7, 2006, 60–61.

30. Ibid.

31. www.ncsl.org/programs/legismgt/about/states.htm.

32. James A. Stimson, "Party Government and Responsiveness," in *Democracy, Accountability and Representation*, ed. Adam Przeworski, Susan Stokes, and Bernard Manin (Cambridge: Cambridge University Press, 1999).

33. On term limits, see John M. Carey, Richard Niemi, and Lynda W. Powell, "The Effects of Term Limits on State Legislatures," *Legislative Studies Quarterly* 23, no. 2 (May 1998), 271–300; and John M. Carey, *Term Limits and Legislative Representation* (New York: Cambridge University Press, 1996).

34. See Lawrence K. Grossman, *The Electronic Republic* (New York: Viking, 1995)

35. John S. Dryzek *Discursive Democracy: Politics, Policy, and Political Science* (Cambridge: Cambridge University Press, 1990), 127.

36. Barber, *Strong Democracy*, 117, 152–53.

37. James Fishkin, *The Voices of the People: Public Opinion and Democracy* (New Haven: Yale University Press, 1997).

38. Nicholas Wood, "Bulgaria Invites Guest for a Day of Intense Democracy," *New York Times*, May 7, 2007.

39. Iris Marion Young, "Activist Challenges to Deliberative Democrats," in *Debating Deliberative Democracy*, ed. James S. Fishkin and Peter Laslett (Oxford: Blackwell Publishing Ltd., 2003), 115, 119.

40. Robert Putnam, *Bowling Alone: The Collapse and Revival of American Community* (New York: Simon and Schuster, 2000).

41. Hibbing and Theiss-Morse, *Congress as Public Enemy*, chap. 8.

42. Jane Mansbridge, *Beyond Adversarial Democracy* (Chicago: University of Chicago Press, 1983).

43. Morris P. Fiorina, "Extreme Voices: A Dark Side of Civic Engagement," in *Civic Engagement in American Democracy*, ed. Theda Skocpol and Morris Fiorina (Washington, DC: Brookings Institution, 1999).

44. Theda Skocpol, *Diminished Democracy: From Membership to Management in American Civil Life* (Norman: University of Oklahoma Press, 2003).

45. Gary C. Jacobson, "Modern Campaigns and Representation," in *The Legislative Branch*, ed. Paul Quirk and Sarah Binder (New York: Oxford University Press, 2005), 115–16.

46. Edmund Andrews and Robert Pear, "With New Rules, Congress Boasts Of Pet Projects," *New York Times*, August 5, 2007.

47. The case was *Nixon v. Shrink Missouri Government PAC*, 528 U.S. 377 (2000), cited in John Cochran and Jonathan Riehl, "Campaign Finance Debate Turns to Courts for Closure," *Congressional Quarterly Weekly Report*, November 30, 2002.

48. K. D. Ewing, *The Cost of Democracy* (Portland, OR: Hart Publishing Company, 2007), chap. 9.

49. Graeme Orr, "Political Finance Law in Australia," in *Party Funding and Campaign Financing in International Perspective*, ed. K. D. Ewing and Samuel Issacharoff (Portland, OR: Hart Publishing, 2006), 102–6.

50. Molly Hooper and Alan K. Ota, "House Votes for Outside Ethics Review," *Congressional Quarterly Weekly Report*, March 17, 2008, 726–27.

51. See Thomas Mann and Norman Ornstein, *The Broken Branch: How Congress Is Failing America and How to Get It Back on Track* (New York: Oxford University Press, 2006).

52. Rossiter, *The Federalist Papers*, No. 10, 84.

53. "Democrats to Watch," *National Journal*, November 18, 2006, 20–34.

Index

Abramoff, Jack, 104, 160–61
Accord Group, 158
allocational responsiveness, 38–39. *See also* earmarks; formulas
administrative state, 177–78
agricultural subsidies, 103–104
Allen, George, 149
American Association of Retired People (AARP), 146, 148, 166, 191
American Civil Liberties Union, 146
American Medical Association, 21, 146
apportionment, 61–64; in Canada, 62, 65; in Chile, 63; in Ecuador, 63; in India, 63; in lower chambers, 63–64; and single member districts, 64; and the United States Senate, 64; in upper chambers, 64
Argentina, 64
Army Corps of Engineers, 93, 99
Athens, 1, 3, 6, 188
Australia, Parliament of: and campaign finance, 197; and constituency focus of members, 114; electoral system, 50, 114; and pork barrel distributions, 111; representation of women in, 74, 81

Baker v. Carr, 61
Barber, Benjamin, 2, 187
Bean, Melissa, 149

Becerra, Xavier, 99
Belgium, 19, 65, 68
Bianco, William, 42
Biggert, Judy, 128, 130
Bipartisan Campaign Reform Act of 2002, 161
Birnbaum, Jeffrey, 94
Blumenauer, Earl, 103–104
Boehlert, Sherwood, 158
Bolivia, 173
Boucher, Richard, 137
Boxer, Barbara, 99, 130
Boyda, Nancy, 96–98, 101, 106, 109
Brazil, Parliament of, 14; and constituency service, 113, 116; and corruption, 165; and role of the president, 116, 175–76
"Bridge to Nowhere," 38, 104, 105
Bulgaria, 138
Bunning, Jim, 137
bureaucracy: oversight of, 179, 196; representativeness of, 178–79; role of, 15–16, 177–78. *See also*, administrative state
Burke, Edmund, 15, 33–35, 47, 120
Bush, George W. 40, 116, 170–71, 179

campaign ads, 133–34, 135, 194
campaign finance, 66, 195; and congressional committees, 153–56; and

incumbent advantage, 149, 151; and independent expenditures, 150, 161; and public funding, 191, 196–97; in 2006 congressional elections, 149. *See also* Bipartisan Campaign Reform Act

Canada, Parliament of, 3; and constituency serviced, 114; and constituency size, 62, 64; electoral system, 51; minority representation in, 65, 74; and political party strength, 139, 140–41; and public funding of campaigns, 197; representation of women in, 81

Chavez, Hugo, 14–15, 180

Chile, Parliament of, 14; and constituency service, 113–14; malapportionment of, 63; powers of, 176

China, Peoples Republic of, 3, 49, 181–82

Churchill, Winston, 194

citizen information, 5, 7–8, 30–32, 170; and accountability, 35–6; and the internet, 185–86

civic engagement, decline of, 189–191

civic virtue, 34, 168, 199

clientelism, 87–88

Clark, Dick, 143

Clinton, Hillary, 136–37

Cohen, Steve, 77–9

collective representation, 48–49, 141–42

Collins, Susan, 127, 131–32

colonial assemblies, U.S., 11, 13, 56

Concurrent Technologies, 106–107, 155

Congress, U.S.: citizen perceptions of, 122, 129, 170–71, 198–99; committee system, 153–54; and constituency service, 89–109; critiques of, 192–95; and ethnic diversity, 67–68, 76; and gender diversity, 67–68, 80–82; and incumbent reelection, 89–90; media coverage of, 171–72; as overseer of the bureaucracy, 179; and racial diversity, 67–68, 69–73; reform of, 195–201; and social class, 83–84

constituency: as a constraint, 37; as ethnic groups, 65–67; and geography, 55, 65, 141; influence of, 37, 142–43; and interest, 65, 141; as interest groups, 65; meanings of, 26–28, 55; population of, 56–57, 61–64; by random selection, 141; and the Senate, 59; size of, 55–57; in the United Kingdom, 61

constituency driven participation choices, 136–38

constituency service, 117; and advertising, 90; and citizen expectations, 91; and citizen satisfaction, 92; and committees, 90; in comparative perspective, 110–117; and credit claiming, 95–96; and electoral systems, 114–15; incentives for, 87–89; and incumbent reelection, 91, 102; and member resources, 90–91; and political parties, 112–13; and term limits, 112–13; types of, 85–87

Constitution, U.S.: deliberations on, 8–11; democratization of, 59–60; and election of the president, 15; and the powers of Congress, 10, 13, 15; and republican government, 2–3; and the Senate, 58–9; and separate institutions, 15, 181

Converse, Phillip, 125

Copeland Lowery, 158

Corsica, 6

Costa Rica, 86–87, 112–31

Courtney, Joe, 101–102

Craig, Larry, 172

crafted talk, 40, 41, 54

Cunningham, Randy (Duke), 106, 108

Cyprus, 66, 83

Czechoslovakia, 138

Daschle, Tom, 135, 137

Da Silva, Luiz Inacio (Lula), 175

Davis v. Bandemer, 73

DeGette, Donna, 200

DeLay, Tom, 160, 161

deliberation, 6–7, 45, 47–49, 186–89

deliberative polling, 187–88

demagoguery, 9, 14, 188

democracy, 1; compared with representation, 17; dangers of, 8–10; strengthening of, 182, 187

Denmark, 6, 139, 164

descriptive representation, 19, 43–46; and constituent satisfaction, 79, 81–82; and electoral systems, 68, 74–75, 83; in France, 76; and gender, 67–68, 76, 80–82; and majority-minority districts, 68–74, 77, 80; and political integration, 79–80; and policy-making, 77–82; and political party strength, 75; and religion, 76; and socioeconomic status, 83–84; in the United Kingdom, 76, 88

Dingell, John, 155

districting, 70–74

divided government, 179–180

Domenici, Pete, 133

Donnelly, Joe, 134

earmarks, 38, 87, 93–117; and campaign contributions, 106–107; in comparative perspective, 110–16; cost of, 104–05, 108–09; criticisms of, 104–09; defenses of, 105, 106; distribution of, 98–100; increasing use of, 98; presidential role in, 115–16; and reelection success, 100–103; and role of lobbyists, 156–58; and role of political parties, 111; in states, 106; and 2007 reforms, 108–09, 162

Ecuador, 66, 173

election of 2006, U.S., 172–73

Egypt, 3

Eightmile Wild and Scenic River Act, 102

Ellison, Keith, 76

Emanuel, Rahm, 94, 98, 128

ethanol, 137

ethics reform, U.S. House of Representatives, 198

expressive voting, 42

Exxon Mobil, 146

FEC v. Wisconsin Right to Life, 161

Fenno, Richard, 26–27, 39, 45, 129

Finland, 139, 164

Fiorina, Morris, 190

Fishkin, James, 187

Flake, Jeff, 105

Fleishman-Hillard, 158

Ford, Harold, 77

formulas, 92–93

France, Parliament of, 3; and constituency service, 86, 88, 89, 110, 112, 114; electoral system of, 50, 75, 114; Estates General, 66; minority representation in, 76; and political party strength, 139, 141; public perceptions of, 122, 177

Fulbright, J. William, 201

General Dynamics, 157

Germany, Parliament of, and constituency service, 115, 140; electoral system, 50, 74, 140; and political party strength, 141; public confidence in, 170; representation of women in, 74; and Weimar, 14

Gerry, Elbridge, 9

Gerrymandering. *See* districting

Hall, Richard, 136

Hamilton, Alexander, 9, 180–81, 192

Harkin, Tom, 104, 155

Helms, Jesse, 44

Herseth, Stephanie, 137

Hibbing, John, 190

Hill, Kim Quaile, 124

Hillscape Associates, 158

Homeland Security, Department of, 92–93

home style, 129–130

Hungary, 14, 138

Huntington, Samuel, 175

Hurley, Patricia, 124

hyper partisanship, 136, 138, 194

Iceland, 139, 170

immigration reform, U.S., 46, 190–91, 194

India, Parliament of, and constituency service, 86, 87, 89; and constituency size, 63; and minority representation, 43, 66

interest groups, 19, 20–21, 28, 53; and campaign finance, 149–153; citizen perceptions of, 145; and committee system, 153–56; 163–64; and corruption, 156–162; economic bias of, 166–68; and electoral systems, 164; functions of, 146–47; 166; and good public policy, 167; and political parties, 162–66; and referenda, 183; techniques of, 147–49. *See also* lobbyists

Internet, role of, 186

Israel, 26, 63

issue publics, 125, 131

issue uptake, 132–33

Italy, Parliament of: and clientelism, 88; and electoral system, 50, 75; and political party system, 49, 139

Jackson, Jesse, Jr., 96

Japan, 74, 187

Johnson, Lyndon B., 179

Kaddafi, Mohamar, 181

Kangas, Paul, 159

Kennedy, Ted, 44

Kenya, 89, 91

Kirk, Mark, 128, 133

Klein, Ron, 99

Korea, Republic of, 89, 91

K Street Project, 160

Lamont, Ned, 136

Landrieu, Mary, 127, 131–32

Leahy, Patrick, 130

Lebanon, 65, 66–67, 83

legislatures: as conservative bodies, 174–77; as checks on executive power, 11–17; critiques of, 21–22, 191–92; dangers of, 10–11; in defense of, 195–201; and democratic transitions, 14; military interventions against, 176–77, 180; origins

of, 11–13; public perceptions of, 170, 177

Lewis, Jerry, 99, 158

Lewis, John, 77–79

Libya, 181

Lieberman, Joseph, 136, 149

liquid coal, 137–38

Livingston, William, 10

lobbyists: and campaign contributions, 150; and congressional staff, 157–160; and earmarks, 108, 109, 156–57; and 2007 reforms, 161–62. *See also* interest groups

Locke, John, 12

Lowery, Bill, 158

Machiavelli, Niccolo, 180

Madison, James, 9, 10, 13, 15, 33–34, 145–46, 147, 168, 196, 199–200

Magliochetti, Paul, 157

Magna Carta, 12

Malone College, 157

Mansbridge, Jane, 42, 44, 47, 75–76, 190

Marcos, Ferdinand, 177

Markey, Edward, 200

Martinez, Mel, 46

Mason, George, 15

McCain, John, 199

McCarthy, Carolyn, 200

McConnell v. FEC, 161

McSweeney, David, 149

Mayhew, David, 95

Medicare Part D, 40–41, 156, 159

Menendez, Robert 46

Mexico, 89, 112–13, 165

Mill, John Stuart, 6, 12, 48, 74, 141, 161

Miller, Warren, 123–24

Mollohan, Allan, 160

Moore, Jeff, 158

Mosley-Braun, Carol, 44

MoveOn.org, 186, 191

Mugabe, Robert, 3, 180

Murtha, John P., 93, 99, 106–107, 155, 157

Myanmar, 180

National Abortion Rights Action League, 146
National Association for the Advancement of Colored People, 166
National Rifle Association, 132, 146,166
Netherlands, 26, 63, 170
New England Town Meeting, 1, 6, 187, 190
New Zealand, Parliament of, 3; and constituency service, 113–15; electoral system, 140; representation of Maoris in, 66, 79–80
Ney, Bob, 160–61
No Child Left Behind, 179
Norton, Phillip, 163
Norway, Parliament of (Storting), 3; committee system of, 164; and constituency service, 89; and political party strength, 139; public confidence in, 170; representation of women in, 19, 81

Obama, Barack, 46, 137
Obey, David, 99
O'Connor, Sandra Day, 70
Office of Management and Budgeting, 94

Pallone, Frank, Jr., 95
Panama Canal Treaty, 143
Pell, Clairborne, 200–201
Peterson, Collin, 103, 155
Pharmaceutical Research and Manufacturers of America, 146, 158–59
Philippines, 88, 177
Pitkin, Hanna, xii, 36–37
PMA Group, 157
Poland, 6, 83, 138, 165
policy representation, 119–143; and campaign tactics, 133–34; and assessing constituency opinion, 126–130; and constituency heterogeneity, 130–32; and electoral risk, 193–94; and electoral systems, 140; and issues, 124–26, 132; and political party strength, 139–141; and

representative decision-making, 142–43; and role orientations, 119–124
Political Action Committees (PACs), 149–152
political parties: citizen perception of role of, 139–140; and committee strength, 163; and interest groups, 162–66; and public policy, 138–141; as representational agents, 52–53; representatives' obligations to, 27–28; strength of, 18–19, 51–52
Political Parties, Elections, and Referendum Act of 2000 (UK), 164
pork barrel. *See* earmarks
Portman, Rob, 94
Presidency, U.S., 14, 15; expansion of powers of, 15–16; selection method, 15, 60
presidentialism, 180–81
proportional representation, 18–19, 27, 29, 50–52; and constituency service, 114–15; and descriptive representation, 74–75, 142; and interest groups, 164; and interest representation, 142
Price, David, 200
Property Casualty Insurers Association of America, 159
public opinion: and attentive publics, 31–32; and congruence with representatives' attitudes, 123–24, 126; and heterogeneous constituencies, 130–32; and intense minorities, 31, 122–3; measurement problems, 31–32, 122; and potential preferences, 40–41; and process issues, 134–35. *See also* issue publics; subconstituencies

Rahall, Nick, 137
Randolph, Edmund, 15
Rangel, Charles, 150
Raytheon, 157
recall, 182–83
referendum, 182–83, 186–87

Reform Acts (UK), 60–61
Regula, Ralph, 109
Rehfield, Andrew, 141
representation, 23–54; and accountability, 25, 33–36, 134–36, 138;
   anticipatory model of, 40, 121; and
   authorization, 25, 28–29; and delegate v. trustee issue, 119–122; as
   deputies, 139; educative function of,
   39–40, 41, 127–28; and electoral
   promises, 33; entrepreneurial model
   of, 47; gyroscopic model of, 42–43;
   principal–agent theory of, 23–36;
   and representative institutions,
   192–95; role of elections in, 49–50;
   as a system, 18–19, 49–53. *See also*
   collective representation; descriptive
   representation; responsiveness; surrogate representation; virtual representation
representative democracy: arguments
   for, 6–8, 10, 17; compared with
   democracy, 2–6, 17; criteria for, 2;
   democratic critique of, 169–173
responsiveness, 20, 36–38
Reynolds v. Sims, 62
R. J. Reynolds Tobacco Company, 183
Rockefeller, John D. IV, 152, 153
rotten borough, 60
Rousseau, Jean-Jacques, 2, 6

Salazar, Ken, 46
Samuels, David, 63, 64
Saudi Arabia, 3, 181
Saxton, H. James, 95
Schlesinger, Arthur M., 16
Schumpeter, Joseph, 8
Schwartz, Joe, 136
Senate, U.S.: and constituency service,
   92; creation of, 11, 57–59; and credit
   claiming, 96; direct election of, 60;
   and formulas, 92–93; job approval
   of members of, 131; malapportion-
   ment, 64; unlimited debate in,
   173,198
Serrano, Jose, 109, 194–95
Shaw, E, Clay, 99

Shaw v. Reno, 70
Shays Rebellion, 9
Sherman, Roger, 10
Shockey, Jeff, 158
Sierra Club, 146, 166
Sieyes, Emmanuel, 8
Simmons, Rob, 101
Singapore, 86
single member districts, 18, 27, 29,
   50–52, 83. *See also* apportionment;
   districting
Skocpol, Theda, 191
Smith, Gordon, 133
Snyder, Richard, 63, 64
Solomon, John, 94
Souter, David, 197
South Africa, 75, 81
Spain, 13–14, 175
State Child Health Insurance Program
   (S-Chip), 94–95, 133–34
Stevens, Ted, 38, 104, 107–08, 109
Stokes, Donald, 123–24
Stupak, Bart, 95
subconstituency. *See* issue publics
subgovernments, 156
surrogate representation, 46
Sweden, 89, 139

Taiwan, 75
Talent, Jim, 158
Tanzania, 63, 75
Tauzin, Billy, 158–59
term limits, 183–85
Thailand, Parliament of: and constitu-
   ency service, 87; and role of the mili-
   tary, 16, 180
Theiss-Morse, Elizabeth, 190
Thomas, Clarence, 125
Trident Seafoods, Inc., 108
trust, 42, 47–48, 54
Tunisia, 3
Turkey, Parliament of: and constituency
   service, 89; and political party
   strength, 139; public expectations of
   members of, 91; and role of the mili-
   tary, 16

Ukraine, 140

Union of Soviet Socialist Republics, Parliament of, 5; and constituency service, 86, 111; and political party strength, 20; representation of workers in, 83

unitary executive, theory of, 180

United Kingdom, Parliament of, 15, 20; and campaign finance, 164; committee system in, 163; and constituency service, 91, 110, 111, 114; and constituency size, 62–63, 64; and electoral system, 51; and interest groups, 163–64; minority representation in, 76; origins of, 12, 55–56; and the personal vote, 112; and political party strength, 51–52; 139; and pork, 111–12; private member bills in, 163; public expectations of, 122; representation of women in, 81

universalism, 92, 174

U. S. Chamber of Commerce, 148

Van Scoyok Associates, 157

Venezuela: and Hugo Chavez, 14, 180; and role of political parties, 115, 165

Virginia House of Burgesses, 12–13

virtual representation, 46–47, 65–66

Voltz, Neil, 161

Voting Rights Act of 1965, 59–60, 69–70; 1982 amendments to, 69

Walberg, Tim, 136

Walsh, James, 99

Warner, John, 133

Webb, James, 149

Weber, Max, 177–78

Wesberry v. Sanders, 61

Williams, Melissa, 44, 45, 167

Wilson, James, 13

Young, Bill, 99, 107

Young, Don, 108

Young, Iris Marion, 84, 188–89

Yugoslavia, 66, 83

Zimbabwe, 3, 180

About the Author

Michael L. Mezey is professor of political science at DePaul University in Chicago. He earned his B.A. from the College of the City of New York and his M.A. and Ph.D. from Syracuse University. He served on the faculties of the University of Virginia and the University of Hawaii before joining DePaul's faculty in 1977 as chair of the Political Science Department. From 1993 through 2005, Dr. Mezey served as dean of DePaul's College of Liberal Arts and Sciences. He has held visiting and adjunct faculty appointments at Thammasat University in Bangkok, Wesleyan University in Connecticut, the University of Chicago, and Loyola University of Chicago. He is the author of numerous scholarly papers, articles, and anthology chapters in comparative legislative behavior, legislative politics, and American politics. At DePaul, he teaches courses on legislative behavior and the American presidency. He is the author of *Comparative Legislatures* (Duke University Press, 1979), *Congress, The President, and Public Policy* (Westview Press, 1989), and co-editor of *Parliaments and Public Policy* (Cambridge University Press, 1991).